WITHDRAWN

FREEZING ORDER

Also by Bill Browder

Red Notice

FREEZING ORDER

ORDER

A TRUE STORY OF MONEY LAUNDERING, MURDER AND SURVIVING VLADIMIR PUTIN'S WRATH

BILL BROWDER

Waterford City and County Libraries

WITHDRAWN

SIMON &
SCHUSTER

London · New York · Sydney · Toronto · New Delhi

First published in the United States by Simon & Schuster, Inc., 2022
First published in Great Britain by Simon & Schuster UK Ltd, 2022

Copyright © Hermitage Media Limited, 2022

The right of Bill Browder to be identified as the author of this work has been
asserted in accordance with the Copyright, Designs and Patents Act, 1988.

3 5 7 9 10 8 6 4

Simon & Schuster UK Ltd
1st Floor
222 Gray's Inn Road
London WC1X 8HB

www.simonandschuster.co.uk
www.simonandschuster.com.au
www.simonandschuster.co.in

Simon & Schuster Australia, Sydney
Simon & Schuster India, New Delhi

The author and publishers have made all reasonable efforts to contact
copyright-holders for permission, and apologise for any omissions or errors in the form
of credits given. Corrections may be made to future printings.

A CIP catalogue record for this book is available from the British Library

Interior design by Paul Dippolito
Hardback ISBN: 978-1-3985-0607-7
Trade Paperback ISBN: 978-1-3985-0608-4
eBook ISBN: 978-1-3985-0609-1

Printed in the UK by CPI Group (UK) Ltd, Croydon, CR0 4YY

FSC
www.fsc.org

MIX
Paper from
responsible sources
FSC® C171272

To my wife and children,
who have stood by me, supported me, and loved me as
the events in this story unfolded. I know it hasn't been
easy, but I'm eternally grateful to each of you.

Author's Note

This is a true story that will surely offend some very powerful and dangerous people. In order to protect the innocent, some names, locations, and details have been changed.

Contents

Freezing Order: A legal procedure that prevents a defendant from moving their assets beyond the reach of a court.

FREEZING ORDER

– 1 –

The Madrid Arrest

SPRING 2018

Madrid was uncharacteristically cool for the end of spring. I'd flown in for a meeting with José Grinda, Spain's top anti-corruption prosecutor. I was there to share evidence about how dirty money connected to the murder of my Russian lawyer, Sergei Magnitsky, had been used to purchase luxury properties along Spain's Costa del Sol. The meeting was scheduled for 11:00 a.m. the following morning, which in Spain counts as an early meeting.

When I arrived at my hotel that evening, the manager scurried over to the check-in desk and ushered the clerk aside. "Mr. Browder?" he asked. I nodded. "Welcome to the Gran Hotel Inglés. We have a very special surprise for you!"

I stay at a lot of hotels. Managers don't typically have surprises for me. "What's that?" I asked.

"You will see. I will accompany you to your room." He spoke in careful English. "Could you please give me your passport and credit card?" I handed them over. He scanned my passport and fed the credit card—a Black American Express Card to which I'd recently been upgraded—into a chip reader. He handed me a room key with both hands cupped in a vaguely Japanese manner and stepped from behind the counter. Holding out his arm, he said, "Please. After you."

I walked to the elevator, the manager following directly behind. We rode to the top floor.

He stepped aside when the doors opened, making room for me to exit first, but once we were in the hall he shuffled past me, stopping in front of a white door. He fumbled briefly with his master key, and then opened the room. I peered inside. I'd been upgraded to the presidential suite. I was pretty sure this wasn't because of who I was, but because of this new American Express card. I'd always wondered what the fuss was with these things. Now I knew.

"Wow," I said.

I walked through the foyer and into a white living room decorated with tasteful modern furniture. On a low table was a spread of Spanish cheeses, Ibérico ham, and fruit. The manager talked about what an honor it was to have me as a guest, even though I doubted he knew anything about me beyond which credit card I carried.

He followed me around the suite, seeking my approval. There was a dining room, its table laid out with pastries, chocolates, and champagne on ice; then came the reading room, with a small private library; then a lounge with a glass-topped bar; then a little office with subdued lighting; and finally, the bedroom, which had a freestanding bathtub tucked under a high window.

I had to suppress laughter. Of course, I loved the room— who wouldn't?—but I was in Madrid on a one-night business trip. It would have taken half a dozen people to eat all the food they had laid out. Moreover, if the manager had known the nature of my visit— talking to law enforcement officials about the sort of Russian gangsters who often booked suites like this—he probably wouldn't have been so enthusiastic. Still, I wasn't going to be rude. When we circled back to the foyer, I nodded appreciatively. "It's very nice," I said. "Thank you."

As soon as he was gone, I called Elena, my wife, who was at home in London with our four children. I told her all about the room, how extravagant and ridiculous it was, and how I wished she were with me.

After our call, I changed into jeans and a light sweater before heading out for an evening walk through the streets of Madrid, mentally preparing for my meeting with José Grinda the next day. Eventually, though, I got lost in the maze-like streets and squares, and had to hail a cab to take me back to the hotel.

The following morning was bright and sunny. Unlike the previous day, it was going to be hot.

At around 8:15 a.m. I checked my papers and business cards and opened the door to go downstairs for breakfast.

I stopped short.

The manager stood on the landing, hand raised in mid-knock.

On each side of him was a uniformed police officer. The patches on their crisp, navy shirts read, POLICIA NACIONAL.

"Apologies, Mr. Browder," the manager said, glancing at the floor. "But these men need to see your identification."

I handed my British passport to the larger of the two stone-faced officers. He studied it, comparing it to a piece of paper in his other hand. He then spoke to the manager in Spanish, which I don't understand.

The manager translated. "I'm sorry, Mr. Browder, but you must go with these men."

"What for?" I asked, looking past the manager.

He turned to the larger officer and rattled off something in Spanish.

The officer, staring directly at me, stated, "Interpol. Russia."

Fuck.

The Russians had been trying to have me arrested for years, and now it was finally happening.

You notice odd things when adrenaline hits you. I noticed there was a light out at the far end of the hall, and that there was a small stain on the manager's lapel. I also noticed that the manager didn't look so much contrite as concerned. I could tell this wasn't for me. What concerned him was that his presidential suite would be unavailable so long as it contained my belongings. He wanted my things out as soon as possible.

He spoke quickly to the officers, and then said, "These gentlemen will give you a few moments to pack."

I hurried through the series of rooms to the bedroom, leaving the officers waiting in the entryway. I suddenly realized I was alone and had an opportunity. If I'd thought the room upgrade was frivolous before, now it was a godsend.

I called Elena. But she didn't answer.

I then called Ruperto, my Spanish lawyer who'd arranged the meeting with Prosecutor Grinda. No answer there, either.

As I rushed to pack, I remembered something Elena had said to me after I'd been detained at Geneva Airport that February. "If something like this ever happens again," she said, "and you can't reach anyone, post it on Twitter." I'd started using Twitter a couple of years earlier, and now had some 135,000 followers, many of them journalists, government officials, and politicians from around the world.

I followed her instructions, tweeting: "Urgent: Just was arrested by Spanish police in Madrid on a Russian Interpol arrest warrant. Going to the police station right now."

I grabbed my bag and returned to the two waiting officers. I expected to be formally arrested, but they didn't behave like cops in the movies. They didn't cuff me, frisk me, or take my things. They just told me to follow them.

We went downstairs, not a word passing between us. The officers stood behind me while I paid the bill. Other guests gawked as they filtered through the lobby.

The manager, back behind the desk, broke the silence. "Do you want to leave your bag with us, Mr. Browder, while these men take you to the police station? I'm sure this will be sorted out quickly."

Knowing what I did about Putin and Russia, I was sure it wouldn't be. "I'll keep my things, thank you," I responded.

I turned to the officers, who sandwiched me front and back. They led me outside to their small Peugeot police car. One took my bag and put it in the trunk; the other pushed me into the back seat.

The door slammed shut.

A partition of thick Plexiglas separated me from the officers. The back seat was hard plastic like a stadium seat. There were no door handles and no way to open the windows. The interior was tinged with the odors of sweat and urine. The driver started the car while the other officer turned on the lights and sirens. We were off.

As soon as the car's sirens started blaring, I was struck by a terrifying thought. What if these people weren't police officers? What if they'd somehow obtained uniforms and a police car and were impersonating police officers?

What if, instead of driving me to the police station, they drove me to an airstrip, put me on a private plane, and whisked me off to Moscow?

This was not just a paranoid fantasy. I had been subjected to dozens of death threats, and had even been warned several years earlier by a US government official that an extrajudicial rendition was being planned for me.

My heart pounded. How was I going to get out of this? I began to worry that the people who'd seen my tweet might not believe it. They might have thought my account had been hacked, or that the tweet was some kind of joke.

Thankfully, the police officers—or whoever they were—hadn't taken my phone.

I pulled my mobile out of my jacket pocket and surreptitiously snapped a picture through the Plexiglas, capturing the backs of the officers' heads and their police radio mounted on the dashboard. I tweeted the image out immediately.

If anyone doubted my arrest before, they certainly weren't now.

 **Bill Browder** ✔
@Billbrowder
···

In the back of the Spanish police car going to the station on the Russian arrest warrant. They won't tell me which station

8:36 am · 30 May 2018 · Twitter for iPhone

Bill Browder, via Twitter. (© BILL BROWDER)

My phone was on silent, but within seconds it lit up. Calls started coming in from journalists everywhere. I couldn't answer any of them, but then my Spanish lawyer called. I *had* to let him know what was going on, so I ducked behind the partition and cupped my hand over the phone.

"I've been arrested," I whispered. "I'm in a squad car."

The officers heard me. The driver jerked the car to the side of the road. Both men jumped out. My door opened, and the larger officer hauled me onto the street. He aggressively patted me down and confiscated both of my phones.

"No phones!" the smaller officer shouted. "Under arrest!"

"Lawyer," I said to him.

"No lawyer!"

The larger one then pushed me back into the car and slammed the door. We took off again, coursing through the streets of old Madrid.

No lawyer? What the hell did that mean? This was an EU country. I was sure I had the right to a lawyer.

I scanned the streets outside, looking for any sign of a police station. None. I tried to convince myself: *I'm not being kidnapped. I'm not being kidnapped. I'm not being kidnapped.* But of course, this could easily be a kidnapping.

We made a sharp turn and suddenly got stuck behind a double-parked moving truck. As the car idled, I panicked and desperately looked for a way out. But there was none.

The truck driver eventually emerged from a nearby building, saw the police car's flashing lights, and moved his vehicle out of the way. We continued to snake through the narrow streets for more than 15 minutes. Finally, we slowed as we came to an empty square.

We rocked to a halt in front of a nondescript office building. There were no people and no signs that this was a police station. The officers exited the car and, standing side by side, ordered me out.

"What are we doing here?" I asked as I stood.

"Medical exam," the smaller officer shouted.

Medical exam? I'd never heard of a medical exam when being arrested.

Cool sweat gathered on my palms. The hairs on my neck tingled.

There was no way I would willingly enter an unmarked building to submit to an exam of any kind. If this *were* a kidnapping, and I was starting to believe it was, I could picture what was in there: a bright-white office with a steel gurney, a little table with an assortment of syringes, and Russian men in cheap suits. Once inside, I'd be injected with something. The next thing I knew, I'd wake up in a Moscow prison. My life would be over.

"No medical exam!" I said forcefully. I clenched my fists as the fight-or-flight instinct took hold. I hadn't been in a fistfight since ninth grade, when I was the smallest kid at a boarding school in Steamboat Springs, Colorado, but I was suddenly ready for a physical confrontation with these men if that meant avoiding being kidnapped.

But at that moment, something shifted in their demeanor. One officer stepped very close to me while the other made a frantic call on his cell phone. He spoke into the phone for a couple of minutes and, after hanging up, typed something. He showed it to me. Google Translate. It read, "Medical exams standard protocol."

"Bullshit. I want my lawyer. Now!"

The one next to me repeated flatly, "No lawyer."

I leaned against the car and planted my feet in front of me. The one with the phone made another call and then blurted something in Spanish. Before I knew it, the car door was opened and I was shoved back inside.

They put on the lights and sirens again. We drove out of the square in a different direction. We were soon stuck in traffic again, this time in front of the Royal Palace, among a throng of tour buses and schoolchildren. I was either being kidnapped or arrested, but the world outside was oblivious, enjoying a day of sightseeing.

Ten minutes later, we pulled onto a narrow street lined with police cars. A dark blue sign reading POLICIA stuck out from the side of a weathered stone-and-redbrick building.

These officers *were* real police. I was in a proper European legal system and not in the hands of Russian kidnappers. If nothing else, I would be afforded due process before any possibility of being extradited to Moscow.

The officers pulled me from the car and marched me inside. There was a palpable air of excitement in the station. From their perspective, they'd successfully tracked down and arrested an international fugitive wanted by Interpol, which probably didn't happen every day at this little police station in central Madrid.

They dropped me in the processing room and put my suitcase in the corner. My phones were placed facedown on top of a desk. One of the arresting officers ordered me not to touch anything. It was difficult. My phones buzzed and glowed with messages, tweets, and unanswered calls. I was relieved to see that my situation was getting so much attention.

As I sat there alone, the gravity of the situation swept over me. I may not have been kidnapped, but I was now in the Spanish criminal justice system on a Russian arrest warrant. I'd been bracing for a moment exactly like this for years. It had been drilled into me how this process would work. The arresting country would call up Moscow and say, "We've got your fugitive. What do you want us to do with him?" Russia would respond, "Extradite him." Russia would have 45 days to file a formal extradition request. I would then have 30 days to respond, and the Russians would have another 30 days to respond to my response.

With the inevitable delays, I was looking at a minimum of six months of sitting in a sweltering Spanish jail before I was either released or sent to Russia.

I thought of my 12-year-old daughter, Jessica. Only a week before, I'd taken her on a long-promised father-daughter trip to England's Cotswolds. I thought of my 10-year-old daughter, Veronica, whom I had promised a similar trip, but who might now have to wait a very long time. I thought about my eldest child, David, a junior at Stanford who was already making a life for himself. He'd dealt with all my Russian troubles so well, but I was sure he was following this ordeal on Twitter, overcome with worry.

I thought of my wife, and of what she must have been feeling at that moment.

Twenty long minutes later, a young woman entered the room and sat beside me. "I'm the translator," she said in English bearing no Spanish accent.

"When can I speak to my lawyer?" I demanded.

"I'm sorry, I'm just the translator. I only wanted to introduce myself." She got up and left. She didn't even say her name.

Ten more minutes crept by before she returned with a senior-looking police officer. He stood over me and presented my charge sheet in English. Under EU law, anyone who's been arrested must be presented with the charges in their native language.

I bent over the sheet of paper. It was all boilerplate except for a little space for whatever alleged crimes I'd committed. The only word there was "Fraud." Nothing else.

I leaned back. The wooden chair creaked. I eyed the officer and translator. They expected some kind of reaction, but the Russians had been accusing me of much more serious crimes for such a long time that the sole accusation of "fraud" had almost no impact. I was surprised they'd opened so low.

Once again, I asked if I could speak to my lawyer. The translator replied, "In due course."

At that moment, a commotion erupted in the hallway. An officer I hadn't seen before burst into an adjacent room packed with people in uniform. The door slammed. The officer and translator who were with me looked at each other and then disappeared, leaving me alone again.

Five minutes later, the door leading to the room full of officers opened. People spilled out. I called for the translator, who ducked into my room. "What's going on?" I pleaded. She ignored me and left.

A few minutes later, the senior officer who'd presented the charge sheet re-entered the room, translator in tow, both with heads bowed. He said something to her in Spanish, and then she turned to me and said, "Mr. Browder, the Interpol general secretariat in Lyon has just sent us a message. They've ordered us to release you. The warrant is invalid."

My spirits soared. My phone buzzed. I stood. "Can I use my phone now?"

"*Sí.*" No translation necessary.

I snatched up the charge sheet along with my phones. I had 178 missed calls. There was a message from the British foreign secretary,

Boris Johnson, asking me to call as soon as possible. Every news outlet—ABC, Sky News, the BBC, CNN, *Time*, the *Washington Post*—all
of them wanted to know what was going on. Same with Elena, David,
and friends from all around the world, including several in Russia. I
texted Elena that I was fine and would call her soon. I did the same
with David and my colleagues at the office in London.

I strode into the open part of the police station. The mood had
swung. They thought they'd caught a modern-day Carlos the Jackal,
but now I was going to walk.

At last I was able to get ahold of my Spanish lawyer. While I'd been
sitting at the police station, he'd been busy calling everyone he knew in
Spanish law enforcement, to no avail.

What saved me was Twitter. My tweets had generated hundreds of
phone calls to Interpol and the Spanish authorities, who soon realized
the mess they'd waltzed into.

As I left the station, the arresting officers sheepishly stepped in
front of me with the translator. "They'd like you to delete the tweet that
has their photo in it. Would that be okay?" she asked.

"Will I be breaking any laws if I don't?" She translated. The officers shrugged. "Then no, I won't." The tweet is still there to this day.

They then offered me a ride to my hotel.

I laughed a little. "No, thank you. This whole ordeal has made me
forty-five minutes late for a meeting—with José Grinda."

When they heard his name, all the color drained from their faces.
They practically fell over themselves to offer me a ride to Grinda's
office.

I accepted. This time, we rode in a much nicer car.

Less than half an hour later, we pulled up to the prosecutor's office.
I was met in the lobby by Prosecutor Grinda himself. He apologized
profusely, mortified that he'd invited me to Madrid to give evidence
against Russian criminals only to be arrested by his colleagues on the
orders of the same Russian criminals.

He led me to his office, where I told him the story about Sergei
Magnitsky, my Russian lawyer, that I'd told so many times before.
I explained how, in 2008, Sergei had been taken hostage by corrupt
Russian officials and ultimately killed in jail as my proxy. I talked

about the people who had murdered Sergei and profited from the $230 million tax rebate fraud he'd exposed. I explained how some of that money had been used to purchase $33 million of property along the Spanish Riviera.

By the glint in Prosecutor Grinda's eye, I could see that he would take what I was telling him seriously. When our meeting was over, I felt confident that we had gained another ally in the West—and that Putin's Russia had lost a few more shreds of its tattered credibility.

2

The Flute

1975

How did I end up in such a mess?

It all started with a flute. A sterling silver flute to be exact. One that I received on my 11th birthday. It was a present from my favorite uncle—also named Bill—who was an amateur flutist and a math professor at Princeton.

I loved my flute. I loved the way it looked, the way it felt in my hands. I loved the sounds it made. But I wasn't all that good at it. Still, I practiced as much as I could, and was able to take the last flute chair in the school orchestra, which held rehearsals three times a week.

School was the Lab School in Hyde Park, on the South Side of Chicago. My family lived in a redbrick townhouse four blocks from the University of Chicago, where, like my uncle, my father was a math professor. At the time, Hyde Park was a rough neighborhood, and the surrounding areas were even worse. As kids, we were taught never to cross 63rd Street to the south, Cottage Grove to the west, or 47th Street to the north. To the east was Lake Michigan. Always concerned about the safety of its professors and their families, the university employed an impressive private police force, and installed security phones on nearly every corner. Combined with the Chicago Police Department (CPD), there were more police per capita in Hyde Park than any other community in the United States.

Because of all this security, my parents let me walk to school on my own every day.

One morning in the spring of 1975, as I was on my way to school,

I was approached by three teenagers who were much bigger than me. One of them pointed at the flute case in my left hand and said, "Hey kid, what's in the case?"

I gripped my flute with both hands. "Nothing."

"I'm sure it ain't nothing," he said, laughing. "Why don't you let me see what's inside?"

Before I could respond, another kid grabbed me, while the third went for the flute. I tried to twist away, but it was no use. There were three of them, and I was only 11. Finally, the biggest one grabbed the case and yanked hard, wresting it from my grip. They turned and ran off.

I ran after them for a couple of blocks, but then they disappeared across 63rd Street and I stopped. I jogged to the nearest university police phone and explained what had happened. Within a few minutes, two university police cruisers arrived, and shortly thereafter the CPD showed up as well.

Two Chicago Police officers drove me home, led me to our front door, and rang the bell. My mother answered. "What's going on?" she asked from the doorway, her eyes darting back and forth between the three of us. I started sobbing.

"Some kids stole his musical instrument, ma'am," one of the officers said. She thanked them for bringing me home and pulled me inside. As she was closing the door, one of the officers asked if I would be willing to give a statement with a description of the boys.

She didn't answer right away. I could tell she didn't want me to. Wiping the tears from my eyes, I insisted. "I want to, Eva." (My brother and I had the strange habit of calling our parents by their first names.) We went back and forth for a few seconds before she gave in, reluctantly leading the officers to our kitchen table.

I answered their questions while one of them scribbled notes on a small pad. After they left, my mother told me that was the last we'd ever hear from the Chicago Police about my flute.

But a month later, the police called. They'd arrested three boys trying to sell some stolen musical instruments at a pawnshop. They fit the description that I'd given. My flute was long gone, but the police wanted to know if I'd be willing to come to the station to look at a lineup.

My mother didn't want any trouble, but I was adamant, and a short while later we were in our old Buick Century on the way to the police station.

When we arrived, a young officer led us through a series of dirty hallways to a small, darkened room with a plate glass window looking onto an adjoining room. The policeman explained that we could see the young men on the other side, but they couldn't see us. "Are any of these boys the ones who stole your flute?" the officer asked.

All three were there, standing with several other kids. One of them was even wearing the same short-sleeved red sweater he'd had on that day.

"Those are them," I said, pointing at each.

"Are you sure?"

"Yes, completely." I would never forget their faces.

"Good," he said, turning toward my mother. "Ma'am, we'd like your son to testify against these individuals."

"Absolutely not," she said.

I tugged on her elbow. "No. I *do* want to." These kids had done something wrong, and I thought they should pay a price.

Two months later, we drove to the Cook County Juvenile Court, a brand-new building off Roosevelt Road, across the street from Chicago's FBI field office. The hearing was in a large modern courtroom. The only people there were the three kids, their mothers, the judge, a public defender, the assistant district attorney, and me and my mother.

The three kids behaved like they didn't have a worry in the world. They were horsing around, and even after the judge began, they continued to whisper and giggle under their breath. However, when the prosecutor asked me to identify them, the joking stopped, and they all glared at me.

They had no real defense. After I explained what had happened, the judge found all three guilty of robbery. But instead of sending them to juvenile detention, the judge gave them each suspended sentences, meaning they wouldn't serve any time behind bars.

I never got my flute back, and the whole incident kind of turned me off music.

But it did turn me on to something completely different: law enforcement.

From that moment, I became obsessed with everything and anything having to do with the police.

On my daily walk to school I passed a Greek diner called the Agora, on 57th Street. I noticed that it always had Chicago Police cruisers parked out front. I often wondered what they were doing in there.

One day, I mustered the courage to go inside and see for myself. I asked the cashier if I could use the bathroom. She said yes. As I approached the toilets, I spotted two groups of police officers sitting together drinking coffee and looking at sheets of paper showing pictures of terrifying-looking men and women.

On the way back from the bathroom, drying my hands on the front of my pants, I tried to steal another glance at the policemen's papers. Who were the people in the photos?

When I got home, I scoured my room for loose change, and the next day, on the way home from school, I stopped at the Agora again. This time, I sat at a table next to the policemen, ordered a root beer, and glanced furtively at the sheets of paper.

I was not very smooth. A heavyset middle-aged cop caught me and said sternly, "Hey, you can't be looking at these. This is classified."

I stared into my root beer and took a long sip.

The officers erupted in laughter. A different one said, "Come over here, kid." I was sure I was in trouble.

But instead he said, "Don't listen to that guy. He's just joking. You want to take a look?"

I nodded timidly. He showed me something he called that day's "rap sheet." One side had license plate numbers of recently stolen cars. The other had mugshots and descriptions of fugitives the Chicago Police were pursuing, along with the crimes they'd allegedly committed. On that day, the rap sheet had two people wanted for murder, one for rape, and two for aggravated assault.

I didn't know what all that meant exactly, but it sounded dangerous. Exciting, too. Every picture was a window into a terrible story I wanted to know more about.

The friendly officer could see I was interested. "You want it?" he asked. I nodded. "It's yours. Come back tomorrow if you want more."

And so I did. I collected another rap sheet. And another and another. By June of that year I had more than a hundred. I was so enthusiastic that one of the officers asked if I wanted to join something called the Chicago Junior Police Patrol.

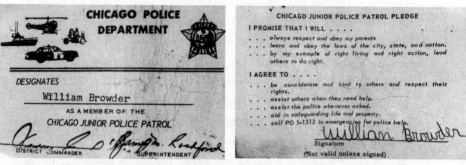

Chicago Junior Police Patrol membership card. (© BILL BROWDER)

Without knowing what it was, I exclaimed, "Yes!"

The following school year, every Thursday afternoon, I would join other kids from the Chicago area for lectures about crime, policing, and careers in law enforcement.

As with other childhood obsessions, my interest fizzled, and, in time, I grew up.

Little did I know that, later on, law enforcement would become a central part of my life.

3

John Moscow

1989–2008

Fourteen years later, I graduated from Stanford Business School. It was 1989, the same year the Berlin Wall came down. Three years after that, I joined the East European desk of the US investment bank Salomon Brothers in London. The opportunities were so great in that part of the world that, in 1996, I moved to Moscow to set up a hedge fund called the Hermitage Fund. I named it after the Hermitage Museum in St. Petersburg, where Russia keeps its most precious art treasures.

Running the fund wasn't smooth sailing. The companies we invested in were being robbed blind by Russian oligarchs and corrupt officials.

My compatriots in the financial markets blandly accepted this as the cost of doing business in Russia, and nobody said a thing. But I couldn't accept that a small group of people could steal virtually everything from everybody and get away with it. It felt like my flute, only on a much grander scale.

I decided to fight back. Instead of just focusing on companies' income statements and balance sheets like normal fund managers, my team and I would research how money was being stolen, how the thieves were doing the stealing, and who pocketed the stolen money. We would then use this information to file lawsuits, launch proxy fights, and brief government ministers on the damage this was doing to their country.

This activism had some impact, but our most effective weapon was to air this dirty laundry with the international media.

I didn't have to put a complete stop to the stealing, I just needed to create enough pressure for marginal change. The share prices of the companies were so undervalued that any improvement would push up their valuations dramatically.

This naming-and-shaming approach turned out to be remarkably profitable, and the Hermitage Fund became one of the best performing funds in the world. At the height of my career, I was responsible for $4.5 billion invested in Russian equities.

But, of course, exposing corrupt oligarchs didn't make me very popular in Russia. And in time, my actions led to a cascade of disastrous consequences.

In November 2005, Putin declared me a threat to national security and expelled me from Russia. In order to protect my clients' assets, my team liquidated the fund's holdings in Russia. I also evacuated my team and their families, including our chief operating officer, Ivan Cherkasov, and our head of research, Vadim Kleiner, to London. This evacuation turned out to be prescient.

Eighteen months later, our office in Moscow was raided by dozens of officers from the Russian Interior Ministry, led by one Lt. Col. Artem Kuznetsov. At the same time, the Interior Ministry also raided my lawyers' office in Moscow. The items they seized included the seals and certificates for our investment holding companies, which proved our ownership. (The seals were mechanical devices used to make embossed impressions on paperwork—you couldn't do any company business without them.) These were then passed to Maj. Pavel Karpov, also at the Interior Ministry. While these items were in his custody, they were used to fraudulently re-register the ownership of our investment holding companies to a group of violent ex-convicts.

Because we'd liquidated our assets, these holding companies were empty, so their theft wasn't a major financial blow. I might have left it at that, but the Russian authorities had opened a criminal case against my colleague Ivan Cherkasov as a pretext for the raids. If Ivan had still lived in Russia, this case would have been disastrous for him. He would surely have been arrested and detained. However, even if he was

Ivan Cherkasov.
(© HERMITAGE)

safe in London, we still had to defend him, or it would come back to bite him.

To do so, we hired a team of Russian defense lawyers. Working together, they quickly found evidence proving that the case against Ivan had been fabricated.

In the process, though, our lawyers made a shocking discovery. The people who had stolen our holding companies had also forged documents to claim those companies owed $1 billion to three empty shell companies. The shell companies then sued our stolen companies in three separate Russian courts for that fictitious $1 billion. Lawyers working for the criminals represented both plaintiffs and defendants, who pleaded guilty. Corrupt judges then approved the fraudulent claims with no questions asked in five-minute hearings.

We didn't know what they would do with these fraudulent claims, but because corrupt police officers were involved in this case, we hoped that once we reported them to Russian law enforcement, they and their criminal partners would be arrested and prosecuted, and the case against Ivan would be closed.

In early December 2007, we filed three separate criminal complaints in Russia, naming the officers involved in the fraud, including Kuznetsov and Karpov. However, instead of launching a real investigation, the Interior Ministry assigned Karpov to the case, effectively to investigate himself. His first "investigative action" was to initiate a criminal case against *me*. He subsequently placed me on Russia's domestic wanted list.

The more our lawyers dug, the worse things got. In June 2008, one of them, Sergei Magnitsky, discovered that the criminals had used our stolen companies and their fake claims to apply for a fraudulent $230 million tax refund. This was the same amount of taxes our companies paid in 2006 after liquidating our holdings in Russia. The refund request was approved in one day, on Christmas Eve 2007, and paid out two days later. A large portion was wired to an obscure Russian bank called Universal Savings Bank. Altogether, it was the largest tax refund in Russian history.

Universal Savings Bank was owned by a shadowy figure named Dmitry Klyuev, and could hardly even be called a bank. It was ranked as the 920th "largest" in Russia, with only one branch and total capital of $1.5 million. It was more like a shell company specializing in money laundering than a legitimate financial institution.

Our lawyers filed new complaints, hoping for a different response. Maybe the Russian government didn't care about a foreigner getting ripped off, but certainly they would be offended by the theft of their country's own money. Instead, there was just more retaliation.

The criminals dispatched two of their associates to London, who went to the DHL office in Lambeth, a neighborhood just across the Thames from Westminster. From there, they sent documents that had been used in the fraud to one of our Russian lawyers in Moscow. They put "Hermitage Capital Management, 2 Golden Square, London, England" as the return address on the package. The goal was to make it appear as if we had sent the fraudulent documents from our office in London to our lawyers in Moscow.

Almost as soon as the package was delivered, the Interior Ministry arrived at our lawyer's office in Moscow and "seized" the documents.

Afterward, our lawyers were summoned for interrogation by the Interior Ministry. The picture was now crystallizing. Our adversaries were going to frame us for the theft of the $230 million, and our lawyers were on the front line. Two of our lawyers quickly fled Russia for London under cover of night, but one stayed—Sergei Magnitsky. We begged him to leave as well, but he wouldn't. He believed Russia was changing for the better and that the rule of law would ultimately protect him.

If he was going to stay and fight, he needed reinforcements.

The world is full of defense lawyers, but what we needed was an attack lawyer. As I searched, four separate people gave me the same name: John Moscow. I laughed every time I heard it.

John Moscow had served at the New York District Attorney's Office for 33 years and was one of their most aggressive prosecutors, having led fights against domestic corruption and international financial crime. He was renowned for being the lead prosecutor against the Bank of Credit and Commerce International, which was at the center of one of the largest money laundering scandals in history. He also led the prosecution against executives at Tyco, a US conglomerate whose CEO and CFO were found guilty of stealing hundreds of millions of corporate funds from the company. In the mid-2000s, John Moscow went into private practice, eventually joining the New York office of the prestigious international law firm BakerHostetler.

I reached out to BakerHostetler in September 2008 to set up a call with John Moscow. His secretary told me that, coincidentally, he was in the UK attending something called the Cambridge Crime Conference. She offered to have him visit us while he was in England.

The man who arrived in our office a few days later didn't look like the vicious crime fighter everyone talked about. He was below-average height, with gray hair and a lazy eye. His demeanor could only be described as awkward.

I tried to make small talk, but he either didn't want to or didn't know how. It was only when I handed him a thick PowerPoint presentation showing the chronology of the fraud that he became animated and started asking questions.

John Moscow.
(© /BLOOMBERG/GETTY IMAGES)

"This Lieutenant Colonel Kuznetsov," he said, his finger resting on a picture of the man who'd led the raid on our offices. "We need to prove what happened in the raid, what he took, and where that stuff showed up afterwards."

"That's no problem," I said. "They actually left an inventory of what they seized."

He smiled. "Is that an official document?"

"It is." Russia is fastidiously bureaucratic. They keep track of everything.

"That's helpful." He flipped through a few more pages of our presentation. "Now, these seals and certificates—"

"Yes, those were used to re-register the companies' ownership."

"If this thing ever goes to trial in the US, you'll need someone who knows Russian law to describe how these corporate seals work. Anyone come to mind?"

I liked the way this guy was thinking. The thought of a trial in America was a lot more than I'd even considered when I first called him.

"I'm sure Sergei Magnitsky would testify," I said. "He's one of the smartest lawyers in Russia."

"Good. The key to any successful prosecution is the quality of the evidence and the credibility of the witnesses."

"Does it bother you that we'd be going up against some really dangerous people?" I asked.

"Bill, I've spent a lot of time locking up bad guys. This is what I do."

I now understood where his reputation came from.

I definitely wanted him on our side.

– 4 –

Footprints in the Snow

SUMMER 2008–FALL 2009

On October 2, the Russian Interior Ministry opened criminal cases against the two Hermitage lawyers who'd fled to London. They were each charged with using false powers of attorney for filing criminal complaints about the theft of our companies. They were told that it was illegal for them to represent our companies, since those companies no longer belonged to us. The Interior Ministry was effectively saying that the only person who had the right to report a stolen car was the person who stole it.

This cynicism so offended Sergei that, five days later, and in spite of the obvious danger, he went to the Russian State Investigative Committee (Russia's version of the FBI) to lay all the facts on the table. In an effort to exonerate his colleagues, he testified that the same criminal group that stole our companies had also stolen the $230 million.*

After his testimony, Sergei made another jaw-dropping discovery. He found documents showing that one year before the $230 million crime, the same criminal group had stolen $107 million of taxes from the Russian Treasury, which had been paid by a different company. If we could show that a similar crime had been committed by the same criminal group a year earlier—a crime that had absolutely nothing to

---

* This was his second trip to the State Investigative Committee. During his first, in June 2008, he testified against Karpov and Kuznetsov for their role in the theft of Hermitage's investment holding companies, mentioning the two Interior Ministry officers by name 27 times.

do with us—then it would make it extremely difficult for them to frame us for the $230 million crime. We needed to make this information public as soon as possible.

I called the Moscow bureau chief of *BusinessWeek*, an Englishman named Jason Bush. I knew him from the Hermitage days, when he'd worked on corruption exposés at companies like Gazprom.

Jason was intrigued and spent several weeks investigating the story. The more he dug, the more shocking it became. The criminal group had sent billions of rubles to shell companies with derelict apartments as their listed addresses. Those companies were often dissolved as soon as the money was transferred out of them.

Before publishing, Jason wanted to speak to the person who had uncovered the scam, so he arranged to meet Sergei in person.

In mid-October, Jason gathered his documents and went to Sergei's office. Over tea, Jason laid out the files and placed a recorder on the table.

"I'm sorry," Sergei said, "but I'd prefer if you didn't record this. I can't be on the record."

Jason slipped the recorder back into his jacket pocket. "Understood."

"I'm a bit scared, to be honest," Sergei said, almost apologetically.

"Of course, of course." Jason turned to the work at hand. "Can we begin by looking at these statements, then?"

"Yes."

They spent the next half hour sifting through the documents. When they got to the ones showing the $107 million tax refund, Jason asked, "Is there any innocent explanation for this?"

"I've looked for one," Sergei said, "but sadly, the most sinister explanation seems to be the only one."

"So this is another tax rebate fraud, just like with Hermitage?"

"Yes."

There *was* no other explanation. The paper trail was definitive. The same criminal group had used the same bank, the same lawyers, the same tax office, the same courts, and the same technique to steal $107 million from the Russian Treasury a year earlier. They had even used some of the same documents, just changing dates and company names.

Jason's article came out a month later. It created a whole new set of problems for our adversaries. They were now at risk of being exposed not just for the $230 million, but for a separate $107 million fraud as well.

Sixteen days after publication, the Interior Ministry raided Sergei's home, arresting him in front of his wife, Natasha, and seven-year-old son, Nikita. Lt. Col. Artem Kuznetsov, the same officer who'd led the raid on our office and whom Sergei had testified against, was assigned to carry out Sergei's arrest.

Up until then, our problems with the Russians had been virtual. But now they had a real-life hostage.

One of my first calls was to John Moscow.

He was sympathetic, but understood the criminal mindset better than most. "They'll use him as a bargaining chip," he said. "Does he have a wife? Does he have kids?"

"Yeah, we're going to support them with lawyers and whatever we need to do."

"You're not planning on going back there ever, are you?"

"No. Of course not."

"Okay, because we're going to be saying things about these people which will make you less than socially acceptable."

"Yeah," I said.

He then laid out his strategy. "I want to know who got the money. Do you remember *Jerry Maguire*? The movie? 'Show me the money.'"

"But the problem is the money got sent from one bank to another to another," I said. "How're we going to get all the way through the trail?"

"Because if it's in dollars, it's in New York."

He explained that we could trace these dollars by using something called a 1782 subpoena. I'd never heard of it, but it sounded promising. His idea was to take advantage of a little-known feature of the international banking system: whenever money is transferred in dollars—even between two banks in Russia—it touches a US clearing bank for a fraction of a second, leaving a permanent record. Those clearing banks are headquartered in Manhattan and under the jurisdiction of US courts.

If we subpoenaed those banks and got their records, we could use that information to begin to reconstruct the money trail.

"We're just going to do it step by step," he said confidently.

"Right."

"The good news is the money is big enough so it should be traceable. One million these days could be delivered in cash, and there you're just out of luck in terms of evidence."

"But this is two hundred and thirty million, so there's—"

"Yeah," he said, cutting me off. "Harder to walk across a field of snow with two hundred and thirty million dollars and not leave a footprint."

His approach was shrewd. If we could find out who had received the money, we'd have leverage to get Sergei out of jail.

But then, on December 11, Bernie Madoff was charged in New York with running the world's largest Ponzi scheme, defrauding investors in his hedge fund of an astonishing $64.8 billion. Why mention Madoff here? Because this scandal was oddly connected to our story.

It was right around this time that John Moscow became almost impossible to reach. I would call him, and sometimes it would take weeks for him to respond. Other times he simply never called back.

At first, I was confused. We've all had friends who've stopped speaking to us for unknown reasons, but John Moscow wasn't a friend. He was my lawyer and I was his client, and I was paying him $600 an hour. My confusion quickly grew into frustration since we needed him. *Sergei* needed him. When he continued to ignore my calls, my frustration grew to outright anger. It was one of the strangest things I'd ever seen a lawyer do. It was like being ghosted by a teenage crush.

Sometime in January, it all became clear. John Moscow's law firm, BakerHostetler, had become the trustee responsible for unwinding the Madoff bankruptcy. The rumor was that BakerHostetler was going to earn $100 million for this work. (At the time of writing, BakerHosteler has actually earned upward of $1.4 *billion* for its work on the Madoff bankruptcy.) Next to that, our paltry $200,000 in legal fees wasn't even a rounding error.

Lawyers, unlike businesspeople, are supposed to be professionals. I had naïvely assumed that once hired, a lawyer, like a doctor, was duty-bound to advocate for their client no matter what. A doctor doesn't drop a patient because another patient might pay them more for a more elaborate procedure. They treat both patients. The same should be true for lawyers.

What made his conduct even worse was that by the late spring of 2009, we were getting bits and pieces of news that Sergei was being tortured in detention. Sergei's jailers put him in cells with 14 inmates and eight beds and kept the lights on 24 hours a day to impose sleep deprivation. They put him in cells with no heat and no windowpanes in the winter in Moscow, where he nearly froze to death. They put him in cells with no toilet, just a hole in the floor, where the sewage would bubble up.

His hostage-takers seemed to have two objectives. One was to compel him to drop his testimony against Kuznetsov and Karpov. The other was to force him to sign a false confession saying that *he* had stolen the $230 million and had done so at my direction.

Sergei was a white-collar lawyer who wore a blue suit and a red tie during the week and enjoyed classical music at the conservatory with his wife and son on the weekend. His torturers surely thought that even the slightest amount of pressure would cause him to buckle. But they misjudged him. For Sergei, the idea of perjuring himself and bearing false witness was more painful than any physical torture they subjected him to. He refused to break.

The torture did affect him, though. After seven months, his health had seriously deteriorated. He'd lost nearly 40 pounds and was suffering from excruciating stomach pains.

We were getting more and more desperate. We had to get him out of jail. We did everything we could think of. We contacted the International Bar Association, the UK Law Society, the Parliamentary Assembly of the Council of Europe, and many other organizations. Many intervened on Sergei's behalf, but as far as the Russians were concerned this was just noise they could easily ignore. I'd never felt more powerless in my life.

We *needed* to find that $230 million.

Before John Moscow ghosted us, he had prepared the 1782 subpoena to be served on the two clearing banks that had performed the dollar payments of the tax rebate fraud: JPMorgan and Citibank. It was time to submit them to the court.

We hired a new law firm to file the subpoenas. By then, Sergei had become seriously ill. He had been diagnosed with pancreatitis and gallstones, and needed an operation, which was scheduled for August 1, 2009.

One week before his operation, his hostage-takers returned to his cell and again tried to coerce him into signing a false confession. Again, he refused. In retaliation, they moved him from a pretrial detention center with a medical wing to a maximum-security jail called Butyrka—a hellhole considered to be one of the worst in Russia. Most significantly for Sergei, Butyrka had no proper medical facilities. There, his health completely broke down. He went into constant, agonizing pain, and was refused all medical treatment.

Our new US lawyers filed the subpoenas with the court on July 28, and the judge quickly granted them.

Two weeks later, as Sergei languished at Butyrka, JPMorgan and Citibank sent us their responses. We were hopeful, but soon realized their responses were horribly incomplete. Both banks had missed entire categories of information and skipped over key time periods, making it impossible for us to get any closer to discovering who had actually received any of the stolen money.

Our lawyers went back to the banks, demanding they do the job properly, but this would take time, and Sergei was running out of time.

We had one last reason to hold on to hope, though. Under Russian law, a person could only be kept in pretrial detention for one year. After 365 days, the Russian government either had to put the defendant on trial or release them. But in Sergei's case, they couldn't risk a trial. If they did, he would have had an international platform to expose the $230 million fraud, the $107 million fraud before it, and all the Russian government officials involved. The court could find him guilty— and it would—but that wouldn't silence him.

They *had* to silence him.

On the night of November 16, 2009, 358 days after his arrest, Sergei went into critical condition. The Butyrka authorities didn't want to have responsibility for him anymore, so they put him in an ambulance and transferred him to a different detention center across town, which had a medical wing. But when he arrived there, instead of putting him in the emergency room, they put him in an isolation cell, chained him to a bed, and eight riot guards with rubber batons beat Sergei until he was dead.

He was only 37 years old.

– 5 –

The Roadmap

FALL 2008–SPRING 2010

I got the call at 7:45 a.m. the next morning.

That call remains the most heartbreaking, traumatic, and devastating moment of my life. Nothing had prepared me for losing a colleague in this way. Sergei had been killed because he had tried to do the right thing. He'd been killed because he'd worked for me. The guilt I felt and continue to feel permeates every cell of my body.

When I was able to clear my mind from the fog of hysteria and sorrow, there was only one thing for me to do—put aside everything else in my life and devote all of my time, all of my resources, and all of my energy to making sure that anyone involved in Sergei's false arrest, torture, and murder, as well as anyone who had received any of the $230 million, would face justice.

Since then, that is precisely what I've done.

After Sergei's murder, we peppered every law enforcement agency in Russia with criminal complaints demanding justice. We had a mountain of evidence. In the 358 days that Sergei was held in custody, he and his lawyers wrote 450 complaints documenting his abuse and mistreatment. His lawyers had provided us with copies of these, and put together, they constituted the most well-documented case of human rights abuse that had come out of Russia in the previous 35 years. The Russians would *have* to do something.

Only they didn't. Instead, the entire system closed ranks and the Russian authorities embarked on a full-scale cover-up. Less than 24 hours after Sergei's murder, the Interior Ministry changed the cause of death from "toxic shock" to "heart failure." The government then refused his family's request for an independent autopsy and denied that Sergei had ever been sick. These lies, along with many others, were repeated from the lowest official right up to the top of the Russian government.

We soon received more details on the cover-up. Two weeks after Sergei's murder, one of Russia's top investigative journalists, Yevgenia Albats, the senior editor of the *New Times Magazine*, reported that a $6 million cash bribe had been paid to officials at the FSB, the successor agency to the Soviet KGB, to arrest Sergei and cover up the $230 million fraud.

Sergei had been murdered for money, plain and simple. We needed to go back to JPMorgan and Citibank and get them to come clean. This wasn't just dirty money anymore, it was blood money.

This time the banks took us seriously and sent us every single dollar payment for dozens of banks in Russia and the former Soviet Union over a 28-month period. It was a windfall. In all, we received a database with over 1.3 million transactions from multiple Russian banks.

Initially, we thought this would be the key to unlocking the money laundering mystery, but when we started looking at it, we realized it was actually *too much* information. We had tens of thousands of company names, account numbers, and amounts, but absolutely no context.

Without some sort of roadmap linking this data to the $230 million fraud, we were lost.

We pivoted. Without a sophisticated way to determine who had received the dirty money, we focused on the most visible perpetrators in Russia: Maj. Pavel Karpov, Lt. Col. Artem Kuznetsov, and Dmitry Klyuev, the owner of Universal Savings Bank, where a lot of the money had been wired following the crime.

We no longer had a money laundering expert like John Moscow on our team, but that didn't mean we were neophytes when it came to financial sleuthing, especially in Russia. Forensic research had been a large part of our business model at the Hermitage Fund, and it didn't feel like a big leap to apply it here.

Aside from our experience, we had two other assets working in our

Vadim Kleiner.
(© HERMITAGE)

favor: my colleague Vadim Kleiner, and the fact that, in Russia, data protection is virtually nonexistent.

Vadim had been an equity analyst at the Hermitage Fund since its inception. He was a Muscovite, six years my junior, with an economics PhD, glasses, and a dark beard. If you spotted him at a cocktail party or conference, you'd probably tag him as an academic or journalist. But Vadim was a top investment analyst, and because of the way we did business, over time he had morphed into one of the world's best forensic financial investigators. This is not hyperbole. Anyone who has ever met Vadim would confirm it. He's a true genius.

Luckily for Vadim, there was a bounty of information for him to work with. While many think of Russia as being completely opaque, it's actually quite transparent. Every time someone does something in Russia, that information gets filed in quadruplicate with four different ministries. The people working at those ministries make only a few hundred dollars a month. As a result, nearly everything is for sale.

Most of this data ends up at the physical epicenter of Russia's information market, a low-end shopping mall just west of the Moskva

Gorbushka Market, Moscow. (© HERMITAGE)

River called Gorbushka. Inside is a chaotic hodgepodge of kiosks selling everything from pirated *Fast and Furious* DVDs to *Star Wars* figures to Chinese cell phones. But if you go into the back of some of these stalls, you'll find disks of government databases for sale. They contain things like salary information, cell phone registries, and travel records, and the most you have to pay for any of these is a few dollars.

At the higher end of the information market were specialized brokers who had nothing to do with Gorbushka. They sold more sophisticated databases like those belonging to the Russian Central Bank or the State Customs Committee. Back when I was running the Hermitage Fund, Vadim and I used these sources to ferret out multibillion-dollar scams at the companies we invested in. Now that we were conducting a money laundering investigation, these resources became invaluable in a completely different way.

Dmitry Klyuev, the owner of Universal Savings Bank, was initially elusive. But the Interior Ministry officers, Pavel Karpov and Artem

Kuznetsov, were not. Shortly after the $230 million was
went on un-self-conscious spending sprees. They bough
Mercedes, and Audis for themselves and their family me
took 5-star holidays to places like Milan, Madrid, London,
They also lived in multimillion-dollar condominiums in Mosc ...ey
seemed totally unconcerned that their $15,000-a-year salaries couldn't
have supported these lavish lifestyles. They were caricatures of corrupt
Russian cops.

We made a pair of YouTube videos about Karpov and Kuznetsov,
in both English and Russian, which went viral right away, especially
in Russia.

In addition to the outrage created among ordinary Russians, these
exposés provided us with an unexpected windfall: a Russian whistleblower named Alexander Perepilichnyy.

Perepilichnyy was a financial advisor, and two of his clients had
been Olga Stepanova, the tax official who had approved the bulk of the
$230 million refund, as well as her husband, Vladlen. Perepilichnyy had
helped the Stepanovs set up and manage their Swiss bank accounts. In
the 2008–2009 financial crisis, his investment advice led to big losses.
Instead of accepting these, the Stepanovs accused Perepilichnyy of
stealing their money. They then threatened him with criminal investi-

Alexander Perepilichnyy.

gations in Russia. To avoid this trouble, he'd fled to London with his family.

As the Stepanovs' financial advisor, Perepilichnyy had evidence showing that $11 million from the $230 million crime had gone to Vladlen Stepanov's account at Credit Suisse in Zurich. Perepilichnyy wanted to share this evidence with us not because he was shocked by their corruption, but because he hoped that by publicizing this information, it might create such a scandal in Russia that the Stepanovs would be prosecuted, lose their power, and make the legal threats against Perepilichnyy disappear.

Perepilichnyy showed us the bank statements for two shell companies containing the $11 million at Credit Suisse. With these, we finally had the beginnings of a roadmap to orient ourselves in the clearing bank data.

When Vadim ran these company names through this database, both popped up. These each led to another shell company. And another, and another. Vadim was ultimately able to trace the path of this $11 million from the Russian Treasury, to Universal Savings Bank, through Moldova and Latvia, and into Switzerland.

As John Moscow had promised, every dollar transfer touched New York for a split second. And even though that money went through 11 different steps, our database picked it up.

If our adversaries thought they'd obscured their footprints in the snow by laundering the money through so many countries and accounts, they were wrong. We'd discovered the power of our dollar payment database, and this wouldn't be the last time we would use it.

6

The Finrosforum

SPRING–SUMMER 2010

Money laundering is typically regarded as a victimless and faceless crime. But in this case, we had a victim, Sergei, and we had the smug, smiling faces of the police officers who'd profited from the crime that Sergei had exposed and was killed over.

When people picture Russian police officers, they envision men in outdated uniforms driving Soviet-era Lada police cars. But that wasn't the case with Maj. Karpov and Lt. Col. Kuznetsov.

They didn't wear uniforms, preferring designer Italian suits and expensive Swiss watches. Karpov was especially blatant. On VKontakte, Russia's version of Facebook, he posted pictures of the parties he attended and the vacations he took in the months after the crime.

Pavel Karpov (left) and friends at a party.
(© TOCHKA.NET)

His arrogance was galling. It was almost as if he was taunting us.

Anyone who watched our YouTube videos wanted to wipe the smug smiles off their faces. One way to do this was to make sure that they and their corrupt colleagues couldn't use their ill-gotten gains to go on fancy foreign holidays or keep their money in Western banks. This idea slowly evolved into a legislative proposal called the Magnitsky Act, which would ban visas and freeze assets of Russian human rights violators, including those who had tortured and killed Sergei.

This idea got immediate traction in Washington when Sen. Ben Cardin, a Maryland Democrat, took it on as one of his top legislative priorities. It would soon have broad bipartisan support, with Senators John McCain, Roger Wicker, and Joe Lieberman coming on board as original cosponsors.

The support for the Magnitsky Act in the United States was gratifying, but corrupt Russian officials spend the majority of their time and money in Europe, enjoying luxury vacations in places like Courchevel, Marbella, and Sardinia. They send their kids to boarding schools in Switzerland, their wives to spas on the Côte d'Azur, and their girlfriends to fashion shows in Milan.

To really hit these people where it hurt, we needed a European Magnitsky Act as well.

Europe was different political terrain than the United States, though. The European Union had 28 member states (this was before Brexit) and was dotted with pockets of support for Putin throughout.

To try to get the Europeans on board, I started at the European Parliament, a legislative body roughly equivalent to the US Congress but that had nearly twice as many lawmakers.

There were so many of them that I wasn't sure where to start, but I quickly found one promising lead: a Finnish member of the European Parliament (MEP) from the Green Party named Heidi Hautala. Heidi was chair of the human rights subcommittee and a well-known advocate for victims of the Putin regime. She had a reputation for attending opposition rallies in Moscow, where protestors were routinely beaten and arrested. She seemed like a brave person and a good prospective ally.

In late May 2010, I went to Brussels to meet Heidi. It was my first visit to the European Parliament, a maze-like warren that felt as confusing as Europe itself. There were modern buildings connected to older ones, escalators and elevators and stairways in every configuration, and the MEPs' offices had an arcane numbering system making them almost impossible to find. It was a little like stepping into a parliament designed by M. C. Escher.

When I finally found Heidi's small office, I was greeted by a 40-something woman with short blond hair and a severe, businesslike manner. (I quickly learned that the Finns pronounced her name "Hay-dee" not "Hi-dee.")

I sat opposite her desk, told Sergei's story, and explained the Magnitsky Act. When I mentioned the momentum building in the United States, she said, "I think this is a wonderful idea. It should be in Europe as well."

"Agreed. Can you help me?"

"I can, but this is a complicated place." She waved her hand to indicate the European Parliament. "To get anything going around here, you're going to need some Russians on your side. Good Russians. Ideally some famous human rights activists."

She was probably too polite to say it, but having an American-born British former hedge fund manager fronting a human rights campaign against corrupt Russian officials would definitely rub some people in Brussels the wrong way. Europe is an intensely egalitarian place where success in business is often frowned upon. In Germany, private equity funds are often referred to as *heuschrecke*—which translates to "locust."

"I'm sorry, but I don't know any human rights activists," I told her.

"That's okay. I do. Come to Helsinki and I'll introduce you."

That July, Heidi was hosting a conference called the Finrosforum at a cultural retreat near Helsinki, bringing together all the great and good from the Russian opposition and human rights community. "Would you like to come and present the Magnitsky Act there?" she asked.

I nodded. "Yes."

I was excited, but also a bit scared of traveling to Finland, which shares an 833-mile border with Russia. This proximity guaranteed there were always a lot of Russians milling about Helsinki.

But I wasn't going to miss this opportunity out of fear. I hired three bodyguards, and along with Vadim, we traveled to Helsinki on July 20, 2010. This was the first time since the early 2000s, during my fights with the Russian oligarchs, that I'd relied on bodyguards.

As soon as we arrived at the conference, I felt out of place. Vadim and I were the only ones wearing suits, and no one else had three large men shadowing them. I looked like an oligarch, which was the exact type of person these activists were fighting against. I'm sure some of them hated me from the moment I walked in. If I'd been them, I probably would have hated me, too.

When I found Heidi among a small group, she greeted me warmly. She introduced me to Russian dissidents, opposition figures, and sundry bloggers, journalists, and NGO representatives.

None of them knew what to make of me and they kept me at arm's length—except for one: a Russian documentary filmmaker named Andrei Nekrasov, a youthful intellectual in his early 50s with a wild mop of gray hair. Andrei was Heidi's boyfriend and was there with a small film crew to document the conference. He told me that he'd recently made a film about the assassination of Alexander Litvinenko, the former FSB agent who had been fatally poisoned with radioactive polonium in central London. Since he had all of his equipment, he asked if he could interview me about what had happened to Sergei. I happily agreed.

Before my speech the next day, I sat with Andrei in a light-filled atrium for a lengthy conversation. His questions were thorough. He touched on every aspect of Sergei's murder, and was outraged by everything the Russian government had done to him, as well as their subsequent cover-up.

Andrei thought this interview could be the basis for a new film and asked if I'd sit for more interviews. He also asked if I could put him in touch with Sergei's widow and mother. My answer to all of this was an emphatic "Yes."

Even if my upcoming speech went nowhere, this chance meeting with Andrei had made the entire trip worthwhile.

After lunch, I went to a large, wood-paneled auditorium and sat at the presenters' table. The room was packed and humming, with an audience made up of people speaking Russian, English, and Finnish. Despite the cool reception I'd received the day before, as soon as Heidi introduced me, everyone quieted down.

The Russians there were familiar with Sergei's story, but not with me. I explained my relationship to Sergei, and when I presented the idea of the Magnitsky Act, the room started buzzing.

The Russian men and women there had experienced every version of human rights abuse, oppression, and injustice that the Putin regime could throw at them. Their friends had disappeared, their families had been targeted, their livelihoods had been taken away, and many had seen the insides of Russian prisons themselves—mostly for the "crime" of speaking out against the regime. No matter how much they had protested, nothing ever changed.

But here I was, a strange hedge fund manager with an American accent, telling them that there might be a way to make Putin and his henchmen pay. Everybody in that room understood that the regime valued money more than human life, and that every corrupt Russian bureaucrat kept their money outside of Russia. They perceived how the Magnitsky Act could strike at the heart of the Putin regime. The best part was that the Kremlin would have no say in these sanctions.

Afterward, I was approached by a tanned 50-year-old man wearing a blue linen shirt and white trousers. He looked like he had just stepped off a sailboat in Capri. I'd never met this man, but I would have recognized him anywhere. He stuck out his hand. "Mr. Browder, my name is Boris Nemtsov."

I could hardly believe it.

Boris Nemtsov was a legend. He'd been deputy prime minister under President Yeltsin, and for a while was considered his potential successor. But after witnessing Putin's corruption and oppression, Boris had become one of the most outspoken critics of the regime. He had been arrested multiple times for organizing banned demonstrations, written reports highlighting Putin's illegitimate wealth, and refused to be bought off or intimidated.

Over the course of a lifetime, any of us might meet five or six people who are charismatic in every way. Boris was one such person.

"This Magnitsky Act of yours is genius," he said. "But how realistic is it?"

"I don't know. This is my first foray into human rights work. Heidi's told me I need voices from the Russian opposition to make it a reality."

"I could be one of those voices, Mr. Browder," he volunteered.

"Please, call me Bill."

He smiled. "Bill, we'll make sure these bastards never forget the name 'Sergei Magnitsky.'"

From that moment forward, Boris Nemtsov became my partner in getting justice for Sergei and advocating for the Magnitsky Act all over the world.

Boris Nemtsov.
(© EVGENIY FELDMAN/NOVAYA GAZETA)

7

The Cambridge Crime Conference

SUMMER–FALL 2010

Having Boris on board exponentially increased our chances of getting the Magnitsky Act passed, not just in the United States, but in Europe as well.

However, I knew that in the best case it would take years for the act to become law. In the meantime, we had something we could move on right away: the millions sitting in a Credit Suisse account in Zurich belonging to Vladlen Stepanov.

We didn't need a new human rights law to go after this money. These were the proceeds of crime, and there were existing money laundering laws on the books that could be used to freeze and seize it. If we could convince the Swiss authorities to take action, it would be a major blow to our Russian adversaries.

The question was how to get the Swiss involved.

Aside from my stint with the Chicago Junior Police Patrol, I had no experience with Western law enforcement—but inexperience had never stopped me before. Back when I started the Hermitage Fund, I didn't know a single person in Russia, didn't speak the language, and had never run an investment fund. I'd overcome these obstacles by diving headfirst into unknown waters. I cold-called business school classmates, read obscure trade journals, attended conferences, and took every opportunity I could to learn about investing in Russia.

Of course, dealing with Western law enforcement was different. Whereas there were practically no rules for investing in Russia after the fall of Communism, law enforcement in the West is built on hundreds of years of rules, traditions, and procedures. Even so, I resolved to take the same approach and see what happened.

I started by looking into conferences I could attend. The only one I'd ever heard of was the Cambridge Crime Conference, which was the event John Moscow had attended in 2008 before coming to our offices.

I Googled it. Its full name was the Cambridge International Symposium on Economic Crime. That sounded perfect. It was held every year in early September on the campus of Jesus College at Cambridge University, less than an hour by train from London.

I downloaded the program. Hundreds of law enforcement officials would be there. Better yet, on the second day, a Swiss federal prosecutor who specialized in money laundering and economic crimes would be giving a keynote address.

I decided to go and try to buttonhole this Swiss prosecutor.

I signed up, paid the fee, and on September 5, 2010, took the train from King's Cross in London to Cambridge. I checked into the Double-Tree next to the university, threw my bag in my room, and picked up my credentials at the opening reception. I slung my nametag over my head and scanned the crowd. The room was full of people drinking, laughing, and shouting to one another as if they were long-lost friends. I hadn't imagined a law enforcement conference could be so festive.

I looked for officials from Switzerland, but it was almost impossible to find anyone specific, so I just moved through the crowd scanning nametags, trying to strike up conversations.

It was a challenge. Everyone there seemed to know each other. My badge read "Hermitage Capital Management," which meant absolutely nothing to them.

As I waited in line at the bar, I noticed that the badge of the woman behind me identified her as a Caribbean financial regulator. That was a long way from Switzerland, but since many shell companies used in money laundering are registered in the Caribbean, knowing her might be useful.

I introduced myself and explained why I was there. She nodded politely. After picking up her drink, she shot a look over my shoulder at someone she actually wanted to talk to and interrupted me midsentence. "Nice to meet you, Mr. Browder," she said, and walked away.

Diet Coke in hand, I wandered around some more, failing to make headway with anyone. Eventually, somewhere in a far corner, a gong rang out. The crowd moved toward the dining hall for dinner. As I entered, it reminded me of reading Harry Potter with my kids—the room was a long, wood-paneled chamber with soaring ceilings and walls covered with oil portraits going back to the 16th century. The meal was open seating, and groups of friends and colleagues formed at different tables.

As I searched for an empty seat, a friendly-looking man smiled and indicated I could sit next to him. I leaned in to read his badge. "Attorney General, Autonomous City of Buenos Aires." We had a nice meal, but there was nothing an Argentinian prosecutor could do to help me.

Dinner was followed by coffee and dessert and another round of mingling, but I was still afflicted by the same awkwardness, and there was still no sign of the Swiss prosecutor. I wasn't worried, though. I knew I'd find him at his keynote address.

The next morning, I silently prepared my elevator pitch over breakfast and then made my way to one of the tents on the college green to attend his lecture. I can't remember what it was about. It was one of the most boring speeches I'd ever heard, but everyone else seemed to like it. I supposed this was their world, not mine.

After he finished, I stood next to the podium and waited for other people to ask their questions. When he and I were the only ones left, I introduced myself.

He clearly didn't want to talk to me, but I'd cornered him. I launched into the story, and finished by talking about the $11 million at Credit Suisse. "Do you think Swiss law enforcement might be interested in opening a case?" I asked.

He responded brusquely, "I appreciate your situation"—he paused to read my badge—"Mr. Browder. But if you have a complaint, then file it with the Office of the Attorney General in Bern." He then walked off.

We didn't even exchange cards. In retrospect, it was naïve to think I could show up as a random person at this conference and get a Swiss criminal investigation launched. This was a conference about the law, and more than anything, prosecutors abide by the rules.

I wandered outside, berating myself for coming to Cambridge in the first place. But as I strolled across the Jesus College campus making plans to return to London, I saw an unexpected, but familiar, face.

John Moscow.

Of course he would be here. This was his domain, and these were his people.

I spotted him before he spotted me. I was still furious at him for abandoning us and Sergei, but there was no way I could avoid him. I was pretty sure he would ignore me, but when we made eye contact he blurted out, "Bill! What're you doing here?" He extended his hand as if nothing had ever happened.

I held down my anger and shook his hand. "I'm trying to meet people who might be helpful on the Magnitsky case."

"I might know a few," he said. It was the last thing I'd expected. Whatever his reasons for making nice, he was a giant in this world, and it would be foolish of me to hold a grudge.

The morning session ended as we chatted. The tents emptied and the lawn filled with lawyers. John looked around and spotted someone, indicating I should follow. We walked up to a man roughly my age wearing what looked like a government-issue blue suit, white shirt, and red tie—obviously American.

John said, "Adam, I want you to meet Bill Browder." I shook the man's hand. "Bill, this is Adam Kaufmann. He's at the DA's Office in New York, where I used to work."

As we spoke, people gravitated toward the dining hall for lunch. Adam invited us to join him.

We found seats in the same grand room as the night before, put our jackets on a trio of chairs, and went to the buffet. The lunch looked barely edible—some college-dorm version of beef Wellington alongside steamed peas, sausage rolls, and overcooked pasta. But I didn't care.

I tried to tell Adam the story over lunch, but we were constantly interrupted by a stream of fellow attendees. Apparently, a lot of other people wanted to talk to him as well. Sensing my frustration, he offered to have a proper meeting in London at the end of the week. I agreed.

I wasn't going to make any more headway in Cambridge, so I left after lunch.

That Friday, back in London, Adam came to our offices on Golden Square. I briefed him on the $230 million fraud and Sergei's murder, and showed him what we'd found in Switzerland.

"If you ever find a connection to New York, I'd be interested," he said.

I had to contain my excitement. As John Moscow had told me at the very beginning, we *had* a New York connection—all the dollar payments that passed through JPMorgan and Citibank, even if they'd only touched New York for a split second.

But when I mentioned these, Adam shook his head. "I'm afraid that's a little too tenuous. But if you find money in accounts in New York, or if anyone bought property there, we'd have a real New York nexus. Then we could do something."

If a New York nexus existed, we were going to find it.

8

Blame the Dead

FALL 2010

It was a warm, late summer evening in Moscow in September 2008. There was nothing remarkable about it. A 57-year-old Russian man, with a hangdog expression and a push-broom mustache, was driven in a chauffeured Mercedes from the city center to a tall, partially built apartment building near Moscow State University. The Mercedes belonged to a close friend of Dmitry Klyuev, the owner of Universal Savings Bank.

The man was met at the construction site by a real estate agent. The two donned orange hard hats and trudged up 17 flights of stairs to the penthouse.

The inside of the building was bare, and not much more than exposed cinder blocks and concrete. There were no windows, no doors, and no railings on the balconies. The details of what transpired there are unknown, but shortly after arriving, the man plummeted 17 stories to the ground, landing in the mud in a twisted, broken heap. The chauffeur, who'd remained with the car, told the police that he hadn't seen the fall. Neither did the real estate agent. The police declared the man's death an unfortunate accident. The man's name was Semyon Korobeinikov.

Six months earlier, a different Russian man had gone to the train station in Bryansk, Russia, a town near the Ukrainian border, to meet four colleagues. All were associates of Dmitry Klyuev, and all were ex-convicts, having served time in Russian prisons for crimes ranging from manslaughter to aggravated assault to larceny. They boarded a train bound for Kyiv and spent several weeks there. In April, the man's four colleagues returned to Russia, but he didn't. He was pronounced dead in Boryspol near Kyiv Airport on April 30. His death certificate cited cirrhosis as the cause. His name was Valery Kurochkin. He was 43 years old.

In 2007, a year before the incident at the apartment building, a third man, a former musician and an out-of-work security guard from Baku, Azerbaijan, who spent his days drinking vodka in the courtyard behind his Moscow apartment, died at his home on October 1. The cause of death was recorded as heart failure. This man's name was Oktai Gasanov. He was 53.

What did these three untimely and seemingly unrelated deaths have to do with us? A lot, according to the Russian authorities.

On November 15, 2010, a day before the first anniversary of Sergei's murder, as I sat in my London office reflecting on all that had happened, Vadim walked in. I was lost in thought and barely noticed him. "Bill?" he said.

I snapped out of it. "What?"

"The Russian government just officially blamed Sergei for stealing the two hundred and thirty million."

Vadim showed me a transcript of an Interior Ministry press conference that had just taken place that morning in Moscow, along with an article from *Kommersant*, a Russian newspaper.

Taken together, these laid out an elaborate conspiracy theory. According to the Russian government, Sergei had prepared the documents used in the illegal tax refund. The government then claimed that Sergei gave these documents to the drunk, Oktai Gasanov, who passed them to their co-conspirators. One of these was the ex-convict, Valery Kurochkin, who signed one of the fraudulent tax refund requests and submitted it to the Russian tax authorities. Once the money was paid, the man who later would fall to his death, Semyon Korobeinikov, used a bank which the Interior Ministry claimed belonged to him to launder the money. That bank was Universal Savings Bank, which we knew in fact belonged to Dmitry Klyuev. There was no mention of Klyuev in the press conference transcript or the *Kommersant* piece.

"Who are all these guys?" I asked.

"I don't know," Vadim said. "But they have one thing in common—they're all dead."

"Fuck! So these guys were killed?"

"No idea, they could have died of natural causes for all we know. But one thing's certain. None of them can defend themselves in court or explain what's really going on."

"We need to look into this Klyuev person," I said.

"I'm ahead of you," Vadim said. "I've already started."

Vadim was brilliant, but disorganized. Nobody at the office wanted to sit next to him. His desk was like a hurricane that scattered papers not only across his workstation but any place nearby. A week after he began his Klyuev deep-dive, I noticed his area was even messier than usual, with several large stacks of interleaved documents in Russian.

"What's all this?" I asked offhandedly.

"This is the Mikhailovsky GOK case file."

"What's Mikhailovsky GOK?"

"A Russian iron ore company. This isn't the first time the Interior Ministry got Klyuev out of a bind. In 2006 he was caught using his Universal Savings Bank to try to steal one-point-six *billion* dollars of shares of Mikhailovsky GOK from a Russian oligarch."

"I can't imagine the oligarch was too happy about that," I said.

"He wasn't. He got a criminal case opened against Klyuev. But guess who the Interior Ministry put on it?"

"No idea."

Vadim grabbed a DVD, came around to my desk, and popped it into my computer. It was a video of a TV report on the Mikhailovsky GOK investigation he'd found online. He paused on a scene showing three young men hunkered over a pile of binders and paperwork. Vadim pointed to the man in the middle. "Recognize him?"

I leaned closer. The man was looking down and I could only make out the top of his head, but his haircut was unmistakable. "That's Karpov!" This was the same high-spending Interior Ministry officer involved in the $230 million fraud.

"Yep. And check this out."

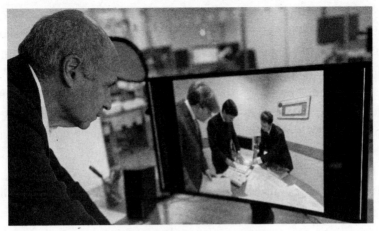

Pavel Karpov (center on screen).
(© HERMITAGE)

Vadim laid out two spreadsheets—travel records for Klyuev and Karpov. He pointed at two items highlighted in yellow. "They flew together to Larnaca, Cyprus, at the same time Karpov was supposedly investigating Klyuev."

"I'm shocked." I wasn't.

Vadim laid out another stack of papers—the court verdict for the case against Klyuev. "Klyuev was found guilty, but he got a suspended sentence. No jail time."

"So nobody went down?"

"No, two guys went down. Klyuev's driver, and some kind of administrative assistant.'"

"Were they actually involved?"

"Who knows? Both died before the trial. One was thirty-nine and the other was forty-six."

"Let me guess. 'Heart failure'?"

"Yep."

This sent a shiver down my spine. Klyuev's modus operandi was to commit crimes and blame those crimes on the dead. We'll never know exactly how these people came to die, and it was entirely possible that each had died of natural causes, but that didn't make Klyuev and his criminal group any less terrifying.

Vadim kept digging. He soon learned that Klyuev had served in the Soviet special forces in Afghanistan as a reconnaissance scout in the late 1980s, and in the late 1990s his name popped up in a police report where he was accused of assault and robbery. A few years later, he showed up in another police report, where he and his wife narrowly escaped an assassination attempt in the parking lot of the Starlite Diner, a 24-hour Moscow eatery popular with expats and well-off Muscovites.

Despite this profile, Vadim could only unearth one picture of Klyuev—an old snapshot showing an unremarkable, even affable-looking, bullet-headed man in his mid-40s.

Dmitry Klyuev.

The trail ended there, so Vadim called one of his most reliable sources in Moscow, a man we called Aslan. He worked at the FSB, but had become embroiled in a feud with some of the same Russian officials who were persecuting us. Aslan often shared information with Vadim. He didn't do this out of the goodness of his heart, but out of Machiavellian necessity. Nearly everything he gave us checked out.

Vadim called Aslan, but as soon as he mentioned the name "Klyuev" there was a long silence on the other end of the line.

Eventually, Aslan asked, "Why do you want to know about him?"

"He seems to be at the center of everything," Vadim said. "Who is this guy?"

"You should understand, just talking about him is dangerous," Aslan said quietly. "He's a big mafia boss. He drives around in an armored Mercedes Brabus, surrounded by three other cars. A heavily armed entourage accompanies him wherever he goes."

"How does he get the Interior Ministry to cover for him?"

"They practically work for him, Vadim. I've heard that uniformed officers line up and salute him whenever he visits, as if he's some kind of general."

Aslan finished with an ominous warning: "They're coming for Browder and the rest of you. I've already told too much. Be careful, Vadim. Be very careful."

9

The Swiss Complaint

WINTER–SPRING 2011

We took Aslan's warning seriously. We knew for sure they were going to blame us for their crimes; we feared that they would attempt to kill us too. I didn't know how to stop mobsters from trying to kill us, and that weighed heavily on me, but I was confident that if the Swiss successfully prosecuted the Stepanovs, the Russians could no longer credibly blame us for their crimes. This might also reduce the incentive to kill us. It wasn't much, but it was all we had.

By early 2011, we had produced a complaint that we were now ready to file with the Swiss authorities. But before sending it to a PO box in Bern and blindly hoping that someone there would read and act on it, I was going to make one last-ditch effort to find someone influential in Switzerland who might be able to help.

I would have that opportunity at the World Economic Forum in Davos at the end of January.

I'd attended Davos every year since 1996, and on January 25, I flew from London to Zurich to make the familiar three-hour train ride up into the Alps. When I arrived in Davos, I found the streets piled high with snow. The Swiss military was out in force, manning barricades and posting rooftop snipers to protect the international VIPs descending on this otherwise sleepy mountain town.

I checked into the Hotel Concordia, a modest 3-star hotel near the conference center that charged an immodest 500 Swiss francs (about $520) a night for a cramped single with a shower. Even so,

I was thrilled. The really unlucky Davos attendees get shunted into hotels in Klosters, the next town down the valley, and a 30-minute drive away.

The official motto of the World Economic Forum is "Committed to Improving the State of the World," but in reality, many attendees are billionaires, dictators, and Fortune 500 executives who have little interest in improving the state of the world. A few are interested in exactly the opposite.

To justify their noble mission, the World Economic Forum regularly invites a handful of people who *do* take their motto to heart. In 2011, one of these was a Swiss criminologist named Mark Pieth. In the early 1990s, he was at the Swiss Ministry of Justice, in charge of the fight against economic and organized crime. Since then, he'd become a professor at the University of Basel and one of the world's foremost experts on money laundering.

Every Davos attendee fills their schedule with meetings to justify the $50,000 entry price. It was almost impossible to get appointments with the likes of Bill Gates or Richard Branson. But not everyone at Davos wanted to meet a money laundering expert—in fact, a lot of attendees probably preferred to avoid Mark Pieth like the plague.

The day after I arrived, I was scheduled to meet Mark at the Meierhof, an old-world Swiss chalet-style hotel just down the Promenade from the conference center. When I got there, he was finishing a meeting with a man I recognized as the CEO of Total, the French oil company which at that time was plagued by corruption allegations. The CEO appeared completely at ease, but must have had some serious enemies, because he was flanked by two large bodyguards in leather jackets.

As soon as Mark was finished, I greeted him and we looked for a table as far away from the Total crew as possible. They weren't Russians, but I still didn't want them to overhear what Mark and I were about to discuss.

We found a quiet table in a corner of the hotel restaurant and ordered breakfast. Mark was in his late 50s with swept-back graying hair and a thin, boyish grin. After introducing myself and explaining the whole Magnitsky affair, which he was only vaguely familiar with, I took out the draft of our criminal complaint and slid it across the table.

I let him thumb through it for a minute, and then directed him to the flowchart showing the money traveling from Universal Savings Bank, through Moldova and Latvia, and into accounts at Credit Suisse. When he saw this, his eyes lit up.

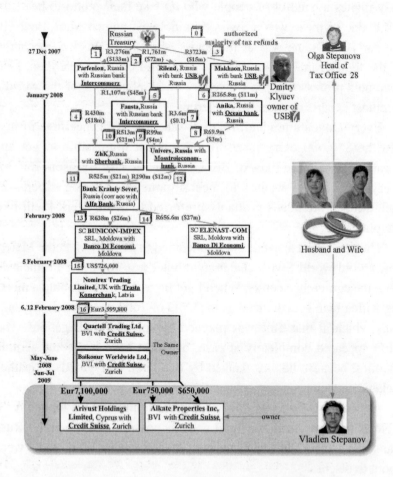

Money flow from the Russian Treasury to the Stepanovs.

(© HERMITAGE)

"Can you substantiate all of this?" he asked.

"Yes. Hundred percent."

"Where does the data come from? I assume Russian law enforcement didn't provide this to you."

"We have a whistleblower who's given us the Credit Suisse statements, and the dollar payments come from a New York subpoena."

"This is impressive work, Mr. Browder."

"Thank you. Most of the credit belongs to my colleague, Vadim Kleiner. I'm planning to file this in Bern, but it would make a big difference if someone like you could represent us and file it on our behalf. Would you consider that?"

He placed his elbows on the table and leaned forward. "Let me read it carefully and think it over. This is just the kind of thing I've spent years fighting. If it's valid, I might very well be interested."

I had a full schedule of other meetings in Davos over the next few days, but this was the main one I cared about. I hoped he would say yes.

After Davos, I traveled to the United States for meetings in Washington and New York to follow up on the Magnitsky Act, which was gaining traction in Congress. While in New York, I got a call from an unknown number with a Swiss country code. I answered. The connection was full of cracks and pops, and I could barely understand the person on the other end. I was about to hang up when I finally heard a man say, "Bill? Bill? It's Mark Pieth. Can you hear me?" The line went clear.

"Mark! What's going on?"

"Sorry for the interference—I'm in the car. I read everything over. It's very compelling. So compelling in fact that I'm ready to join your cause."

"You are?" If I could have hugged him through the phone, I would have.

"With your permission, I'd like to file it right away."

Of course, I agreed. The next day, he called me back and said, "The bomb's been dropped. Let's see where it explodes."

Mark's involvement was a boon, but it still didn't guarantee the

Swiss would act. In general, prosecutors open cases that they're al-most certain to win. Although the evidence was irrefutable, the Swiss knew that any case involving Russians was sure to be excruciating. The Russians are notoriously uncooperative, they throw up constant smoke screens, and they lie at every turn.

I needed to do whatever I could to make it impossible for the Swiss to bury this case. So I decided to get the press involved.

After John Moscow's conciliatory gesture at the Cambridge Crime Conference, he'd introduced me to an old friend of his, a *Barron's* reporter named Bill Alpert, whom he described as one of the best in-vestigative reporters in New York. Bill's day job was as a market re-porter covering health care and technology stocks, but he also wrote long-form, hard-hitting investigative pieces exposing corruption and malfeasance.

Before returning to London, I arranged to meet Bill for lunch in the lobby lounge on the 35th floor of New York's Mandarin Oriental Hotel, overlooking Central Park. As soon as he walked into the restaurant, zipped into a worn blue parka and wearing old sneakers, I realized he might not have been comfortable in such a swanky place.

"You Bill?" he asked as he approached the table.

"I am. Are you?"

He snickered. "Guilty."

He was completely unbothered by the setting. Between his appear-ance and his nonchalance, he reminded me of a modern-day Detective Columbo. I liked him immediately.

We made small talk, and soon realized we shared more than a first name—we were both related to famous Communists. My grandfather, Earl Browder, had been the general secretary of the American Com-munist Party from 1932 to 1945; and Bill's distant cousin, Maxim Litvinov, had been Stalin's foreign minister in the lead-up to World War II (Litvinov was eventually replaced by Vyacheslav Molotov, of cocktail fame). Somehow Bill and I both ended up as far from Com-munism as we could get—Bill as a Wall Street reporter, and me as a Moscow hedge fund manager.

Before becoming a reporter, Bill trained as a lawyer—he'd gradu-

Barron's reporter Bill Alpert. (© BILL ALPERT)

ated from Columbia Law School in the '80s—and one of his hobbies was poring over legal documents in search of corporate scandals. His bosses at *Barron's* weren't particularly enthusiastic about his investigative pet projects, but so long as he filed his regular stock market stories on time, they let him pursue them.

As we ate, I walked him through the Swiss complaint. His reaction was similar to Mark Pieth's, even if he came at it from a different angle. Bill saw it as a huge scoop. It had everything—murder, Swiss bank accounts, whistleblowers, corrupt Russian officials, and a Kremlin-led cover-up.

He told me he definitely wanted to work on it.

However, when I returned to London and our lawyers learned about my meeting with Bill, they were emphatic that I put the brakes on the story. They reasoned that publicizing the complaint would anger and alienate the Swiss prosecutors, who, in response, could sit on it interminably, or even reject it outright.

I talked to Bill about this, and he agreed that holding off until the Swiss made a decision was the right call.

After that, I waited for the response from Bern. That's the hardest part about filing criminal complaints. Weeks went by with no news. I called Mark in mid-March to ask if he knew when we might hear anything, but he replied, "Bill, you just have to be patient. These people work at a different pace than we do."

But then, on March 22, 2011, something did happen—just not in Switzerland. In Moscow, the Russians named a new actor in the $230 million tax fraud. It was another ex-convict—a burglar named Vyacheslav Khlebnikov—but this one was alive.

The Interior Ministry claimed that Khlebnikov was one of the principal organizers of the fraud. In mafia terms, he was a "stand-up guy," someone who would willingly take the fall for his and his associates' crimes. In addition to pleading guilty to being a central figure in the theft of the $230 million, he "verified" that Sergei and the three other dead men had assisted him in committing the crime.

The Interior Ministry buttressed this "confession" with a sprawling case file, trying to make the whole thing appear legitimate; but this file was squirreled away at the Tverskoy District Court in Moscow, where we couldn't access it.

Khlebnikov was found guilty solely on the basis of his confession and sentenced to five years in a penal colony (the minimum possible sentence) with no fine or requirement to reveal the money's whereabouts. The authorities concluded that Olga Stepanova and several other tax officials who had authorized the illegal refund had been "tricked" and were, in fact, victims of the crime. The authorities conveniently ignored the fact that after the fraud, Olga's husband had received $11 million at Credit Suisse in Zurich from the tax refund she'd authorized. They also ignored the Stepanovs' $28 million prize-winning mansion outside of Moscow that was registered under the name of Vladlen's pensioner mother; and their $3 million vacation villa in Dubai. (All of this on a combined annual income of just over $38,000.)

Nor was there any reference to the earlier $107 million tax rebate fraud, which Stepanova had also approved. For everyone involved, it was as if this had never happened.

I thought, *To hell with it. These guys can't keep adjusting their cover-up with no fight-back. We're not going to wait for the Swiss.*

I discussed it with Bill, and on April 16, 2011, *Barron's* published

The Stepanovs' Moscow mansion.
(© ANDREI MAKHONIN)

"Crime and Punishment in Putin's Russia." It was a 2,800-word exposé describing the money laundering trail and how some of it had ended up at Credit Suisse, showing pictures of the Stepanovs' "country home" outside Moscow, describing Klyuev's involvement, and ending with a challenge to the Swiss to take all of this seriously.

A week later, on April 23, the Swiss announced that they had done exactly that. They froze the $11 million the Stepanovs held at Credit Suisse. This was the first freezing order in the Magnitsky case.

It would not be the last.

– 10 –

Alexander Perepilichnyy

SUMMER 2011–SPRING 2012

After opening the case, the Swiss prosecutor, Maria-Antonella Bino, summoned me to testify in Lausanne.

Switzerland is renowned for its neutrality. That may sound nice, but often it's not. Yes, the Swiss bring together warring countries to sign peace treaties, and Switzerland serves as headquarters for multilateral organizations like the World Health Organization and the UN Human Rights Office, but they also abuse their "neutrality" to support some of the world's most heinous dictators. Rarely a year goes by when you don't hear about a scandal involving some African potentate or Central Asian kleptocrat hiding hundreds of millions of dollars in Swiss banks. The Swiss almost take pride in the fact that they welcome everyone—good or bad, it doesn't matter so long as the country continues to accrue the economic benefits.

I was worried this kind of Swiss neutrality might come into play with us. Fortunately, after Bill Alpert's story, the Swiss media became interested in our case. When SRF, the Swiss national broadcasting company, heard I was coming to Lausanne, they sent a reporter to interview me there.

On May 16, I flew to Geneva and took the train to Lausanne. The one-hour trip skirts the edge of Lac Léman, with the snowcapped Alps rising in the distance. I'd never been to Lausanne. The town was picture-postcard Switzerland—winding streets, old buildings with tiled roofs, frequent church steeples, and medieval-looking towers dotting the skyline, all with the lake never far away.

The next day, I went to the prosecutor's office, which was not as charming as the surrounding town. In fact, it was the opposite of charming—a five-story utilitarian office block that looked like it had been built in the 1970s, with shops on the ground floor and a parking lot out front.

The TV crew met me there, and we set up under an arcade to shoot a short segment. The reporter asked what I expected of the Swiss investigation and whether I would be bringing any new evidence. I kept it general, predicting this thread would eventually unravel the whole money laundering network used by the criminals who had stolen the $230 million.

As we wrapped up, a 40-something woman wearing a gray suit approached us. "Are you Mr. Browder?" she asked.

"Yes."

"I'm Prosecutor Bino," she stated. She glanced at the cameraman and reporter. "You're not allowed to film here." Her English was perfect.

"I'm sorry. We were just finishing up." I waved at the crew. "They're not coming inside."

She raised her eyebrows. "Please follow me."

We entered the building, I presented my passport at reception, and she led me to the elevator. As we rode up, standing shoulder to shoulder, she said, "These proceedings are confidential. I hope that's clear. Don't do that again."

I may have gotten off on the wrong foot with her, but I'd made my point. If the Swiss tried to stay neutral on this case, the world would know.

The hearing room was like a small courtroom, with Prosecutor Bino sitting on a dais and me sitting below her at a witness table. We were surrounded by clerks, a bailiff, and a translator. Under Swiss law, the whole procedure had to take place in one of their official languages—in this case, French. Prosecutor Bino conducted the interview in French, which was translated into English for me. I then answered in English, and the process was repeated in reverse. What should have taken at most an hour-and-a-half ended up taking five hours.

The substance of the hearing was unremarkable, consisting mostly of me rehashing the allegations in our complaint—with one notable exception. Prosecutor Bino wanted to know the identity of our Russian whistleblower.

As part of our arrangement with Alexander Perepilichnyy, we'd committed to keeping his identity confidential, so I didn't name him. I simply called him a "person" who'd contacted us. He'd taken a big risk in giving us his evidence, and I wasn't going to increase that risk any further.

Prosecutor Bino let it go, and the interview ended a short while later.

My caution surrounding Perepilichnyy turned out to be for naught. Our Russian adversaries had been keeping tabs on the Swiss proceedings, and on that same day in Moscow, Olga Stepanova's husband published a full-page paid ad in a Russian business daily that outed Perepilichnyy. "I'm confident Alexander Perepilichnyy played a role in my 'notoriety,'" he wrote, "since only he knew certain details and nobody else." Stepanov promised to "seek redress."

The next day, an SRF reporter confronted Russian president Dmitri Medvedev about our case at a press conference in Moscow. (Medvedev served as the Russian president from 2008 to 2012, while Putin served as prime minister. Of course, Putin retained all the power behind the scenes.) The reporter asked, "Mr. President . . . regarding the case of Hermitage Capital and Sergei Magnitsky. The Swiss Federal Prosecutor's Office is investigating the case at the request of Hermitage Capital, and it involves charges of tax fraud in Russia and possible laundering of those funds in Switzerland. Will Russia cooperate with Switzerland on this matter?"

Medvedev dodged the substance of the question, but said he was taking the case seriously and that he'd discussed it with the heads of the FSB and the Russian State Investigative Committee. But then he showed his true colors. "Things are not as simple as the media sometimes portrays," he said, "and we must find out the truth and identify the circle of persons involved both in Russia and in other countries." Translation: our cover-up will continue, and people like Bill Browder, his colleagues, and Alexander Perepilichnyy are included in this "circle of persons in other countries."

A few weeks later, Medvedev dispatched Russia's most senior law enforcement officer, General Prosecutor Yuri Chaika, to meet with the Swiss attorney general in an attempt to shut down the case. Chaika's office subsequently filed two mutual legal assistance requests (MLAs) with the Swiss, formally asking for access to the case file.*

I've seen the Russians make a lot of crazy moves, but to have Russia's president and most senior law enforcement officer now openly and directly involved in covering up organized criminal activity in Russia and abroad was truly amazing.

These interventions didn't seem to work, though. The Swiss did not shut down the case, nor did they share the file with the Russians at that juncture.

If the Russian authorities couldn't stop the Swiss case from going forward, their next best option was to stop Perepilichnyy.

To do so, the Russians promptly launched a new criminal case targeting him. Then, in early September, a man named Andrei Pavlov, the consigliere and personal lawyer to Dmitry Klyuev, started communicating with Perepilichnyy over Skype.

Pavlov suggested there might be a way to resolve Perepilichnyy's issues if the two men could meet in person. Since there was no way Perepilichnyy was going to return to Moscow, they agreed to meet at Zurich Airport.

Early on September 6, Perepilichnyy flew from London to Zurich. The two men had never met, so Perepilichnyy wore a bright orange jacket. He made sure he was beyond Immigration and safely on Swiss soil before Pavlov arrived. Although a kidnapping in broad daylight in the middle of Zurich Airport was highly unlikely, he wasn't going to leave it to chance. He found a Starbucks near check-in at Terminal 2 and waited.

Pavlov texted Perepilichnyy just before 8:30 a.m. He was adamant that they meet near the departure gates, but Perepilichnyy stood his ground. Pavlov ultimately relented, and they found each other about 20 minutes later. They sat and began their discussion.

---

* MLAs are based on international treaties and are intended to allow prosecutors and investigators access to evidence and information in criminal and civil cases. They are almost always honored.

Perepilichnyy's goal was to have the criminal cases against him in Russia closed. But the train he had set in motion by providing dirt on the Stepanovs had not had the desired effect, and in fact had backfired. The Stepanovs were as powerful as ever. That Pavlov was sitting across from him was proof of that. Perepilichnyy knew he had miscalculated, and was now ready to cooperate.

Pavlov's goal was to get Perepilichnyy to go on the record, asserting that the Stepanovs' money at Credit Suisse had not come from the tax rebate fraud, but from legitimate business activity. Pavlov probably hoped this would compromise the Swiss case, and he knew it would be helpful with the cover-up narrative in Russia. The implied quid pro quo was that if Perepilichnyy made a statement that exonerated the Stepanovs, his problems in Russia would disappear.

Perepilichnyy apparently agreed that he would sign such a statement, and the men went their separate ways.

By the time Perepilichnyy returned to London, however, he realized that Pavlov's proposal would get him into an even deeper mess. His problems in Russia might go away, but their agreement would create serious problems for him in Switzerland. If he claimed the Stepanovs *hadn't* benefitted from the $230 million crime, the Swiss would have to conclude that Perepilichnyy wasn't a sympathetic whistleblower but rather a tarnished co-conspirator. Perepilichnyy might then find himself with a Swiss criminal case targeting him, just like Stepanov. Perepilichnyy was in a bind. He faced a Russian prosecution if he didn't cooperate with Pavlov, or a Swiss prosecution if he did.

A short while later, Pavlov sent a statement to Perepilichnyy for him to sign. But when Perepilichnyy refused, Pavlov became agitated and insisted on another meeting, this time at Heathrow in London.

This meeting did not go well. About two weeks afterward, the Russian Interior Ministry summoned Perepilichnyy's brother-in-law in Moscow for interrogation.

Whatever they were trying to get out of the brother-in-law didn't work, either. On November 19, Pavlov messaged Perepilichnyy. "The interview went very badly," he wrote. "You shouldn't have done it this way. . . . There's a real possibility that if you don't show up for interrogation, they'll prepare a pro forma indictment against you so they can get you by detaining you at the border."

All of this weighed heavily on Perepilichnyy over the Christmas and New Year holidays, and in early January 2012, he contacted Vadim. They met at the Polo Bar at the Westbury Hotel and sat at a low table near the window.

Perepilichnyy—a stocky 43 years old with thick black hair—was usually upbeat with a good sense of humor, but that day he was twitchy and uneasy, constantly looking over his shoulder as they spoke. "What's going on?" Vadim asked.

Perepilichnyy set down his drink and let out a sigh. "I think someone wants me dead."

"How do you know?" Vadim asked.

"My family got a call from the anti-terrorism police in Moscow. They'd recently searched a hit man's house in another investigation, and found a file on me."

"A hit man?"

"Yeah. Some Chechen."

"How do you know this is even real? They've been trying to scare you for months."

"Because they had all kinds of details about me and my family and our lives in the UK. The only thing that gives me any comfort is that the home address they have for me is an old one."

"That doesn't sound very comforting," Vadim said.

Afterward, it emerged that the hit man was Valid Lurakhmaev, a well-known Chechen assassin who went by the street name of "Validol"—the Russian translation for Valium—a not-too-subtle play on the idea that he was good at calming his victims by killing them.

There wasn't much Perepilichnyy could do to protect himself, so he began researching large life insurance policies in the UK. At least his family would be taken care of if the worst were to happen.

Whatever his fears, they didn't prevent him from testifying. That spring, he made the same trip I had to Lausanne. On April 26, 2012, Perepilichnyy sat with Prosecutor Bino and gave a formal witness statement in the money laundering case targeting the Stepanovs.

The die was now cast.

– 11 –

The Honey Trap

SUMMER 2012

On July 4, 2012, I flew from London to Nice, in the South of France. As my British Airways flight banked over the Mediterranean, the red tile roofs of Nice in the distance, I was envious of the people around me—they wore shorts and sandals, smiles already on their faces, their vacations just beginning.

I was wearing a suit.

I was headed to the annual meeting of the Parliamentary Assembly of the Organization for Security and Cooperation in Europe (OSCE PA). The OSCE PA was made up of hundreds of parliamentarians from 57 countries who met regularly to discuss human rights, democracy, and security. That year, they were meeting in Monaco, a short drive from Nice. I was going because they would be voting on a resolution urging all OSCE member states to pass Magnitsky Acts in their home countries.

I'd been invited by the Parliamentary Assembly's secretary general, a gregarious Texan named Spencer Oliver. He thought it would be helpful for me to host a side event about the Magnitsky Act. Usually these side events are staid affairs where NGOs present policy papers, but I thought I would spice things up by presenting a short YouTube video we'd recently made about Dmitry Klyuev. It was in a similar style to the videos we'd made about Karpov and Kuznetsov, and this would be the film's international premiere.

No single person was more emblematic of the merger between Russian organized crime and the Russian government than Klyuev, which made him the perfect person to explain the necessity for a Magnitsky Act.

Politically, this event was a golden opportunity, but personally, I was not looking forward to visiting Monaco. Since 2008, I'd been on Russia's domestic wanted list. It was only a matter of time before they placed me on their international one as well. When that happened, I wouldn't find out about it until I was arrested at some border crossing. For this reason, whenever I crossed an international border, my heart always beat a little faster. This fear was particularly acute in Monaco.

Prince Albert, Monaco's head of state, was notoriously chummy with Vladimir Putin. He was the only foreigner on the 2007 Siberian hunting trip that produced the infamous picture of a shirtless Putin on horseback. Because of their friendship, Prince Albert enthusiastically supported the Russian president and occasionally did his bidding. I'd

Prince Albert (center, in hat),
and Vladimir Putin in Siberia, 2007.
(© DMITRY ASTAKHOV/AFP/GETTY IMAGES)

heard stories about Putin's enemies checking into Monaco hotels, presenting their passports, and finding themselves arrested within minutes by the local police.

I had a workaround, though. Since there's no border control between France and Monaco, I could stay on the French side without hitting any legal tripwires. I chose a hotel in Roquebrune-Cap-Martin, a French town only 15 minutes from Monte Carlo. It was still a bit risky for me to set foot in Monaco, but because I would be attending an international government symposium, I presumed it would be too scandalous to touch me at the actual event.

On the morning of July 5, I met my colleague Mark Sabah for breakfast at my hotel. Mark was an enthusiastic 35-year-old and my right-hand man for political lobbying in the justice campaign. He had an Arabic-sounding surname, but was actually Jewish, from North London. He'd worked on several British political campaigns before joining me.

Mark was practically made for lobbying. He was a natural extrovert who had no reservations about striking up a conversation with anyone. More often than not, people warmed to him quickly.

After breakfast we took a taxi to Monte Carlo's convention center, the Grimaldi Forum, a huge, glass-and-concrete structure sitting on a low bluff above the Mediterranean. The soaring entry hall was so blindingly bright that many of the people—Mark included, but not me—wore sunglasses inside.

We made our way to a large conference room deep in the building's interior, arriving 20 minutes early for our screening. People filed in as we checked the equipment, and by the time the lights were dimmed, the room was packed. There were easily 100 people in attendance, including roughly 50 members of parliament from more than a dozen countries.

The film began. I watched their faces as they absorbed the Klyuev story. It highlighted his criminal record, his miraculous avoidance of jail time in the Mikhailovsky GOK case, his coziness with the Interior Ministry and Maj. Karpov, and the fact that he and his associates were surrounded by dead men who'd conveniently been blamed for their crimes.

I was the first to speak after the movie finished. I made my pitch for the Magnitsky resolution, and concluded, "As you can see, there's now no difference between the Russian government and organized crime."

Following my comments, a string of MPs clamored for the microphone. There was universal support for the upcoming Magnitsky resolution, but a number of them thought I had gone too far in asserting that the Russian government was so thoroughly criminalized.

As the event ended, a Belgian MP invited us to a cocktail reception hosted by Monaco's prime minister at the Hotel Le Méridien that evening. We thanked him and told him we'd be there.

At around 6:00 p.m., Mark and I jumped in a taxi and went to Le Méridien. As we walked through the lobby, I noticed that nearly every person we passed spoke Russian. It was extremely unnerving.

The end of the lobby opened onto a sprawling, crescent-shaped swimming pool with little footbridges connecting walkways surrounded by cypress trees. The Mediterranean sparkled in the distance. As we scanned the crowd, we were approached by a friend of Mark's, an American OSCE staffer named Anna Chernova. "Why are all these Russians here?" Mark asked.

Anna responded in a whisper, "For most politicians, this is work. But for the Russians it's a holiday and the government pays for everything." Russia was also a member of the OSCE, along with other non-European countries like the United States and Canada, but they had sent an unusually large delegation.

Anna pointed at a group of overweight, middle-aged men perched at the bar. "Those are the Russia MPs." She nodded at a bunch of gaudy women wearing too much jewelry and high-end clothing milling around the buffet. "And those are the wives." Then she swung toward the far end of the pool, where there was a gaggle of bikini- and caftan-clad blondes, none of them older than 25. "And those are the mistresses. The kids are all up in their rooms on their iPads."

The whole scene was a caricature, and it was too much. I wanted to leave. But Mark pushed back. "There're a lot of important people here, Bill. This is a good opportunity."

Reluctantly, I agreed to stay.

Anna left us as Mark and I mingled through the crowd, drifting from one conversation to the next. Mark was in his element. As he chatted up people, I was overcome with hunger. It had been such a busy day that I hadn't had time for lunch.

I headed for the buffet. The government of Monaco had spared no expense—there were piles of fresh shrimp, crab legs, and trays brimming with French charcuterie. I joined the end of the line.

As I thumbed through my BlackBerry, I felt someone push into my back. I moved forward to make room, but then it happened again. I glanced out of the corner of my eye and realized it was a woman bumping into me. I turned to find a stunning, six-foot blonde with full red lips. She smelled like sandalwood. She wore a simple black cocktail dress and high heels. She smiled warmly. In English with a slight Russian accent she said, "Hello. I'm Svetlana. Are you here for the conference?"

"Yes I am. And you?"

"I live in Monaco and I'm volunteering at the OSCE. It's a very interesting event, don't you think?"

I nodded. The line inched forward. I grabbed a plate and a napkin rolled with silverware. Svetlana did the same and continued to make conversation. "I normally work in fashion. But I find politics to be so fascinating."

Given that earlier in the day I'd accused the Russian government of having merged with Russian organized crime, I wasn't too keen to engage further with any Russian, let alone a beautiful woman who "normally" worked in "fashion."

I reached the food and filled my plate, then shuffled off to a bar table to eat on my own.

When I went to get dessert, though, Svetlana sidled up to me again. This time she asked, "Are you speaking at the conference?"

"I am."

"What's your topic?"

"Human rights."

"Oh! Human rights are *very* interesting. Do you have a visit card?" She touched my arm with her fingertips and let them linger for a moment too long.

Just then, a pair of MPs who'd been at the screening approached and began peppering me with questions. Svetlana lingered among them. A few minutes later, both MPs asked for my contact details. I pulled out my business cards and passed them to the MPs. Svetlana held out her hand expectantly. I hesitated, but it would have been awkward not to give her a card as well, so I did.

Mark and Anna joined me, and the group dispersed, Svetlana slipping away. Mark asked, "Who's the hot blonde?"

"A Russian girl interested in fashion and human rights," I answered flatly. Mark smirked.

I was exhausted and didn't stay at the reception much longer. I took a cab back to my French hotel, leaving Mark to work the crowd. Once in my room, I checked my email. As I scrolled through the messages, a new one arrived. It was from one "Svetlana Melnikova."

"Dear Mr. Browder," it read, "I very much enjoyed meeting you earlier this evening. I thought we had a very strong connection. I was wondering if you'd like to meet for a drink at your hotel? Where are you staying?" She signed it, "Kisses, S."

Strong connection? We'd spent all of two minutes standing in line together, what was she talking about? I didn't respond.

An hour later, as I was getting into bed, another email arrived. "William, are you still awake? I am. I can't stop thinking about you. I'd really like to see you this evening. More kisses, S."

I had to laugh. I'm a five-foot-nine middle-aged bald man. Six-foot, busty blond models don't throw themselves at me. This couldn't have been a more blatant honey trap.

But as I lay in the dark, my mind spun. Our adversaries were actively framing us for their crimes in Russia. I was a wanted criminal there. Alexander Perepilichnyy was a known target of a Chechen assassin. And now here I was at a conference in Monaco getting hit with a honey trap. Sure, it was ham-fisted and clumsy, but it meant that I had been standing next to an FSB operative that very night.

The honey trap hadn't worked, but the Russians knew I was in Monaco. As I tried to sleep, I realized I couldn't go back there.

At first light, I grabbed my things, stuffed them into my bag, and went down to the hotel lobby to order a taxi.

The night manager offered the cab waiting outside, but I refused.

"Please call a new one." He didn't understand why I was being so fussy, and I didn't explain. He did as I asked.

A few minutes later, a black Mercedes pulled up. I got in and instructed the driver to go to Menton, a French town in the opposite direction from Nice Airport. The good thing about being up so early was that there was nobody on the road, so it would be clear if someone was following us.

I kept looking out the back window as we headed toward Menton. There was nobody on our tail, so I told the driver to turn around and head back in the direction of Nice.

I called Mark, waking him. I told him what had happened with Svetlana and my fear that the FSB knew our whereabouts. I told him to meet me at the British Airways desk at Nice Airport. "It's not safe here. We've already shown our film. We can do the rest from London."

"Bill, you're way overreacting. They're not targeting me. And I won't go with any Russian girls—promise. Let me finish what we came here to do." I gave in.

I returned to London alone, and for the next couple of days, Mark systematically worked his way through the European delegations, making our case for the Magnitsky resolution and encountering few headwinds.

But then, on the day of the vote, Mark got a call from a man named Neil Simon, the press officer for Spencer Oliver, the secretary general of the Parliamentary Assembly. Neil had previously worked on the Magnitsky Act in the US Senate, and knew Mark well.

Just as Mark answered his phone, Neil blurted, "You won't fucking believe this. Dmitry Klyuev and Andrei Pavlov are meeting with Spencer in his office right now!"

"*What?*" Mark choked.

"Klyuev is here with Spencer and—"

"Doing what?"

"He's trying to convince Spencer to take the Magnitsky resolution off the agenda."

"Dmitry Klyuev? *Our* Dmitry Klyuev?"

"Yes!"

Mark was speechless.

Dmitri Klyuev (left) and Andrei Pavlov in Spencer Oliver's
office in Monaco, July 2012. (© HERMITAGE)

The Russian FSB had a lot of things in their tool kit, but to dispatch
a major organized crime boss to personally lobby the head of an international political organization? That was a new one.

Mark asked Neil to send him a picture. Within seconds, a photo
popped up on Mark's phone showing Klyuev and Pavlov sitting on a
couch in Spencer Oliver's makeshift office at the Grimaldi Forum. It
was the best picture Mark or any of us had ever seen of Klyuev.

Mark called Neil back and said, "We need more!" If we could get
more images of Klyuev—or even better, a video—we could use them
to help bring Dmitry Klyuev to life.

Neil hedged. "It's too risky. I'll get fired."

Mark ran over to the Forum's press center, desperately looking for
anybody who could help. The lounge was empty, except for a Georgian
TV crew drinking coffee. Mark jogged over to them and stopped short
in front of the female correspondent, Ketevan Kardava, whom Mark
knew. "Ketevan, I need your camera!"

The cameraman, who looked more like a rugby player than a technician, gruffly asked, "Why would I give you my camera?"

"You guys were at our film the other day, right?"

"We were," the cameraman replied.

"Dmitry Klyuev is *here*."

"What?"

"He's here. The star of our film. Right now. Meeting with Spencer Oliver!"

The Georgians looked at one another in disbelief. "No way," Ketevan said. Mark scrolled though his phone and held out Neil's picture at arm's length.

Her eyes widened. The crew spoke among themselves in Georgian for a few seconds and then Ketevan said, "Let's go." (Russia had invaded Georgia in 2008, and the emotional and physical wounds were still fresh—there was no love lost between Georgians and Russians.)

Mark and the Georgians rushed to the escalators in the Forum's main lobby. They set up and waited. Within a few minutes, Dmitry Klyuev, Andrei Pavlov, and two members of the Russian Foreign Ministry emerged in the hall. Klyuev and Pavlov wore official OSCE badges around their necks. These had been provided to them by the Russian delegation, even though neither of the men had any official position in the Russian government.

The Georgians started filming. Klyuev tried to ignore them. He slouched slightly and looped his badge's lanyard over his head, then stuffed the badge in his pocket. He glanced around nervously, stepped onto the escalator, and went upstairs toward the exits.

Dmitri Klyuev accompanied by a member of the Russian delegation, at the OSCE PA in Monaco, July 2012. (© KETEVAN KARDAVA / GEORGIAN TV)

The Georgians only got about a minute of video, but that was all we needed.

After Klyuev had left the building, the crew went back to the press center, downloaded the footage, and sent a link to Mark.

Klyuev's unexpected presence in Monaco was almost too good to be true. There was no way that Spencer Oliver would have agreed to meet with Dmitry Klyuev unless the Russian government had formally asked Spencer to take the meeting. All of this proved our point: the Klyuev Organized Crime Group and the Russian government were one and the same.

With only hours before the vote, Mark swiftly made the rounds, showing the Klyuev clip to MPs throughout the Assembly.

Any of the doubts aired at our screening had now evaporated. When the Assembly convened, the vote on the Magnitsky resolution wasn't even close. It passed 291–18. The only delegations to vote against it were from Russia, Belarus, and Kazakhstan.

The Russians had spectacularly overplayed their hand. In fact, they had done our job much better than we ever could have done it ourselves. Not only had they failed to stop the Magnitsky resolution, but their actions cemented their defeat. Moreover, we'd succeeded in forcing Dmitry Klyuev out of the shadows.

Mark came home triumphant, but then the news got even better. Based on the reporting coming out of Monaco, Swiss law enforcement had taken it upon themselves to freeze Klyuev's Swiss bank accounts.

This was the second freezing order in the Magnitsky case. It too would not be the last.

The Moldovan File

SUMMER 2012

Right after Monaco, as I was getting ready for work in London one morning, Bill Alpert called. I hadn't heard from him in a while.

"I've found something in New York!" he exclaimed.

Since his story about the Swiss accounts, he'd become obsessed with the Magnitsky case. As he searched for more sources and pulled at threads, he'd gained access to a database containing all the wire transfers for a bank called Banca di Economii, located in Moldova, a tiny former Soviet republic wedged between Ukraine and Romania.

The database had been obtained by a newly formed NGO called the Organized Crime and Corruption Reporting Project (OCCRP). They were a loose confederation of investigative journalists focusing on corruption in Eastern Europe and Russia. It was run on a shoestring from head offices in Sarajevo and Bucharest. When I first heard of them, they'd sounded more like a front for money launderers than an anticorruption organization, but it turned out they were the real thing.

The OCCRP had a man in Chisinau, the Moldovan capital, who had succeeded in obtaining a police file containing Banca di Economii's wire transfer database, which the OCCRP then shared with Bill Alpert and us.

This file was a crucial discovery. On our end, Vadim had previously only been able to trace the money up to the Russian border, with two exceptions: the $11 million that had ended up in Switzerland; and a much larger $55 million chunk that had gone to two Moldovan companies with accounts at Banca di Economii. After that, the trail had gone cold.

When Vadim searched the Moldovan file, though, he could see where this money went afterward. Since these transfers were in dollars, some of them even showed up in our New York subpoena database.

We now had more of a roadmap. Vadim used the Moldovan file to follow the money from Moldova to places like Cyprus, Lithuania, Latvia, and Estonia. Unfortunately, neither we nor the OCCRP had police files for these countries, and as EU member states, they all had good data protection, meaning we couldn't just purchase the information we needed like we had done in Russia.

Our team in London started working on criminal complaints that we would eventually file in each country that had received the dirty money. Hopefully, these complaints would lead to criminal cases being opened, as well as to new vistas on our map.

Yet there was another way to use this data, one that Bill Alpert had come up with. Instead of connecting the dots linearly, following the money from Russia, through all the transit countries, to wherever it ended up, which could take years, he developed a clever data-mining strategy.

The Moldovan file contained references to dozens and dozens of shell companies with meaningless names like Dexterson LLP, Green Pot Industrial Corporation, Prevezon Holdings, and Malton International. Bill decided to run these names through every New York property database he could get his hands on, operating on the idea that one or more of the thieves might have bought Manhattan real estate using some of the $230 million.

For many nights, after he was done writing his stock market reports, Bill would stay up late, dutifully slogging through databases and decoding arcane legal jargon in the hope that something would pop up.

Now, it seemed, something had.

"One of these companies hit," he told me on the phone that morning. "Prevezon. Whoever it belongs to has been grabbing New York property like candy."

"I can't believe it."

"Neither can I. I just found it today—I mean tonight. What time *is* it?" It was 8:00 a.m. in London, making it 3:00 a.m. in New York. "Look," he said, "I'm going to get some sleep and visit the properties tomorrow, but I wanted to let you know right away."

"While you're sleeping, I'll have Vadim look into Prevezon."

"Great. Talk to you later. This is good stuff."

When Vadim got to the office that morning, he soon found Prevezon Holdings in our copy of the Moldovan file. Two Moldovan shell companies had sent $857,764 from the stolen $230 million to Prevezon, which was registered in Cyprus. This was a lucky break. Unlike places such as the British Virgin Islands or Panama, where beneficial ownership of shell companies is secret, Cyprus has an open registry. All you have to do is go online, punch in a company's name, and you'll find out who it belongs to.

When Vadim did this, he learned that Prevezon Holdings was owned by a Russian man named Denis Katsyv.

In a typical money laundering scheme, ownership is like a Russian Matryoshka doll. You open one shell company to find another, and that leads to another and another and so on. Whenever you do land on an actual name, ninety-nine times out of a hundred it belongs to an unemployed alcoholic or a peripatetic yoga instructor or some other random person willing to hand over their passport in exchange for a few hundred dollars. Little do they know, they then become nominal owners of shell companies that can launder millions, and sometimes billions, of dollars.

At first, Vadim presumed Denis Katsyv was just another of these nobodies. But when Vadim entered his name into Yandex, Russia's version of Google, he discovered that Denis Katsyv was the son of Piotr Katsyv, a senior Russian government official.

That evening, Bill Alpert got back to me. "These places are pretty nice. They've got apartments in the old JPMorgan building downtown at 20 Pine Street. Building looks like Rockefeller Center, even has as a pool table in the old vault. Concierge services, roof deck, everything— *really* nice." As a kicker, he discovered that Prevezon had bought the properties from Lev Leviev, a Russian-Israeli diamond tycoon.

I was speechless.

In total, Denis Katsyv had used Prevezon to purchase roughly

$17 million worth of real estate in New York. This was far more than the $857,764 we'd traced from the $230 million—and we had no idea why he'd received it—but it was a major breakthrough to discover that the son of a senior Russian official was linked to the stolen $230 million.

"I assume you're going to make a big deal about this in *Barron's*," I said.

"Yeah, the thought did cross my mind," he said.

Barron's and the OCCRP agreed to coordinate their respective stories. *Barron's* would publish in print and online, and the OCCRP would publish on their website, both on August 12.

As the date approached, I grew more and more excited. Based on how the Swiss had reacted to Bill Alpert's earlier reporting, I couldn't help but picture US law enforcement doing the same. With any luck, by the end of summer, a freezing order would be placed over all of Denis Katsyv's New York assets, and a criminal money laundering investigation would be opened against him.

The night before the story was supposed to break, I called Bill. "How's it going?" I asked, expecting him to launch into an enthusiastic blow-by-blow of how Denis Katsyv had denied everything when Bill went to him for comment.

Instead, he said glumly, "I'm sorry, Bill, but the story's been spiked. The lawyers refuse to run it."

"What? Is there any way to get them to change their minds?"

"No," he said. Apparently, *Barron's* in-house counsel didn't want to risk a lawsuit even if the story was iron-clad. "I can't go into more detail, but safe to say I'm even more pissed than you are."

I hung up, crestfallen. With no US story, there would be no US legal action against Prevezon.

Thankfully, the OCCRP was not intimidated, and they ran their story. Even though their website only got 1/1,000th the traffic of *Barron's*, and hardly anyone in the United States read the story, one person *did* read it: a compliance officer at UBS in Zurich, the bank where Prevezon held $7 million. After reading the article, the compliance officer filed something called a suspicious activity report (SAR) with Swiss law enforcement. These are routinely filed by banks whenever they come across anything dubious regarding their clients. In theory, SARs absolve banks of responsibility if their clients later turn out to be criminals.

Globally, thousands of SARs are filed every day, and nearly all of them are ignored. But not this one. Shortly after it was submitted, the Swiss authorities placed freezing orders over Prevezon's $7 million at UBS.

This was the third freezing order in the Magnitsky case.

New York *had* to be next.

Adam Kaufmann wanted a New York nexus, and now we had one.

13

Hôtel Le Bristol

FALL 2012

Three months later, on November 9, 2012, Alexander Perepilichnyy flew to Paris to meet his mistress, Elmira Medynskaya, a 28-year-old, six-foot Ukrainian. She looked like a caricature of a Barbie doll—dyed blond hair, puffed lips, and impossibly long legs.

They met at the Hôtel Le Bristol, one of Paris's most opulent and prestigious hotels, where he'd booked the "Romance" package for €1,400 (approximately $1,600) per night. When they arrived, the bed was sprinkled with rose petals, and a bottle of Champagne sat chilled in an ice bucket next to a tray of French patisserie.

Perepilichnyy was aiming to impress—but also to escape his problems. That afternoon, they'd had lunch at the Hôtel George V, and then went to a pharmacy to buy a box of condoms. They spent the rest of the day in bed. That night, they went to dine at L'Ecrin, a Michelin-starred restaurant at the Hôtel de Crillon.

The next afternoon, Perepilichnyy took Elmira shopping on the rue Saint-Honoré. They visited Yves Saint Laurent, Louboutin, and Prada, where Perepilichnyy spent thousands on a handbag and a pair of high-heeled shoes. He tried to buy her a fur coat as well, but she thought that was too much and refused.

On the last night of their trip, they went to the Buddha Bar in the 8th Arrondissement, where they ordered sushi and tempura. Perepilichnyy had been relaxed throughout the trip, but on this last night he was agitated, nervously scanning the room. Halfway through the meal, he sent some of his food back, complaining it was spoiled.

Elmira Medynskaya.
(ELMIRA MEDYNSKAYA / INSTAGRAM /
VIA INSTAGRAM: @ELMIRAMEDINS)

When they returned to their room, Elmira poured herself a glass of wine and put her feet up on the sofa. Perepilichnyy wanted to join her but couldn't. He spent most of that night in the bathroom, vomiting. Eventually, he crawled into bed.

The next morning, he felt well enough to eat a full English breakfast. Afterward, they packed their bags and shared a taxi to the airport, where they discussed meeting again. They embraced, and went their separate ways.

At Heathrow, Perepilichnyy was met by his regular driver, who took him to his home in a gated community in St. George's Hill, Surrey, an affluent London suburb. His wife served him one of his favorite Ukrainian dishes, sorrel soup.

At lunch, his daughter complained that her computer was malfunctioning. When he finished eating, he took her to PC World at the local

Brooklands Shopping Centre to see if they could fix the computer. When they returned home, he changed out of his street clothes, put on his shorts and running shoes, and went out for a jog. Midway through his run, his breathing became heavy. He then collapsed.

The first person to find him was his neighbor's chef, who rushed outside dialing 999 (the British emergency services number). The chef, who had been in the British Special Forces, knew CPR. He dropped to his knees to try to save Perepilichnyy. Between chest compressions and mouth-to-mouth, green foam started bubbling from Perepilichnyy's lips. The chef wiped his face and spat onto the ground. He later reported that it had tasted like battery acid.

Within minutes, an ambulance arrived. The EMTs pushed the chef out of the way and knelt around Perepilichnyy. His body was cold, wet, and unresponsive.

They called the time of death at 5:52 p.m. on November 10, 2012.

Another witness in the Magnitsky case was now dead.

14

The New York Nexus

WINTER 2012–2013

I received news of Perepilichnyy's death six days later, on the third anniversary of Sergei's murder—which happened to be the same day the US House of Representatives was voting on the Magnitsky Act in Washington.

We'd been working on this legislation for over two years, and it was finally coming to fruition. Boris Nemtsov had made good on his Helsinki promise and had advocated for the US Magnitsky Act multiple times on Capitol Hill. In large part due to Boris's involvement, the Magnitsky Act passed the House that day, 365–43. It would head to the Senate within weeks, and was certain to be signed into law by the president soon afterward.

I should have been elated—and part of me was—but Perepilichnyy's sudden death cast a dark shadow over this success in Washington. Perepilichnyy wasn't a friend or colleague like Sergei, but he had played an important role in our money laundering investigation. Whatever his motivations or background, he had taken a huge risk, and now he was dead.

His death was not only tragic—it was also terrifying. It appeared the Russians were sending assassins to the West to retaliate against people exposing Russian government corruption in the Magnitsky case.

If there ever was a moment to get the US authorities involved, this was it.

I traveled to New York on December 4, carrying a thick manila envelope containing a six-page criminal complaint, along with 166 pages of supporting documents and exhibits. It described the connections between Prevezon, Denis Katsyv, and the stolen $230 million, and I intended to hand it directly to Adam Kaufmann at the New York District Attorney's Office.

On December 5, I went to Adam's office at 1 Hogan Place in lower Manhattan. The granite facade was stately and impressive, but the lobby was grim and menacing. I followed a group of men and women who looked like detectives or low-paid public defenders. We took turns filing through metal detectors guarded by surly officers who barked instructions in thick New York accents. No one looked happy. There was an air of resignation and low-simmering aggression all around. Everyone *had* to be there; no one *wanted* to be there.

Except for me.

The first thing I noticed about Adam's office was that it was littered with moving boxes. I ignored these as I greeted him. "Have a seat," he said warmly. "Let me get some of my colleagues."

He returned a minute later, introducing me to Duncan Levin, head of the asset forfeiture division, and another colleague. "This guy's got a crazy story," Adam said, sticking his thumb in my direction. "I'm sure you'll want to hear it."

We gathered around a battered conference table in mismatched chairs. "Last time we met," I said, "you told me if I ever found a New York nexus I should come to you. Well, I've found one." I reached into my bag and pulled out the complaint, pushing it across the table toward Adam. "We've discovered almost a million dollars from the Magnitsky case that was used to buy property in lower Manhattan."

The mood in the room suddenly changed. I think Adam had assumed this was going to be another superficial meet and greet, but now he realized there might be something substantive here. I showed them pictures of the properties and guided them through the schematic of the money trail.

"Where does all this come from?" Adam asked.

"Some of it comes from Russian databases, some from a Moldovan police file, and some from public records right here in New York."

Duncan, the asset forfeiture specialist, made a low sound. He was impressed.

This was much more than they were accustomed to getting. Normally, when someone walks into the DA's office to report a crime, they say something to the effect of "I've been robbed! Please do something!" They don't come in and say, "I've been robbed! Here's the robber's car, here's their license plate number, here's where they live, here's where they fenced the stolen goods, and here's what they bought with the proceeds."

Effectively, that's what I'd just done.

Adam and his team would still have to investigate and gather evidence, but they could use our complaint as the foundation for a solid money laundering case in New York.

Adam jabbed the complaint with his finger. "This we can work with."

"Great," I said. "When can you start?"

"Well . . ." Adam said slowly. "*I* can't start. You see these boxes?"

"Yeah," I said.

"I'm headed to private practice. You caught me only a few days before I'm out of here for good."

"Uh . . . congratulations?"

He laughed a little. "Don't worry, Bill. Duncan isn't going anywhere. If everything you have here checks out, he'll run with it." Duncan nodded reassuringly.

This was exactly the reaction I had been hoping for.

The next day, the US Senate passed the Magnitsky Act 92–4, and President Obama signed it into law on December 14, 2012.

I felt like the tide was turning.

During the Christmas holidays, I heard from Duncan. "Bill, I'd like to put you in touch with an agent from ICE."

"*ICE?*" I asked, unsure of what he meant.

"Immigration and Customs Enforcement," he explained.

That sounded odd. Whenever I thought of US immigration officers, I pictured uniformed agents at JFK checking passports, or men in jeeps patrolling the US-Mexico border, not financial investigators. "Does that mean you guys aren't going to pursue our complaint?" I asked.

"I just want him to have a look at it. ICE also investigates money laundering."

"Okay, sure. Send him my way."

It took a few weeks, but in January, I received a call from Special Agent Todd Hyman at ICE. My first impression was that he didn't sound much like a "special agent." He had an outer boroughs accent, called me Bill, and his tone was warm and conversational. He told me he had an MBA from Baruch College in Manhattan and had worked at Deloitte & Touche before moving into law enforcement. He reminded me more of one of my hedge fund service providers than a federal agent with a badge and gun—at least I assumed he carried a gun.

At the end of our conversation, I asked if they would be opening a case. He politely but firmly said, "I can't tell you that. We'll be in touch."

But afterward no one was in touch.

At the same time, the Russians had revved up a retaliatory rampage against the passage of the Magnitsky Act.

This was the first time the United States had sanctioned Russia since the Cold War, and Putin was apoplectic. His immediate response was to ban the adoption of Russian orphans by American families. This sounded terrible on the surface, but it was even more heinous when you looked at the details. The orphans Russia put up for adoption to foreigners were the sick ones, suffering from things like Down syndrome, spina bifida, and fetal alcohol syndrome, and often wouldn't survive in a Russian orphanage. By banning Americans from adopting these children, Putin was effectively sentencing some of them to death to protect his own corrupt officials. This was exceptional, even by his own depraved standards.

Putin also got personally involved in the cover-up of Sergei's murder. At his annual press conference, Putin pronounced that Sergei had never been tortured and that he had simply died "from a heart attack." This meant no one would ever be prosecuted for Sergei's torture or murder in Russia.

There *were* prosecutions forthcoming, however. At the same press conference, Putin mentioned both Sergei and me by name in connection to our alleged "economic crimes." A week later, a Moscow court set a date to put me on trial in absentia.

And I wouldn't be the only defendant.

Sergei would be tried alongside me—posthumously. This would be the first trial of a dead person in the history of Russia. They weren't going to dig up the body and prop it in the defendant's box like some medieval courts used to do in their posthumous cases—but the Russian authorities did try something similarly pernicious. They attempted to put Sergei's widow in the defendant's box in his place. Thankfully, only a short time before, I'd evacuated Natasha and her young son, Nikita, to the UK, where they were safely out of harm's way.

The trial against Sergei and me was set to begin in early March 2013.

Putin was using the full weight and force of the Russian government to crush anyone associated with me and the Magnitsky case, up to and including murder. The only way to make this a fair fight would be to bring in strong allies, and the best possible ally was US law enforcement.

But it didn't look like that was happening. Adam Kaufmann had gone to private practice; Duncan Levin seemed interested but then shuffled me off to Special Agent Hyman; and, after interviewing me, Special Agent Hyman had disappeared.

At that moment, I felt like we were completely on our own.

The SDNY

WINTER–FALL 2013

But then Duncan finally called. He asked if I could come to New York to meet the asset forfeiture division of the US Attorney's Office for the Southern District of New York (SDNY).

It turned out that we *weren't* on our own. Something was cooking.

It was one thing to talk to New York State prosecutors, but an entirely different thing to talk to US federal prosecutors. The fact that it was the Southern District of New York—which was colloquially known as the "Sovereign District"—meant this had the potential to be even bigger than I'd hoped.

I flew to New York, and on a cold, gray February day I went to the SDNY at 1 St. Andrews Plaza. There was no way to drive directly to the building, so the cab dropped me at Foley Square, a triangle of patchy grass and barren sycamores in the midst of a confusing concrete jungle of law enforcement buildings. I was soon lost. First, I walked into the Federal Courthouse. Then the Metropolitan Correctional Center. After 10 minutes, I at last found the SDNY, an ugly, fortress-like structure that didn't match the grandeur of the other nearby government buildings.

By then, I was late. I checked in. A secretary escorted me to a large, windowless conference room on the eighth floor, containing a long table and rows of shelves filled with red-spined law books. At the far end of the room was the seal of the SDNY. Although everything was government-issue and worn, I knew I was at the center of one of the most powerful law enforcement bodies in the world.

The room could hold about 20 people, and I was surprised to find it half-full. I walked around the table and introduced myself. There was Duncan Levin and one of his assistants; Todd Hyman and a colleague from the Department of Homeland Security; and Sharon Levin, head of the asset forfeiture division (no relation to Duncan), along with two lawyers who worked for her.

There were two others present as well, but they didn't hand out cards and remained conspicuously anonymous. I'd been to enough US government meetings to know that when people didn't identify themselves and never talked, it usually meant they were spooks.

Duncan opened the meeting by explaining why he had passed the case to the SDNY. If his office were to bring a money laundering case under New York State law, they would have had to prosecute a physical person. This meant Denis Katsyv would have to be brought to the United States and put on trial in New York. Since the United States and Russia have no extradition treaty, and there was no way Denis Katsyv would willingly surrender to New York authorities, that would be impossible.

However, Duncan explained, under *federal* law there was no need for a physical defendant. Federal prosecutors could simply go to court, file an asset forfeiture case, and try to seize the property that had been purchased using illicit funds. Nobody would go to jail, but it would be a lot better than anything we had at that moment.

As I began my presentation, a new person rushed into the room. "Sorry I'm late," he said, out of breath. "I just ran over from court."

"Bill, this is Assistant US Attorney Paul Monteleoni," Sharon said. "I've asked him to take the lead on this case."

Paul was in his mid-30s, tall, with clean-cut brown hair and a runner's build. Although he was the same rank as the other assistant US attorneys in the room, and Sharon was his boss, he commanded the respect of everyone there. It was as if Sharon was the head coach and Paul her star player.

He found a seat and I resumed my briefing. Initially, Paul seemed a bit disengaged. But as I spoke, he leaned back in his chair, closed his eyes, and grabbed the armrests. Every now and then he would open his eyes, stare at the ceiling, and ask a pointed question. Some were quite technical. I answered as best as I could.

The meeting lasted well over an hour. When we finished, I went around the room shaking hands. When I got to Paul, he said, "This has been great, but is there someone on your side who can help me understand everything better?"

"Yes. You need to talk to my colleague Vadim Kleiner. He's our expert."

"Can he come here?"

"Absolutely."

I returned to London and told Vadim he was headed to New York.

A few weeks later, Vadim arrived at the SDNY with his laptop and a Samsonite rolling bag bursting with papers. Vadim went to Paul's office, and was greeted by another roomful of people. Evidently, when you meet with a federal prosecutor, they're always accompanied by other prosecutors or government agents.

Vadim worked with Paul and his team until 9:00 p.m., long after everyone else in the building had gone home. He returned the next morning at 8 a.m., stayed late again, and the pattern repeated itself for the next three days. By the end of the week, there wasn't a stone left unturned or a question left unanswered.

Or so we thought.

Two weeks after returning to London, Vadim came into my office with a worried look on his face. "When I was in New York, I told Paul it was possible to get the lowest intermediate balance for every account along the money laundering chain. Now he's asking me to actually do it."

I had no idea what he was talking about—Vadim's grasp of how money laundering works was far more sophisticated than mine—but this sounded like a good development to me. "So what's the problem?"

"You don't understand, Bill," Vadim said. "To do that, I'd have to comb through literally tens of thousands of transactions at more than fifty companies in a dozen international banks. Some of them are just a few hundred dollars. It would take weeks."

"Vadim, if you told them you can do it, then you have to do it."

He turned and left, dejected. For the next two weeks, Vadim was the first in the office every morning, and would often stay past midnight. By day eight, Vadim, usually impeccably dressed in suit and tie, had bags under his eyes and had ditched the tie. Often, around dinnertime, I would overhear him arguing with his wife about why he wasn't home with her and their three boys.

He was finally finished at the beginning of April. Haggard but satisfied, he sent his analysis to the SDNY, and looked forward to a bit of respite.

Only he didn't get it. Hardly a moment passed before the SDNY made another request of him. This was followed by another. And another. And another. The SDNY's appetite was voracious and bottomless.

When we'd started this process, I viewed every question from the SDNY as confirmation that the case was moving forward. But after months of giving and giving, I began to worry that this was turning out to be no more than some kind of government fact-finding exercise that would lead nowhere.

All of this was made even more upsetting by what was going on in Moscow.

On March 6, a Russian state-controlled television station, NTV, aired a 45-minute "documentary" called *Browder's List* in a prime time slot. According to the film, not only had I evaded taxes, but I'd stolen $4.5 billion of IMF bailout funds from under the noses of all international authorities and the Russian government, and I'd killed my former business partner, Edmond Safra, who'd died tragically in a fire at his house in Monaco in 1998.

These types of "documentaries" were pro forma leading up to any major political show trial, with the aim of convincing the Russian public that the defendant was a truly heinous individual.

The trial against Sergei and me started the following week. In May, while it was in full swing, Russia issued its first Interpol Red Notice for my arrest. This had been inevitable, but it still came as a shock. I had finally been upgraded to Russia's international wanted list.

Fortunately, after my lawyers intervened, Interpol deleted this Red Notice from their system for being politically motivated. But that wasn't going to stop the Putin regime. This weaponization of Interpol, which is notoriously lax in vetting arrest warrants issued by authoritarian states, was harrowing. After that, every time I crossed an international border, there would be a very real risk of being arrested and extradited to Russia.

With these developments, I needed the United States on my side more than ever. But whenever I asked Paul where the SDNY stood on the Prevezon case, he would never give me an answer.

I planned to be in New York in June on other business and would just ask him face-to-face. Maybe he would answer me then.

I returned to St. Andrews Plaza on a hot summer day and met with Paul and Sharon Levin. After some pleasantries, I asked them point-blank, "This is leading somewhere, right?" But all I got were perfect, sphinx-like poker faces.

I flew back to London having no idea about where this was headed. And the information requests just kept coming.

While Vadim continued to slave away, the Russian trial against Sergei and me concluded. On July 10, 2013, we were both found guilty of criminal tax evasion. They'd already killed Sergei, so there was nothing more they could do to him, but I was sentenced to nine years of hard labor in absentia. Conviction in hand, Russia requested a second Red Notice for my arrest. This was also rejected by Interpol.

I was now truly desperate to know what was happening at the SDNY, but at the beginning of August, they went silent. No more emails, no more information requests, nothing. I didn't know what to make of this. I felt like our only chance of evening the scales was slipping away.

August passed. September began. Still no legal action from the SDNY.

Then, on September 10, 2013, I received an email from Paul Monteleoni. There was nothing in the body, not even a "Hello" or a "Best wishes." All it contained was a cut-and-pasted press release titled, "U.S. Attorney announces civil forfeiture complaint against real estate corporations allegedly involved in laundering proceeds of Russian tax refund fraud scheme."

It was finally happening.

The SDNY's complaint included an application to freeze the four luxury condominiums bought by Prevezon that Bill Alpert had found in the old JPMorgan building on Pine Street.

But not only these properties. During those many months when Paul and his team had been bombarding Vadim with questions, Special Agent Todd Hyman had been methodically turning over every stone in New York City. In the process, he found an apartment on East 49th Street, a retail unit on 7th Avenue, and a whole series of accounts held at Bank of America, all belonging to Prevezon.

The Department of Justice was asking the court to issue a worldwide freezing order over Prevezon's assets. This order included approximately $20 million of real estate and cash in New York, along with €3 million (approximately $3.5 million) of assets held in the Netherlands.

The total was more than 27 times the $857,764 we'd originally traced from the stolen $230 million going to New York. The US authorities were going after everything they could find, with the intention of seizing all of the $230 million, provided they could locate it.

The SDNY's filing was a complete and independent vindication of everything we'd been saying since 2008. The Department of Justice had laid out the facts in black-and-white and was now ready to stand by them in a US federal court.

The next day, the court approved the government's application. This was the fourth freezing order in the Magnitsky case.

The complaint against Prevezon was so damning I thought the Russians wouldn't even bother to show up and defend themselves.

That turned out to be one of the most naïve assumptions I'd ever made.

John Moscow Returns

FALL 2013–SUMMER 2014

About a month later, as I was walking home from work, an email arrived from Bill Alpert. The title read, "My Idol!" There was no message, just an attachment from the New York court naming who would represent Prevezon in New York. Surprisingly, the Russians *were* going to defend themselves. And their lawyer?

John Moscow.

I called Bill. As soon as he answered, I said, "Is this *our* John Moscow?"

"The one and only."

"That *can't* be true."

"It is. I'm devastated," he said sincerely. Aside from John Moscow's towering reputation, Bill had been close to him for decades. The two had regular breakfasts together at a Greek diner in SoHo, and Bill had gone to John Moscow's going-away party when he left the New York District Attorney's Office. Bill had even employed John Moscow's son as an intern at *Barron's*.

This development was potentially devastating for me and my colleagues. Of the 57,000-or-so lawyers licensed to practice law in New York, the Russians had chosen the only one who had represented us on this exact same matter. After befriending us, working for us, ghosting us, and coming back to help, John Moscow was now working for the other side. It was unbelievable.

You don't have to be a legal expert to know that lawyers are not permitted to switch sides. I felt like this was a complete betrayal. But more than that, it was extremely dangerous. John Moscow *knew* us. He'd been our lawyer. We'd had countless conference calls with him; we had shared evidence, aspirations, and worries with him. He knew our security details. He knew every member of our team—hell, he'd even been on a conference call that had included my wife!

I understood why the Russians would want to hire him—they could get access to our inner sanctum. What I couldn't understand was why he would agree to work for them. As a longtime criminal prosecutor, he knew what the Russians were capable of. When he first started working for us, he warned me about how dangerous Russians could be. Besides, he had a reputation to protect. That would evaporate in an instant if he followed through with this.

There was, however, a way we could tackle this problem head-on. John Moscow was an American lawyer working at a major international law firm, not some shady Russian protected by powerful and corrupt officials. Perhaps he was prepared to do this, but BakerHostetler, a firm that billed more than $600 million every year, wouldn't allow it to happen.

We sent a letter to the managing partners of BakerHostetler, reminding them that we and Sergei were victims in the $230 million fraud, and that BakerHostetler had previously worked for us in tracking down who had received that money. Now they were representing one of those recipients! This was a clear conflict of interest, making their client, in legal terms, "adverse" to us. We also pointed out that when we'd worked together we'd given them confidential information. The Bar Association explicitly forbade this type of disloyalty, and we requested that BakerHostetler recuse themselves and John Moscow without delay.*

It was so straightforward that we expected to hear from them

---

* Rule 1.9 of the New York Rules of Professional Conduct states: "A lawyer who has formerly represented a client in a matter shall not thereafter represent another person in the same or a substantially related matter in which that person's interests are materially adverse to the interests of the former client unless the former client gives informed consent confirmed in writing."

within days, apologizing and committing to drop Prevezon right away.

But we didn't hear from them for over two weeks.

When we did, instead of being contrite, BakerHostetler doubled down. Their response came from a lawyer in their DC office named Mark Cymrot, who defiantly said they were *not* going to recuse themselves.

He justified this by claiming that we weren't victims of the crime at all. Since the $230 million had been stolen from the Russian Treasury, he argued that only the Russian government had been victimized and had an interest in this matter.

He then stated that the firm didn't "believe" they had any confidential information of ours because "more than 3,000 pages" about us were "available from public websites" and everything we had told them or given to them must therefore already be in the public domain. Besides, he "assured" us that even if they did happen to possess some confidential information, they hadn't "reviewed" it or "disclosed" it to Prevezon.

Finally, he insisted there was no way Prevezon could be "adverse" to us because we weren't "a party" to the case. He argued that only defendants and plaintiffs in the same case could be "adverse" to one another. Therefore, we didn't have any grounds to ask them to step away.

For many, the words "lawyer" and "ethics" are mutually exclusive. As we all know, lawyers have become the brunt of countless jokes. (What's the difference between a lawyer and a jellyfish? One is a spineless, poisonous blob. The other is a form of sea life. Why won't sharks attack lawyers? Professional courtesy.) But I thought this disrespect was mostly reserved for ambulance chasers with one-room offices in strip malls, not Ivy League attorneys in glass towers in midtown Manhattan. I was surprised that BakerHostetler, a firm that had been around since 1916, with clients like Ford and Microsoft, would conform to this lowest stereotype.

The rules against attorneys who step out of line are explicit, however, and it doesn't matter whether they operate out of strip malls or offices in Manhattan. If BakerHostetler weren't going to recuse themselves, then we would make sure the rules forced them to.

On December 6, we filed a complaint with New York's Attorney Grievance Committee, the body that polices lawyers' conduct, laying out how John Moscow and BakerHostetler had switched sides. It was one thing for them to try to snow-job us with legalese, but another for them to be scrutinized by the Grievance Committee and risk punishment, up to and including disbarment. It would be much easier for them just to walk away from Prevezon.

But once again, BakerHostetler surprised us. They responded to the Grievance Committee by repeating their previous spin from the letter to us, but they went further, claiming they were "not engaged by Hermitage to 'trac[e] the proceeds of the stolen $230 million and identifying beneficiaries of this fraud.'"

When I read this, I thought they'd backed themselves into a corner. We had copies of the subpoena requests to the US banks that John Moscow had drafted specifically looking for the $230 million. This was as clear-cut as you could get. There was no way they could squirm out of this. All we needed was a hearing.

Only we didn't get one. Throughout the whole winter, and leading into the spring of 2014, we didn't receive *any* response from the Grievance Committee.

When I complained to a lawyer friend in New York about the delay, she said, "The Committee has—what?—half a dozen people to police every dirty lawyer in New York? You know how many scumbags we have in the legal profession here?"

"Fifty-seven thousand?" I said.

"Sounds about right," she said with a chuckle. "Besides, this isn't a straightforward case. The straightforward cases are the ones where lawyers murder their clients and steal all their money."

I hoped she was wrong, but if they only had six attorneys to deal with every ethical violation in New York, I could see how it might take them some time to get around to us.

But then, one day in early April, my secretary burst into my office clutching a thick DHL package. "This just came in from New York," she said. "I think it's from the US court."

Finally, a response from the Grievance Committee, I thought. She handed it to me and I tore it open. But as I scanned the first few pages, I realized it wasn't from the Grievance Committee.

It was a subpoena from Prevezon, and it was addressed to me.

I had never been subpoenaed by a US court before. I stared at the words. "YOU ARE COMMANDED to appear at the time, date, and place set forth below." It compelled me to show up in five weeks' time at an office in Rockefeller Center and sit for a deposition. It also demanded I produce 21 categories of documents, including all of our communication with the OCCRP; all of our correspondence with whistleblowers, journalists, and politicians; and all of our confidential discussions with any law enforcement agency investigating the stolen $230 million.

They were going after all "employees, consultants, agents, representatives, or persons acting on [my] behalf." They wanted our "writings, drawings, graphs, charts, photographs, sound recordings, images, and other data" stored in our office or anywhere else.

Basically, they wanted everything.

We knew from working with John Moscow that one of his specialties was using subpoenas as weapons unto themselves. When he first pitched us, he boasted that he liked to identify his opponents' sensitivities and then demand everything they were uncomfortable handing over. Now, he was turning this on us. Except that he didn't need to identify our sensitivities—he already knew them from the time we had worked together.

I knew that once John Moscow got his hands on this information, he would pass it to his client—the son of a high-ranking Russian official—and from there it would most likely be available to all sorts of bad guys in the Russian government. This wouldn't just jeopardize us, it would also place all of our sources and collaborators in Russia in grave danger.

The Russians didn't need to hire someone like Validol to surveil us and gather intelligence—they were simply entering the front door of a US court and demanding all sorts of confidential information.

This subpoena had to be stopped.

Pacing my office, I put on my phone's headset and frantically called my London lawyer.

"What's going on, Bill?" he asked. I spoke so quickly that he interrupted, "Whoa, whoa. Slow down and start from the beginning." As I explained the subpoena, he interrupted again, using a calm, lawyerly tone. "Before you go on, let me see the document."

I scanned it and sent it over. He called me back in no time. "Bill, you haven't been subpoenaed," he said. "You're here in London—they didn't hand it to you in person in New York. Therefore, you haven't been served. End of story."

"Are you serious?"

"Yes. As long as they don't serve you personally, this is just their wish list. Nothing more, nothing less."

I was hugely relieved, but I knew this was just John Moscow's opening gambit.

My lawyer in London was good, but if this carried on I needed to bring on some heavy firepower in the United States, and soon.

I made a list of 10 of the most powerful law firms in New York and contacted each. Six immediately said they weren't interested. None explained why, but I knew the reason. Russians were throwing around legal fees like confetti in New York. They were suing each other, getting divorces, buying luxury properties, applying for visas, and setting up bank accounts. And their US lawyers were loving it. Why would any of these firms jeopardize this gravy train by working with someone as toxic to the Russians as me?

The remaining four firms were willing to meet, and I went to New York in May 2014. The first three were barely distinguishable. Each parked me in a well-appointed conference room in their midtown Manhattan office; each trotted out senior partners known for their litigation prowess; and each of these partners was surrounded by well-dressed, fresh-faced associates a few years out of law school. I knew that as soon as I signed an engagement letter, I'd never see the senior partner again. The entire case would be run by one of these young associates.

My last meeting was with Randy Mastro, head of litigation at Gibson, Dunn & Crutcher. In another professional life, he'd been a deputy mayor of New York under Rudy Giuliani (this was long before Giuliani had self-immolated). Randy had a reputation for being one of the fiercest litigators in New York. When I Googled him, he was described as someone "you don't want to meet in a dark alley—and you really don't want to meet him in a lighted courtroom." Someone else said that going against him would be like "wrestling with an alligator."

I couldn't wait to meet him.

I arrived at Gibson Dunn's offices in the MetLife building above Grand Central Station and went up to the 47th floor. Coming out of the elevator, I walked into a soaring, two-story lobby with white marble floors, walls with dark wood paneling, modern furniture, and a large contemporary mural by the receptionist's desk. My immediate reaction was *I can't afford this.*

Randy's secretary came to the lobby, took me up a flight of stairs, and led me to his corner office. It looked directly over the Chrysler Building and its famous eagles, with a view south all the way to Wall Street and New York Harbor. Randy was on a call, but he waved me to a chair opposite his desk while he finished up.

Randy, who appeared to be in his late 50s, was not like the other lawyers I'd met in New York. He had a shock of long white hair (long for a lawyer, at least) and a well-kept beard. He wore a gray suit but no tie, just an open-collared shirt. I couldn't remember the last time I'd met with a male lawyer not wearing a tie.

His office was decorated with baseball paraphernalia, including a Roberto Clemente memorial patch on his desk and a prominently displayed wooden bat. I laughed to myself that a litigator would keep a bat handy. Next to the patch on the desk was a small rubber alligator.

Five minutes later he hung up his call and introduced himself. "What can I do for you, Bill?"

I told him the story. He listened carefully. When I was finished, he shook his head in disbelief. "I know John Moscow. He was one of the top guys under Morgenthau," he said, referring to one of New York's most famous district attorneys. "It's a damn shame. . . . How can I help?"

"They're going to come after me again. When they do, I need someone who can hit back hard."

"You came to the right place."

"And the Russian angle doesn't bother you?"

"Nope. Not in the least." He reached across his desk, a card in hand. "Here's my personal number. You can call me anytime, day or night."

I returned to London satisfied that when John Moscow struck again, I would be ready.

17

The Aspen Stakeout

SUMMER 2014

A few weeks later, after a business lunch near Parliament, I strolled along Birdcage Walk by St. James's Park, reflexively checking my BlackBerry. Among a backlog of messages was one from Paul Monteleoni. I'd barely heard from him since the US government filed their case against Prevezon. He was blunt: "Call me. Urgent."

I'd never received this kind of message from Paul before.

I ducked into a doorway and punched in his number. He picked up almost before it had a chance to ring. "Hi, Paul. It's Bill. What's going on?"

"Oh, hi." He took a moment before continuing, as if he had to step out of a meeting. "I, uh, I don't want to alarm you, and I can't be a hundred percent sure about this, but we've received intelligence that some individuals are soliciting funds to hire a team to locate you and bring you back to Russia."

Bring me? "Which people?" I asked.

"It involves Russians."

"Which Russians?"

"That's all I can share with you. We're notifying the British authorities, but I wanted to let you know so you can take whatever precautions you think are necessary."

I hung up and stood in the doorway, looking out at the lush green of St. James's Park. Buckingham Palace was in the near distance to the west, and, though it was blocked from view, Parliament was only a few blocks to the east. In spite of being in the middle of London, in an area with more security cameras per square foot than anywhere in the United Kingdom, I suddenly felt vulnerable.

I stepped onto the sidewalk, hypersensitive to my surroundings, and walked briskly through the park. Being told by the US government that there was a rendition plot against me crystallized all of my fears. If this intelligence was reliable, and I had to assume it was, then I was no longer safe in London. It didn't matter how many CCTV cameras there were—they had never deterred the Russians before.

On top of that, there were more than 300,000 Russians living, working, or traveling through London at any given time. They're like lampposts or red double-decker buses—totally ubiquitous and taken for granted.

Except I never took them for granted. Aside from my Russian wife and mostly Russian staff, I avoided them altogether. If I heard any-one speaking Russian when I walked down the street, I instinctively moved away. When I was invited out for drinks or dinner, I made a point of avoiding the fashionable bars and restaurants that Russians frequented.

The British government, however, *did* take Russians for granted. I was almost certain that after Britain received the US government's warning they would do nothing. And worse, if I was actually kidnapped by the Russians, there would be no real consequences.

This had been the case after Alexander Litvinenko, an FSB defector, was assassinated in central London by two Russian agents using radio-active polonium in 2006. In spite of it being established that Litvinenko's murder was an act of Kremlin-sponsored terrorism, the only things the British government did was expel a handful of Russian diplomats and issue some meaningless arrest warrants for Litvinenko's assassins that Russia would never honor. This lax attitude had given Putin the impres-sion that he could operate with impunity in the UK.

Now, with the very real possibility that I could be snatched at any moment, I ratcheted up my security. I hired a team of bodyguards who'd worked for clients in countries like Mexico and Afghanistan, where kidnappings are rife. However, despite their expertise and intim-idating presence, they didn't make me feel much calmer. At the end of the day, the biggest market for bodyguards in London is Russians (who are afraid of other Russians). With all that money sloshing around, I realized I couldn't fully trust any of these people.

To be as safe as possible, I therefore had to rely on myself. I started by asking—if I were trying to kidnap me, what would I do?

Planning such an operation would involve surveillance, monitoring my habits, and looking for any exploitable pattern. This meant I could no longer have habits, and my life could follow no discernible pattern.

I began varying my routine, starting my day at different hours, sometimes very early, other times closer to lunch. I varied my routes to work, often going out of my way. I took a taxi one day, a bus the next, the Tube the day after. Sometimes I walked, or took the Tube only one stop, or dipped into a café before continuing. Sometimes my bodyguards would walk with me; other times they would hold back to see if I was being tailed or watched.

Most importantly, I migrated my entire calendar to a hard copy and went offline as far as any forward planning was concerned.

It was exhausting to do all of this, and even more stressful to be in a constant state of alert. There was no way I could have kept up either indefinitely. Thankfully, I didn't have to. In mid-July, Elena, the kids, and I were going to Aspen, Colorado, for a long vacation, where I would be able to resume a more normal life.

We landed there on July 14. The moment I got off the plane, it felt like a different world. Aspen has a small airport, and you disembark the way people did in the 1950s: you walk outside and descend a set of movable stairs to the tarmac. The air was clean and dry. I could already smell the dark pines that reached up the mountainsides, mixing with aspens and cottonwoods.

I love Colorado. I grew up in Chicago, but I'd spent the first year of high school at a boarding school in Steamboat Springs, where I skied practically every winter day. During those formative years, I fell hard for the Rocky Mountains. After high school, I went to the University of Colorado in Boulder for two years, and since then I've returned to the Rockies every chance I get. By 2014, it wasn't just me who loved being there—my whole family loved it.

It took a few days for my nerves to settle, but they did. I fell into a comfortable routine: biking with my kids, going to outdoor concerts, and visiting friends for dinner. It felt great to be free and not constantly looking over my shoulder.

The vacation was centered on my family, particularly Elena, who bore the brunt of the whole situation. Not only did she have to deal with the stress of her husband possibly disappearing at any moment, but she had to put on a brave face for our children. Somehow, she was able to convince them that all fathers fought with Vladimir Putin, and that our lives were completely normal.

Still, I had some work to do. In late July, I was invited to the Aspen Institute to give a talk about the Magnitsky Act. The Institute is an international think tank and conference center that regularly brings together activists, entrepreneurs, politicians, and journalists to discuss issues of all kinds. Its campus along the Roaring Fork River is one of the most idyllic places you'll ever see. For this particular gathering, I brought along my 17-year-old son, David, hoping he would be inspired.

There was a cocktail reception at the end of the first day at the Doerr-Hosier Center, the main reception hall of the Aspen Institute. David, who was about to start at Stanford, was excited to rub shoulders with a handful of famous Silicon Valley entrepreneurs, and I was excited just to spend time with David.

As the party wound down, the skies began clouding over. A big Rocky Mountain afternoon storm was brewing, and the Aspen Valley would soon be engulfed.

I nudged my son, who was chatting with a young venture capitalist. "Sorry, David, but we have to go."

By the time we reached the front door, the rain had started.

I called my friend Pierre, who was visiting from Belgium. He'd dropped us off earlier and then gone to town to do some shopping. "Pierre, are you anywhere near the Institute? With all this weather, we could use a ride."

"You're in luck! I'm a few blocks away. I'll be there in five."

The Doerr-Hosier Center is tucked down a footpath away from the road, so Pierre couldn't pull right up. He texted a few minutes later when he was in the cul-de-sac. We made our way out. We hadn't brought umbrellas, so David and I broke into a jog, our arms shielding our heads from the fat raindrops.

Suddenly, out of nowhere, a woman rushed toward me, shouting, "Mr. Browder! Mr. Browder!"

Her tone was harsh. David and I stopped momentarily in our tracks. I squinted through the rain. I didn't recognize her and noticed that she didn't have an Aspen Institute badge hanging around her neck like everyone else at the conference.

I was suddenly hit with a shot of adrenaline. My fight-or-flight instincts kicked in, and all the bad feelings from a month earlier in London flooded back. Whoever she was, I could tell she didn't wish me well.

I grabbed David and dragged him into a run.

She started running too, and shouting more. But I wasn't focusing on her words. My only thought was getting David and myself into the car.

David pulled ahead of me. I glanced over my shoulder. The woman had been joined by a man, who'd also taken up pursuit.

Just then, the skies opened and the rain came down in sheets.

David reached the car first and turned to me, a questioning look on his drenched face.

"Get in!" I yelled. He opened the front passenger door and jumped inside. A second or two later I reached the car, practically crashing into it. I opened the back door and climbed in. Pierre was casually scrolling through his iPhone, completely oblivious to what was going on.

"Pierre, hit the gas!" I blurted.

He glanced back at me, wondering if I was serious.

"*Go!*" I shouted.

He got it. Dropping his phone in the center console, he put the car in gear and began to drive.

The Aspen Institute is essentially a pedestrian zone, and we couldn't just peel out. As we left the cul-de-sac, the man who had joined the chase reached the car and threw something onto the windshield. It got stuck under the wipers, which danced back and forth furiously. Pierre had to stop the car. Between the cascade of gray rain and the object on the window, he couldn't make out the road.

Without either of us telling him, David jumped out, flung the object to the ground, and got back in.

"What was that?" I asked.

"I don't know," David said.

We then drove away in earnest, leaving the Institute behind and racing through the wet Aspen streets.

As I looked over my shoulder to see if we were being followed, Pierre asked, "What the hell is going on?"

"I don't know," I said. "Something really shitty, though." Whoever they were, I was relieved they hadn't gotten to us. But the fact that my enemies had now tracked me down in Aspen was seriously bad news.

We drove straight to the house, and I told Elena what happened. Even though these people had sounded American, I knew they were connected to the Russians.

"If the Russians know we're here," I said, "then we need to clear out." I had plans to fly back to London the next day to meet with my British publisher and organize the UK rollout of my book, *Red Notice*. But now I didn't want my family to be there without me, and told Elena to pack up so we could all go.

Elena kept her cool. "Of course we don't need to 'clear out,' Bill," she said.

When we first met in Moscow, Elena had been a high-flying crisis manager for an American PR firm—a nearly impossible position for a young woman in a country as patriarchal and stifling as Russia—and she never got flustered.

"In that case, I'll cancel tomorrow's trip," I said.

"No," she said. "The book is too important. You need to go. Besides, Pierre is here, David is here. And we can always call Steve." Steve was a local friend and an avid hunter with an impressive collection of rifles. "Go to London."

She was probably right. I've always felt that marrying Elena was like marrying a doctor who specialized in treating a rare tropical disease, and that I had come down with that exact rare tropical disease. I couldn't have chosen a more capable partner for handling this ordeal.

The next day I flew to Denver, where I had a connecting flight to London. I called Elena during my layover. She put her phone on Face-

Time. It was a beautiful, sunny day and the kids had set up a sprinkler in the driveway. They giggled gleefully as they chased each other back and forth through the water.

I boarded my flight to London an hour later, and with the image of the kids playing in the driveway I was able to drift into a deep sleep on the overnight flight.

When I cleared customs at Heathrow just before noon, I texted Elena to let her know I'd landed safely. It was barely dawn in Aspen, so I didn't expect her to respond, but the phone rang almost at once.

"Bill, they approached the kids!" she said hysterically.

"Who did? When?"

"Two men came to the house yesterday afternoon when the kids were playing outside. One asked, 'Is your daddy home?'"

"*What?*"

"Veronica told the man, 'No.' And he then asked, 'Where is he?' She got scared and ran inside with the others. The man shouted after them. Then he rang the bell over and over, but we hid in the basement." After a pause she said, "I don't feel safe here anymore."

In our 15 years together, I'd never heard her so upset.

I checked the flight schedule. The first plane back to Colorado wasn't until the next day. Until then, I needed to get some help.

My first call was to Steve. He lived at a small ranch in the foothills west of town. After hearing what happened, he said, "I'll grab a couple buddies. We'll get over to the house right away and keep watch. Don't worry, Bill, nothing will happen to your family."

Next, I called Paul Monteleoni in New York. As a prosecutor, he couldn't do much himself, so he got Special Agent Hyman involved, and he in turn reached out to the Aspen chief of police (he would have called a local counterpart at Homeland Security, but the closest field office was in Centennial, Colorado, a four-hour drive away).

I regularly read the police blotter in the *Aspen Times*. The local police department was pretty quiet, and the most excitement came from the occasional DUI, shoplifting, and bar fights. The chief certainly didn't want Aspen to become the backdrop for a major international incident involving Russians, and he called me right away.

"I've been briefed on your situation, Mr. Browder," he said with a mountain twang. "I'll visit your wife in the next hour, and I've instructed my officers to conduct regular patrols of the house." He gave me his personal number and told me to call him for any reason.

I then spoke to Elena, who still sounded shaken.

"Sweetheart, I'm coming back," I said. "I'll be on the first flight tomorrow."

I went home to change clothes, cancel my meetings, and book my flights back to Aspen.

However, when I checked back with Elena a couple hours later, her tone had changed. "Steve and a friend are out front sitting on the hood of his truck with rifles. I also met with the police chief, and one of their cars comes around every fifteen minutes. I think we'll be fine. You should finish your work."

I was glad to hear she'd settled down. I reluctantly stayed in London for the next couple of days, but the more I thought about what had happened, the angrier I became.

The Russians knew my family's whereabouts, and I suspected that this was because of John Moscow. It was one thing for him to switch sides in a legal case and align himself with the Russian government, but he had completely crossed the line by involving my wife and children.

18

Judge Griesa

SUMMER–FALL 2014

When the dust settled, we learned that the people chasing me had not been kidnappers or poisoners, but process servers hired by the Russians. The object they'd tossed on my car's windshield was a subpoena. John Moscow was indeed behind all of this.

This latest subpoena was even more troubling than the first.

In addition to the swath of information they'd previously demanded, John Moscow and his team now wanted eight years of my personal security details; copies of my passports and visas for the previous 20 years; all of my communications with Interpol and the European Union; and all sorts of personal information about my colleagues Vadim and Ivan.

If we handed all of this over to BakerHostetler, our Russian adversaries were sure to get ahold of it, enabling them to plan any number of sinister moves against us. With all the dead bodies racking up, this was genuinely terrifying. To me these subpoenas looked more like a Russian intelligence gathering operation than anything having to do with a US court case.

As if to confirm this, within days, TASS, the official Russian state news agency, ran the headline "William Browder Summoned to New York for Questioning." The ensuing story included a quote from Prevezon's legal team: "If Mr. Browder does not appear for questioning, he may be subject to punishment up to and including arrest." The Katsyv family lawyer in Moscow, a woman I'd never heard of named Natalia Veselnitskaya, even tried to make it sound like *I* was the defendant, not Prevezon.

If I'd ever needed an alligator on my side, it was now.

In mid-August, I put the expensive modern art and white marble floors at Gibson Dunn out of my mind and called Randy Mastro on the personal number he'd given me. He agreed to represent me, and after signing his engagement letter, the first thing I did was send him documents connected with the case so he could figure out what we should do.

In September, I flew to New York to meet with Randy.

This would be the first time I'd sit with him as my lawyer, and I was more than a little anxious. It was a bit like going to the doctor after a battery of tests. Randy and his team had studied our case file, and now had a diagnosis. I was afraid he'd conclude that there was no hope and I'd have to hand over everything to John Moscow and BakerHostetler.

We met at the Regency Hotel on Park Avenue for breakfast. The maître d', who knew Randy well, led us through the small restaurant. It was surprisingly busy considering it was only 7:30 a.m. Randy seemed to know everyone there, greeting people as we walked to our table. I quickly realized this was some kind of New York institution, a power-breakfast spot where people in finance, media, and law gathered every morning.

We took our seats. I must have looked uncomfortable, because the first thing Randy said was "Relax, Bill. We've got this under control."

"What do you mean?"

"I mean we're going to quash this subpoena. They messed up on jurisdiction, they messed up on service—not to mention this is the most overbroad subpoena I've ever seen. Truly."

"That's a relief," I said.

"But I don't want to stop there. I've never seen a clearer example of a lawyer having a blatant conflict of interest. John Moscow needs to be kicked off this case."

"But we already tried that with the Grievance Committee," I lamented.

We'd finally heard from them in early August, when, in a single paragraph, they baldly stated that they weren't going to do anything.

"Forget about the Committee. We're going to file a motion to disqualify him with the court," he stated.

"Why will that be any different?"

"Because this time we get to argue in front of a judge instead of just leaving it to some guys who're deciding off a bunch of papers. Trust me, we have a good case."

Randy filed the motion to disqualify on September 29, and a hearing was set for October 14.

In the interim, John Moscow and BakerHostetler filed their reply. They tripled down on everything they'd told us when we requested they recuse themselves. They started by saying, "Browder was *never a client of BakerHostetler*" (emphasis theirs), trying to argue that because Hermitage—and not I personally—had paid their bills, attorney-client privilege didn't apply.

They then pointed out that neither Hermitage nor I had a financial stake in the US government's case against Prevezon—win or lose, we wouldn't get any of the seized money. Therefore, they claimed, we couldn't be "adverse" to their client, and no conflict of interest existed.

This was patently absurd. Since 2009 my main mission had been to bring Sergei's killers and anyone who'd benefitted from the crime he exposed to account. They knew this. The whole world knew this. What was going on here practically defined the word "adverse." For them to attempt to thread this needle wasn't just dishonest, it was the height of cynicism.

They finished with a claim that would have made Franz Kafka proud: "Browder is seeking to inflict reputational harm on John Moscow, who served New York State honorably for over 30 years as one of its most prominent anti–money laundering attorneys." They were trying to convince the judge that John Moscow—who was now *defending* alleged money launderers—was the victim, not Sergei or I.

I could barely contain my outrage. This disqualification decision was going to be a cakewalk for the judge. Our day in court couldn't come soon enough.

Then, as the hearing drew nearer, we learned which judge had been assigned to the case, and I became even more excited. The Honorable Thomas Griesa would be presiding. Judge Griesa had a reputation for being tough and taking controversial decisions. Prior to our case, he had forced Argentina into default over delinquent interest and principal payments on Argentine debt in a dispute with Elliott Management, a New York hedge fund. (Griesa was so reviled in Argentina that they burned effigies of him in the streets of Buenos Aires.)

And there was another reason to be optimistic. Years earlier, Randy's colleague at Gibson Dunn, Richard Mark, had been one of Judge Griesa's favorite law clerks. The plan was to have Randy introduce the motion, and have Richard argue the case. In theory, things like this shouldn't matter, but judges are human beings like anyone else, and speaking to a trusted former colleague is always better than speaking to a stranger.

Late on the morning of October 14, Randy and Richard went to room 26B of the Daniel Patrick Moynihan Courthouse on Foley Square, right around the corner from the SDNY. Randy knew the courtroom well— he'd argued hundreds of cases there. It was picturesque and stately, with wood paneling, cushioned chairs, a jury box, a witness stand, and a large public gallery that seated up to 100 people. On the wall behind the judge's bench was the seal of the US Department of Justice.

When Randy and Richard arrived, there was already a large group of people milling around. There were six attorneys from three different law firms representing Prevezon, including John Moscow and Mark Cymrot, the attorney from BakerHostetler's DC office who wrote the first letter refusing to recuse the firm from this case. Cymrot, who had a head of thinning white hair and a thick gray mustache, would be the lead attorney. This team was accompanied by an entourage of associates, paralegals, and other hangers-on sitting in the gallery. This was clearly an important hearing for Prevezon.

Judge Griesa entered the room from his chambers, ascended the bench, and gaveled in the proceedings at 11:15 a.m.

He had been appointed by President Nixon and was 83 years old, but he looked even older. Though tall, he appeared to suffer from some kind of spinal curvature that caused him to stoop. This affliction made it nearly impossible for him to look up from his desk. Any movement appeared painful.

Randy spoke first and then handed the reins to Richard. As Richard began, Judge Griesa asked him to speak into the microphone—it seemed the judge was also having trouble hearing. Richard went to the lectern and resumed, but within moments, Judge Griesa interrupted. He was confused about why we were making this motion. It quickly became apparent that he hadn't read any of the hundreds of pages of filings from either side.

A good lawyer is prepared for this type of thing, and Richard calmly walked Judge Griesa through the whole story. Richard appeared to be doing well, but then the judge started asking questions.

Over the course of the next hour, Judge Griesa mixed up the purpose of the hearing. He couldn't keep track of who I was or how I was related to John Moscow. He couldn't follow how Prevezon had ended up with some of the stolen money. At one point, he couldn't even remember that the original fraud had taken place in Russia.

Richard drew on all of his patience and knowledge of Judge Griesa to try to get through this fog, but nothing seemed to work.

It wasn't any easier for Cymrot. He argued that since I routinely gave speeches about Sergei and posted YouTube videos and Power-Point presentations about the $230 million fraud, I had long ago waived any right to attorney-client confidentiality.

Judge Griesa couldn't follow any of this. "Who's making speeches again?" he demanded.

"He gives speeches publicly," Cymrot explained.

"Who?"

"Mr. Browder."

"Who is putting things on the Internet?"

"Mr. Browder and Hermitage. They have a website, Your Honor . . . and they give speeches all the time, every month."

"Who gives speeches to whom?"

Even Cymrot seemed exasperated. "Mr. Browder gives speeches," he said slowly into the microphone, "talking about Mr. Magnitsky, the $230 million fraud, and why the Russian state is a criminal enterprise."

Although completely confused, the judge seemed to sympathize with John Moscow. When the lawyers were done arguing, Judge Griesa announced, "To take [John Moscow] off the case so that he can't do a very different job, I don't even know why Hermitage would want to do that. Frankly, it's kind of a mean thing to try to do."

Judges aren't supposed to rule on whether things are "mean" or not—they're supposed to rule on the law.

It was plain that we were going to lose. Randy intervened at the last minute, asking Judge Griesa for a meeting in his chambers. The judge agreed, and Randy, Richard, John Moscow, and Mark Cymrot assembled in his office.

Richard presented the judge with the transcript of the call I'd had with John Moscow on the day Sergei was arrested—the call in which John Moscow talked about tracing the $230 million as it left "footprints" in the "snow"—along with some other private, attorney-client conversations between us. The materials disproved John Moscow's claim that he never helped trace the $230 million, as well as Cymrot's assertion that I hadn't shared any confidential information with them.

This closed-door session went on for well over an hour. In the end, Judge Griesa wasn't convinced, but he agreed to allow a second hearing, which was scheduled for October 23.

The whole thing was infuriating, but I also couldn't help feeling a little sorry for Judge Griesa. My father, who was roughly the same age, had won the National Medal of Science and had been one of the world's preeminent mathematicians. At the height of his career, he solved some of the most complex nonlinear partial differential equations in existence, but now, in his mid-80s, simple tasks like paying utility bills or setting the burglar alarm were a challenge. Witnessing the indignity of his aging had been one of the saddest experiences of my life.

The reality was that Judge Griesa no longer had any business being in that courtroom. We'd run into a peculiarity of the American justice system—there is no mandatory retirement age for federal judges. They can literally carry on until the day they die. I'm sure Judge Griesa had been a lion of the bar earlier in his career, but now he was a shadow of his former self, and we were paying the price.

I fixated on this during the week between hearings and grew increasingly worried. I spoke to Randy on the eve of the second hearing. He could tell I was concerned, but he remained calm and confident. "Don't worry, Bill. I'll bring him around."

The following afternoon, all the lawyers reassembled in room 26B.

Randy argued this time, relying on common sense more than complicated legal arguments to sway the judge.

But the more Randy spoke, the more frustrated Judge Griesa became. It seemed like he was angry with himself for not being able to do what had previously come so effortlessly. He simply could not follow. He couldn't see how John Moscow's prior work for us was in any way connected to the current work he was doing for Prevezon.

Shamefully, as Randy argued, John Moscow stage-whispered from across the courtroom, saying things like, "That's not true!" and "Randy, how can you say that?" It was one of the most unprofessional things Randy had ever experienced, but Judge Griesa wasn't going to put a stop to it since he couldn't hear what John Moscow was saying.

Randy spoke for nearly an hour and a half, patiently trying to work through Judge Griesa's frustration. Cymrot went next. Realizing he'd all but won, he spoke for barely ten minutes.

The game was over. But at the last second, Paul Monteleoni intervened, asking to be heard. He wanted to make a last-ditch effort to clear up the judge's confusion. He stood, went to the microphone, and spent the next few minutes explaining that Hermitage and Prevezon were on opposite ends of the same crime.

Still confused, Judge Griesa asked, "Are you claiming that Prevezon was somehow working with Hermitage to perform the money laundering?"

"No," Paul exclaimed. "Prevezon certainly wasn't working with Hermitage. Hermitage was the victim."

I'm sure every lawyer in that courtroom could barely believe their ears. After hundreds of pages of filings, two hearings, and a lengthy session in chambers, Judge Griesa *still* could not understand the basics of the case.

At this point, he ruled from the bench, saying he saw "no reason whatever why Moscow cannot represent Prevezon, his new client, in this new action." He carried on, "This new action is a different animal. . . . Thank you very much."

And that was that. John Moscow and BakerHostetler would remain on the case.

In Russia, our adversaries were ecstatic. Within an hour, Natalia Veselnitskaya, the Katsyv family lawyer, published a lengthy Facebook post. It was contorted and difficult to follow, but on one count she was surprisingly honest. Dubbing the US vs. Prevezon case "Browder vs. Russia," she waved away the entire argument that BakerHostetler had just made. We were absolutely adverse to Prevezon.

The title of her post said it all: "Today is a significant day. 1–0 for Russia."

19

The Daily Show

FALL 2014–WINTER 2015

After our failed bid to disqualify John Moscow and BakerHostetler, Randy lost a bit of his swagger. He was confident he could still quash the Aspen subpoena—and he eventually did—but he was emphatic that I not come to New York while the Prevezon case was live. "If you get served here, it's a whole different ball game," he warned.

But not going to New York was easier said than done. I was regularly there for business and personal reasons, since my parents lived in Princeton, New Jersey, which wasn't far away.

That fall, during Thanksgiving dinner, I got a call from Natalie, the live-in nurse who looked after my parents at their home.

"Bill, your mother's not well," she told me. "We've taken her to the emergency room. I think you need to come home."

My mother was 85 and had been unwell for years. In her mid-70s she had suffered a major stroke that left her partially paralyzed and wheelchair-bound. At 83, she was diagnosed with Alzheimer's disease and since then had suffered one setback after another. As a child, she'd fled Vienna and traveled alone across the Atlantic to the United States to escape Hitler and the Holocaust—but she could not escape the ravages of Alzheimer's.

I'd lived outside the United States since she was 60. For many years, when my parents were well, we found ways to see each other, either in America or the UK. But when my mother's health deteriorated, all that changed. Not being close to her filled me with guilt.

When my mother had been in a similar position decades earlier, she'd been racked by guilt too. Her mother, Erna, had broken a hip in her mid-80s, incapacitating her. Unable to live on her own, she ended up in a dismal nursing home in Alameda, California, paid for by Medicaid. She went through a long and degrading decline. It was painful to watch, and my parents, who lived on a professor's salary, didn't have the means to improve her living situation or bring her home to New Jersey.

I was 24 at the time and in business school. I was the only family member on the West Coast, so I visited my grandmother as regularly as I could. I hated seeing her deteriorate in such a cold, uncaring place. My grandmother eventually died alone in an unfamiliar setting, far from those who loved her. Even I wasn't able to be there when it finally happened.

Following Erna's passing, I made a silent promise: I would have the means to make sure this never happened to my own parents, or anyone I loved. Twenty-six years later, I'd made good on this promise. When my parents were similarly frail, I was fortunate to be able to ensure that they could live at home being attended to by caring aides and nurses.

After speaking to Natalie that Thanksgiving night, I booked myself onto the first flight to Newark. Even though Princeton is in New Jersey and not New York, going there meant I would be ignoring Randy's warning. A US federal court's jurisdiction doesn't stop at state lines but rather just beyond a 100-mile radius from the court, and Princeton is roughly 50 miles from New York City.

But there was no way I was going to let John Moscow or the threat of any of his subpoenas stop me from seeing my mother when she was gravely ill.

After clearing customs at Newark the next afternoon, I rented a car and drove straight to the Princeton Medical Center, a modern hospital on the outskirts of town. When I arrived, I discovered that my mother's condition was far worse than I'd expected.

The doctor came by and explained it was likely she wouldn't pull through. As a matter of protocol, he asked if I intended to authorize a do not resuscitate order for her.

Back in the days when she was still lucid, she'd made me swear not to go to any Herculean efforts to keep her alive in a situation like this, and I wasn't going to go back on that promise now. I told the doctor I would authorize the DNR.

It was one thing to talk about these issues in the abstract years before, but now that it was real, it felt terrible. I called my brother, Tom, who lived in Hawaii. He needed to be there as well. He arrived the next day, and we sat at our mother's bedside for the rest of the week, waiting, praying, and hoping. My father wanted to be there too, but sadly he wasn't well enough to leave home.

Miraculously, however, on the fifth day, my mother's condition improved. Her blood pressure stabilized and her breathing became less labored. One by one, the nurses removed the machines attached to her. Three days later, she was stable enough to be discharged, and was sent home in an ambulance.

It wasn't her time after all.

Tom and I spent one more night with our parents. The next morning, after saying goodbye to Tom, I sat with my mother, holding her hand as we looked out on the backyard, watching the squirrels search for acorns. I talked to her, even though she had no idea who I was or what I was saying. I told her what her grandkids were up to and where David was going to college; I even talked to her about the Magnitsky Act.

Before leaving, I pulled Natalie aside. "I'm having trouble with some Russians," I said. "If anything unusual happens around here, please let me know." Natalie was originally from Georgia—the country in the Caucasus, not the US state—and she knew from her country's hard experience what Russians were capable of. She promised to keep her eyes open.

I returned to London. For the time being, my mother was well enough that I didn't need to be by her side. But I had a real dilemma coming up in the new year. *Red Notice* was set to be published in early February, and I was slated to be in New York to launch it. There was no way I'd be able to stay under John Moscow's radar on that trip.

When Randy heard about the book tour, he was adamant I not come to New York. I might have taken that advice if my only concern had been minimizing the subpoena risk, but there was a lot more at stake. The Russians had invested so much in creating a false narrative about Sergei that it was essential I share the true story of what happened as far and wide as possible. I could brief lawmakers and prosecutors until I was blue in the face, but there would be no substitute for a bestselling book.

My editor at Simon & Schuster, Priscilla Painton, thought we had a real shot. But books don't sell themselves, especially from first-time authors, and the only way to hit the bestseller list was to take every interview and go on every TV show that would have me.

I *had* to go to New York.

Just before Christmas, as Elena and I wrapped presents for our kids in the bedroom, Natalie called again.

Her tone was different this time. "You wanted me to call if I saw something."

"Yes. What's happened?"

"There were two men walking around the house in the snow trying to peek in as I was making dinner tonight." The house was on a cul-de-sac—it was practically in the woods—and anyone lurking around had no business being there.

"Did you get a good look at them?"

"No. It was too dark. But I've made sure all the doors are locked and the alarm is on. What should I do if they come back?"

"Call 911. Then call me."

This news was jarring. I couldn't be certain that John Moscow was behind these mysterious men, but if he was, it would be beyond the pale. Moreover, if he was this committed and well resourced, it would be a lot harder for me to promote the book in New York and not have him track me down.

Somehow, I needed to find a way to do this book tour without incident.

I mostly relied on Sophie de Selliers, who worked for me on the Magnitsky campaign, to figure out how to do this. Sophie was a graduate of Edinburgh University in Scotland and took law classes at night. Although only 29, she was mature beyond her years and highly vigilant.

She plotted my schedule to the smallest detail, asking each producer and journalist in New York to provide alternative ways for entering and exiting their buildings to avoid being ambushed. Most of them understood my reasons—those who didn't probably hadn't read the book.

As Sophie put the finishing touches on my New York itinerary, I got another call from Natalie. She sounded even more agitated. "Bill, you need to come home. I think this is it." She explained that my mother had stopped eating and drinking entirely. If this continued, she only had a few days left.

I put everything on hold and returned to New Jersey. Sadly, my brother, Tom, couldn't make the trip, and Elena had to stay in London with the kids. It was just me, my father, and Natalie sitting vigil next to my mother's bed.

This time my mother was at home, not in the hospital. My parents had an old-style family doctor who made house calls. He came by on the day I arrived, and when I asked what we could do to make her eat or drink, he answered simply, "Nothing. She's decided now is her time." He knew as well as I did that she didn't want her life artificially prolonged. He explained that her body would slowly shut down but that she wouldn't be in any pain or discomfort.

For the next few days I sat with her, reminiscing and reassuring her that she wasn't alone. I'd hold up my iPad and put her on FaceTime so Tom, Elena, and David could each talk to her.

I'd take breaks every now and then to walk around the house and clear my head, using the stairs for exercise. My father had about 35,000 books in orderly shelves in the finished basement, by authors ranging from Aristotle to St. Thomas Aquinas to Gogol, on subjects from geophysics to art history to topology. The books were in English, French, and Russian, and were organized like a college library. He had read them all. Whenever we visited, the kids would play hide-and-seek and get lost among them, sometimes for hours. As I wandered the basement that week, I thought about how impressive it all was—but also about how much my mother hated my father's book-collecting obsession.

For the most part, I was able to concentrate on my mother in those final days, but whenever I passed a window overlooking the yard, John Moscow invaded my thoughts. I filled with rage that there was even a possibility that he and his subpoena would intrude at a moment like this.

Four days in, my mother's breathing became slower and slower.

Two hospice nurses came that afternoon. They promised that if there were any indication she was in pain they would give her morphine. However, when they saw her, they reassured me that she wasn't in any distress.

Toward evening, she was close to the end. I held her hand and told her I loved her. Then she breathed her last breath and was gone.

People always use the expression "rest in peace." And when she passed I could see that she genuinely was in peace. She wasn't struggling, and the years of pain and suffering were finally over.

Later, after she was taken to the funeral home, I drove to nearby Carnegie Lake. There was a pull-out where I would sometimes sit in the car as I shuttled between my parents' home and the hospital, just to think and be alone. Looking over the still water, I reflected that the process of her dying at home was much less upsetting than any of the times I'd visited her at the hospital when she was alive and hooked up to all those machines. Yes, losing my mother was devastating, but being there in her last moments somehow made it more bearable.

This was the second significant loss in my life after Sergei Magnitsky. My mother's natural, peaceful death at home and among people she loved made his murder that much more awful. In addition to being robbed of decades of life, Sergei had spent his last moments alone without any loved ones, in a cold isolation cell, being beaten to death.

As I flew back to London, I realized that the best way for me to mourn my mother *and* right the injustice of what had happened to Sergei was to convert my sorrow into righteous action. In two weeks, I would return to New York.

And I would promote the hell out of *Red Notice*.

*   *   *

I was back in Manhattan on February 2, 2015. My first interview was with *Fox & Friends* at 6:45 a.m. Sophie had asked the producers not to pre-announce my appearance, so John Moscow and his team would have no idea I was there until I was actually on-air.

We entered the Fox building through the loading dock on West 48th Street, about 150 yards from the main entrance on 6th Avenue. Our car pulled in next to an idling delivery truck. There were some maintenance workers milling around smoking cigarettes. One of them said loudly, "You guys're in the wrong place! You gotta go around front."

"No, no," Sophie said. "We're in the right place. It's all been arranged."

The maintenance guy was about to say something else when a door opened and two burly security guards appeared. "You Mr. Browder?" one of them shouted. I nodded. "Come with us." We followed them through a maze of hallways to the greenroom, which was also on the building's ground floor.

During a commercial break, the producer guided me to the couch on-set where I was greeted by the show's three co-hosts. The Russians had been in the news a lot. They'd invaded Ukraine, shot down a passenger plane, and cheated in the Olympics—and it seemed like the hosts wholeheartedly agreed that Putin was a malign influence on the world. I told Sergei's story just as I had many times before, but now I was able to back it up with a hardcover book that sat on the coffee table in front of us. The interview was over in less than five minutes, but it couldn't have gone better.

Sophie and I left the way we came in, with no problems. As the car crossed town, I pictured John Moscow watching the interview and making frantic phone calls, trying to figure out where I would appear next.

The next interview was at *Slate*. There was no way John Moscow could know I was there because we were taping a podcast and it wasn't live, but Sophie and I used a side door anyway.

After that, I did two interviews for print, one at the *Wall Street Journal* and another at *Business Insider*, before going back to the hotel to do several radio interviews from my room. When I was done, I took a break, had a late lunch, and prepared for the biggest interview of the trip—*The Daily Show*.

Having lived in London for the previous 26 years, I knew very little about *The Daily Show*, a satirical news program then hosted by Jon Stewart, a comedian with a smart and incisive wit. I was nervous to go on a comedy show, but my friend Juleanna Glover, a Washington, DC, insider who had been instrumental in helping to get the

Magnitsky Act passed, assured me that going on this show practically guaranteed *Red Notice* would be a bestseller. She was so enthusiastic that she took the train up from DC that afternoon to accompany me and Sophie.

But there was a rub. *The Daily Show* wasn't only the most rewarding event, it was also the riskiest. It was their policy to publicize every guest in advance with no exceptions—including me. John Moscow was sure to know I would be there.

For this reason, we took extra precautions. We arrived at the studio's side entrance on West 51st Street well over an hour before the show began. We scanned the street in both directions before exiting the car. Nobody was within 50 feet of us, so Sophie called the producer. Within a minute, the side door opened. We hustled out of the car and security brought us inside.

We went to the greenroom and got settled. A few minutes before the show started, Jon Stewart rushed in to welcome me. He took me through the running order and asked if I had any questions.

I only had one. "Am I supposed to be funny?" I had no idea how to be funny on command, and certainly not about such a serious subject.

"No, no. Just be yourself and answer like you would on any other show," he said. "I'll be telling the jokes. That's my job." He smiled, turned on his heel, and left.

A short while later, I heard the muffled roar of laughter from the studio audience. The show had begun. I was suddenly more nervous than I'd ever been to appear on TV. The producer then came in and told me it was time. Moments later, I was onstage.

It was a large room. All the surfaces were painted black, and all the lights were pointed at the stage, so I couldn't see the audience. But they cheered, and Jon Stewart stood to welcome me. As expected, it was unlike any interview I'd done before. Jon Stewart clowned around, but never about me or Sergei, only about Putin and his cronies.

Toward the end of the interview, as we discussed banks and money laundering, he interjected, "But if the banks know this is dirty money, shouldn't we just put the banks also on the [Magnitsky] list?"

This drew the biggest cheer of the night. Nobody likes banks.

A few moments later I got the plug every author dreams of when Jon Stewart propped the book on the edge of his desk and said, "Unbelievable story. *Red Notice*. It's on the bookshelves now. Bill Browder."

The music started and I shook his hand. Before I knew it, I was back in the greenroom. Sophie was beaming and Juleanna gave me a big hug. "That was amazing, Bill."

In the rush of it all I had completely forgotten about John Moscow and his process servers, but as we moved to exit the studio through the same side door, a member of *The Daily Show*'s security team stepped in front of me and said, "Let me check if the coast is clear, Mr. Browder." He went outside. The sun had set since we'd entered, and it had begun snowing. A few seconds later, the security guard popped back in and gave me, Juleanna, and Sophie the thumbs-up.

As we crossed the sidewalk to our car, two large men suddenly emerged from the shadows and barreled toward us. Juleanna spotted them first, grabbed my arm, and shouted, "Bill, get in the car!"

Getting "served." Sophie (second from left), process server
(center), Juleanna (second from right), and me (right).
The person at left in the white coat is unknown. February 2015.
(U.S. COURT DOCKET NYSD)

One of the men actually shoved Juleanna out of the way just as I dropped into the back seat. He forced himself into the small space between the car and the door, and no matter how hard I pulled, I couldn't close it.

Realizing I was losing this tug-of-war, I slid across the back seat, opened the other door, and exited into the icy, snow-filled street. I jogged away, weaving through traffic toward the West Side Highway. I needed a cab but couldn't find one, as any New Yorker will appreciate. I kept going, doubling back around the block on 50th Street, and finally spotted a cab on 11th Avenue. If the man was chasing me, he was nowhere in sight.

I got in the cab and barked, "Midtown!"

The driver half turned in his seat. "We're *in* Midtown, mister."

"The Sheraton, then." It was the first hotel that popped in my head, even though I wasn't staying there.

"Got it."

As the cab crawled across the Theater District, I kept peering through the back window to see if anyone was following us. It didn't look like it, but there were so many cars that I couldn't be certain.

We pulled up to the Sheraton 15 minutes later. I went straight to the bar and ordered a drink. I waited for a half hour, and when I was certain I hadn't been followed, I stepped outside and took another cab to my real hotel. No suspicious characters appeared to be there, either.

Once back in my room, I called Randy. He was not impressed. "I told you not to come to New York, Bill."

"Have I been served? I think the guy threw something in the car, but he definitely didn't hand me anything."

"It's hard to say. But this isn't good."

The next morning, I learned that John Moscow's latest subpoena had arrived at Randy's office. We would contest it, but we were going to have to appear in front of Judge Griesa again.

I did get some comfort that morning, though. *Red Notice* had broken Amazon's top 20 bestseller list. At least I had achieved my main objective. A lot more people would soon know the true story of what had happened to Sergei Magnitsky.

But because of John Moscow, I had no idea at what cost to my safety, or that of my colleagues.

20

Boris Nemtsov

WINTER–SPRING 2015

One upside to the *Daily Show* incident was that Sophie and I no longer had to obsess about process servers. For the rest of our stay in New York, there was no more sneaking through side doors or loading docks, and I could focus entirely on promoting the book.

Over the next couple of weeks, *Red Notice* hit the *New York Times* bestseller list in the United States and the *Sunday Times* bestseller list in the UK. People weren't just buying it and putting it on their bedside tables. They were actually reading it—and enjoying it.

After promoting the book in the United States and Britain, I headed to continental Europe. It hadn't been much of a stretch to convince an Anglo-American audience that Putin wasn't a good guy, but in Europe it was a different story. Despite our consistent efforts, there was no Magnitsky Act anywhere in the European Union. And on the law enforcement side, while several money laundering cases had been opened—including a prominent one in France—their pace was glacial and a few were even stalled altogether. I hoped *Red Notice*, which was being published in 12 European countries, would change all that.

Our main difficulty was that, in contrast to the United States, Europe had a smattering of political factions that were nakedly pro-Putin, and they had infected the mainstream debate.

In France, for example, Marine Le Pen, the leader of the far-right National Front party, openly took millions of euros from a Kremlin-connected bank to fund her political party. In return, it appeared that she supported most of Putin's anti-Western policies.

In Germany, former chancellor Gerhard Schröder had taken a lucrative position at a subsidiary of Gazprom, the Russian gas behemoth, almost the moment he left office. Even though he was a longtime Social Democrat, a party committed to freedom and social justice, Schröder became one of Putin's most vocal supporters in Europe.

In Hungary, the autocratic prime minister, Viktor Orban, regularly intervened on Putin's behalf in the EU, making no attempt to hide his sympathies.

There was, however, at least one EU country that was clear-eyed about Russia at that moment—the Netherlands.

In the summer of 2014, Malaysian Airlines flight MH17, en route from Amsterdam to Kuala Lumpur, was shot down by a Russian surface-to-air missile over Eastern Ukraine, killing everyone on board. Of the 298 victims, 193 were Dutch. The Kremlin had tried to deflect blame, but the evidence pointed overwhelmingly to official Russian involvement.* For Holland, a country of only 17 million people, this act of terror was their equivalent to September 11, and the blame fell squarely on Putin's shoulders.

Because of this, there was more media interest in *Red Notice* in the Netherlands than in any other European country.

I flew to Amsterdam on the morning of February 26 and went straight to my publisher's office in an 18th-century townhouse on the Prinsengracht canal. Instead of running around Amsterdam to each media outlet as I had in New York, my publisher sat me in a conference room and a different journalist cycled through every 30 minutes.

This went on for two days. My media blitz in Amsterdam culminated with an appearance on *Jinek*, one of Holland's most popular evening TV talk shows, with a million nightly viewers. *Jinek* had the same power in Holland to turn a book into a bestseller as *The Daily Show* had in the United States.

---

* This was confirmed in 2018 when a Dutch-led investigation concluded that MH17 had been downed by a single Buk surface-to-air missile belonging to the Russian 53rd Anti-Aircraft Brigade based in Kursk, Russia. The mobile unit had been moved into Donetsk, Ukraine, used to shoot down the passenger jet, and then moved back to Russia. Vladimir Putin continues to deny any Russian involvement in this act of terror.

I arrived at the studio half an hour before show time. *Jinek*'s green-room was unlike any I'd been in. It was more like a hip nightclub, with loud music, a bar, waiters bringing food and drinks, and tables and couches everywhere. The room bustled with young, trendy-looking people. When I asked someone if it was always like this, they said, "Not exactly. It's the last show of the season. I guess you could say the after-party's already begun."

I went to the bar and ordered a drink. As I waited, I looked to my left, and was surprised to find the Dutch prime minister, Mark Rutte, standing next to me. I'd been so busy over the previous two days that I hadn't had time to look up who else would be on the show that night. Apparently, he was the lead interview.

We chitchatted for a few minutes. Rutte wasn't my favorite politician by any stretch. In 2011, long before the MH17 atrocity, the Dutch Parliament had unanimously passed a resolution calling on their government to enact a Magnitsky Act, but Rutte had blocked it. Like many other European leaders, he had been reluctant to offend Putin. Dutch companies were among the prime beneficiaries of the construction of the multibillion-dollar Nord Stream 2 Pipeline, among other things, and Rutte didn't want to upset the flow of money.

That night, however, perhaps due to recent events, Rutte was only too happy to stand shoulder to shoulder with me, smiling for pictures as he held up a copy of my book.

A few minutes later a producer escorted Rutte and me, along with the other guests, to the studio. The show was live, and the stage was in the middle of the audience on a circular platform. It had the same casual, party-like atmosphere as the greenroom, almost as if there were no distinction between the two.

The show's host, a blond 30-something named Eva Jinek, had been born in Tulsa, Oklahoma, spent her early childhood in DC, and then moved with her family to the Netherlands at age 11. She was the go-to interviewer for any newsworthy American in Holland. She sat in a chair to the left of a huge semicircular couch, which was reserved for guests. Rutte went to the couch while I sat in the front row among the studio audience. Since the show was in Dutch, I was handed a headset so I could listen to a live translation.

With Dutch prime minister Mark Rutte in the
Jinek greenroom, February 27, 2015. (© BILL BROWDER)

Eva started her interview by asking Rutte about a scandal involving the misuse of a few hundred euros by a member of his political party. It was hard for me to feel anything about this. In my estimation, Putin had stolen billions from the Russian people. I couldn't understand why a few hundred euros would even warrant a mention. As Eva continued to grill Rutte, I lost interest and started checking messages on my phone.

As I scrolled, I came across a text that stopped me cold. It was from Elena Servettaz, a Russian reporter with Radio France Internationale in Paris. It read, "Nemtsov is killed in Moscow!"

I stared at the words, my thumb frozen over the glowing screen. This couldn't be true. I furiously typed "Nemtsov" into Google. Multiple media reports confirmed it. Boris Nemtsov had been shot dead, within feet of the Kremlin, only minutes before.

My heart began to race.

Since meeting Boris in Helsinki, he had become not just an indispensable ally, but a friend. The more I got to know him, the more my admiration for him had grown. Like every other high-level Russian official, he'd had the opportunity to stick his snout in the trough and get fat off corruption and malfeasance. But he rejected this greedy, gluttonous life. He'd taken the difficult and righteous path of standing up for ordinary Russians and speaking out against those abusing power.

After the Magnitsky Act was passed in the United States, he was often asked, "Isn't this an anti-Russian law?" And he would respond, "No. This is the most pro-Russian law passed in the United States in the history of our countries."

For this stance he was reviled in official Russia. Once, following a trip to Washington where he had presented a list of Putin's cronies to US senators to be added to the Magnitsky List, Boris was physically attacked inside Sheremetyevo Airport by members of a pro-Putin youth group called Nashi. That attack hadn't surprised me.

But to kill him was unimaginable.

Emotions stormed within me as I sat on that TV stage in Amsterdam. All I wanted to do was get out of there. But right at that moment, the audience applauded. Rutte's segment was over. A short video featuring Sergei and me began playing. Dazed, I took my spot on the guest couch. The video ended. Eva Jinek switched to perfect American English and introduced me.

She went through Sergei's story. I tried to appear engaged as I answered her questions, but I couldn't stop thinking of Boris. I had to find some way to discuss what had just happened.

"You're sitting here recognizable as yourself," she said, toward the end. "There's no way that can be safe for you."

"There's no way it *is* safe. They've threatened to kill me. They've threatened to kidnap me. I should say that just a couple of minutes ago I got terrible, terrible news from Russia that Boris Nemtsov, who is one of the leaders of the opposition, was gunned down and killed on Red Square."

"Just now?"

"Just, literally, a few minutes ago." The audience gasped. A moment later, the producers put an image of Boris on the screens around the stage.

"Do they have any idea by whom?" Eva asked, startled by this breaking news.

"I just got the headline. But I can't not mention that on this show right now."

The interview ended a few minutes later. I was still desperate to leave but felt I couldn't, so I took my seat next to the prime minister and, for the next 20 minutes, endured lighthearted segments on 3D printing and some Dutch hip-hop group.

As soon as the show ended, I rushed outside and hailed a cab back to my hotel. As the taxi wound through the streets of Amsterdam, Elena Servettaz texted again. "I spoke to Vladimir KM. He's there next to Boris . . . he's destroyed." She was referring to Vladimir Kara-Murza, Boris's 33-year-old protégé who, like him, had been standing up to Putin in Russia and advocating for Magnitsky Acts around the world.

I called Vladimir. He was inconsolable. Between sobs, all I could gather was that Vladimir was on the bridge near the Kremlin, only a short distance from the ambulance that held Boris's body. I tried to get more details, but Vladimir could barely speak.

I spent the whole night on the phone and computer, and eventually was able to piece together some of what had happened.

That night, Boris had given an interview at Echo Moscow Radio about an upcoming anti-Putin demonstration he was organizing. Afterward, he met his girlfriend at a restaurant in Moscow's GUM shopping arcade. When they'd finished dinner, they walked home, arm-in-arm. They strolled past Red Square toward Boris's apartment on the other side of the river. As they crossed Bolshoy Moskvoretsky Bridge, a large snowplow rolled alongside them. At that moment, an assassin jumped from a darkened stairway on the side of the bridge and shot Boris six times. Boris died instantly. His girlfriend escaped unscathed.

Boris lay on his back, his legs twisted and his shirt hiked to his armpits, exposing his stomach and chest. There he remained for a long time, before being zipped into a black body bag and loaded into an ambulance. As the news spread, his ex-wife, Raisa, and his daughter, Zhanna, rushed to the scene. They arrived at the same time as Vladimir Kara-Murza. The three of them were initially forced to remain behind a police barrier, but they were so visibly upset that the police eventually let them through. They begged to see Boris, but their pleas fell on deaf ears.

The authorities cleared the scene, and a street cleaning truck ar-

Boris Nemtsov's body on the Bolshoy Moskvoretsky Bridge,
February 27, 2015. (© EVGENIY FELDMAN/NOVAYA GAZETA)

rived. It sprayed water across the bridge, erasing any chance of a proper forensic investigation.

The next morning, I returned to London. I was completely hollowed out, but I still went to the office. When I arrived, there was more incomprehensible news. The Russian government had announced that all CCTV cameras surrounding the Bolshoy Moskvoretsky Bridge had been switched off for "maintenance" the night before. This was utterly implausible. Boris's murder occurred just next to the Kremlin, the most heavily surveilled piece of real estate in all of Russia. The only working camera filming the bridge belonged to a television station called TV Centre, which was half a mile away. However, the snowplow blocked its line of sight at the exact moment Boris was shot.

Everything the authorities did following his murder showed they had no intention of getting to the truth. Instead of chasing proper leads, they raided Boris's apartment and office, seizing his files, computers, phones, hard drives, and anything connected with his political activities. They were more interested in knowing who was assisting him in his opposition to Putin than establishing who had killed him.

The authorities may not have been interested in the truth, but the Russian people were. Two days after his assassination, more than 50,000 of them took to the streets, stretching for miles along the Moscow River. What had been planned as an anti-Putin march before Boris had been killed was now a mass demonstration of public grief, one that demanded justice. Thousands of flowers had been placed on the spot where Boris was assassinated. The authorities swiftly removed these, but people kept coming back to put down more. This happened again and again and again. To this day, flowers still mark the location as a semi-permanent memorial to Boris Nemtsov.

Boris's murder caused such a furor that the Kremlin had to do something, so the authorities arrested five Chechen men (a sixth died in an explosion just as he was about to be arrested). One of these men confessed, but later it transpired that he had been tortured before his confession. Another of the men turned out to be an active member of the Russian Interior Ministry.

Eventually, all five would be sentenced to long prison terms for

Boris Nemtsov's funeral. (© OLGA MALTSEVA/AFP/GETTY IMAGES)

Boris Nemtsov's makeshift memorial on Bolshoy Moskvoretsky
Bridge. (© ANADOLU AGENCY/GETTY IMAGES)

their involvement in Boris's murder. These convictions served the
bigger purpose of allocating blame. No senior officers were ever
questioned, and, as expected, Putin was never implicated in Boris's
murder.*

I had no doubt that Putin had ordered Boris's assassination. And
I wasn't alone. When public opinion pointed to Putin as having the
strongest motive to kill Boris, the president's press secretary, Dmitri
Peskov, insisted that Boris "did not pose any threat to the current Russian leadership" and that "Boris Nemtsov was just a little bit more than
an average citizen."

This was a remarkable statement. It was as if the Kremlin was
suggesting that if Boris *had been* a threat—which, as everyone knew,
he was—then it would have been perfectly appropriate for them to
kill him.

Besides, Putin knew that Boris was no "average citizen." Tens of
thousands—perhaps hundreds of thousands—of people were already

---

* A February 2020 report by the Parliamentary Assembly of the OSCE argued that Putin
more than likely ordered Boris's assassination.

behind Boris. If Putin had allowed that popularity and respect to grow, Boris's momentum would have eventually become unstoppable.

Perhaps the thing that most upset Putin about Boris was his work on the Magnitsky Act. In Putin's mind, this was an unforgivable betrayal.

But beyond all of this was the message that Boris's murder sent to people like Vladimir Kara-Murza and me. A year earlier, in an appearance on CNN, Boris had said, "I'm a well-known guy, and this is safety because if something happens to me, it will be a scandal not only in Moscow, but throughout the world."

I had said nearly identical words about myself many times. And even though his death was scandalous, these words were now meaningless.

Boris's murder showed that Putin did not care.

21

Arrow in Your Neck

SPRING 2015

Boris's murder made the *Daily Show* subpoena that much more dangerous. If the Russians were able to get any of the confidential information BakerHostetler had requested, then the Kremlin would have a detailed roadmap for how to harm my colleagues, our sources in Russia, and me.

There was a slight chance the subpoena could still be stopped, though. A hearing had been scheduled for March 9 to determine if it was valid. I was in disbelief that we were even in this situation. We'd spent years upgrading our cyber defenses and the physical security of our offices to prevent the Russians from learning these types of details. Now it looked as if they were just going to waltz into a US courthouse and take all our confidential information with the explicit support of a federal judge.

In the lead-up to the hearing, I asked Randy, "How can they do this? What do my security arrangements and travel records have to do with Prevezon's defense?"

"Nothing," Randy replied. "But even if the subpoena is granted, we'll make sure the court doesn't allow them to ask for stuff like that."

"Except Judge Griesa doesn't understand anything," I protested. "If he doesn't see John Moscow's conflict of interest, there's no way he'll see why this subpoena is so dangerous."

"Even if he rules the subpoena is valid, we'll get a chance to narrow it," Randy said calmly. "Overbroad subpoenas like this are never just granted. And the process of narrowing it won't happen in front of

Judge Griesa. He'll hand it off to someone called a magistrate who specializes in this type of thing."

On the afternoon of March 9, 2015, Randy returned to court. For nearly an hour, Randy took the judge through a series of legal arguments for why the subpoena shouldn't be valid. He also stressed that granting it would place me in even greater personal danger.

But the longer Randy spoke about me, the more annoyed Judge Griesa became. He didn't care about whether any Russians were going to come and kill me. All he cared about was that the Prevezon case had been stalled in his courtroom for a year and a half. From his perspective, I was the bottleneck. And he wanted that bottleneck cleared.

Judge Griesa got so worked up that when the time came for his decision, he quickly and summarily ruled against me, declaring the *Daily Show* subpoena valid.

But then he did something truly extraordinary. Instead of sending the subpoena to a magistrate to work out the details, he granted it *in full*. There would be no narrowing of the details, as Randy had promised. The Russians would get every single thing they'd asked for. Judge Griesa was so angry that he told Randy not to "file letters and other documents. No paperwork. We have had enough of it and we don't need any more about Mr. Browder."

With this decision, I would now effectively have to hand over the entire Hermitage computer server, all of my old laptops, and every mobile phone I'd ever carried. As soon as that happened, the Kremlin would know about every person I'd ever met, every place I'd ever been, every correspondence we'd had with every source in Russia, every law enforcement agency we'd ever contacted—and a whole lot more.

Equally alarming, the judge also granted BakerHostetler's request that I sit for a deposition on April 15. Not only would I have to give them all the information from the subpoena, I'd have to answer questions about it too.

I had to hand it to the Russians. They'd failed to get me into their own court system for years, but now they were using a US court proceeding, in which they were the target, to do the exact equivalent.

Conventional lawyering clearly wasn't working. We had a judge who couldn't understand legal arguments and a shameless adversary. I really liked Randy and I knew he was a great lawyer, but if I had any chance of coming out of this, I needed a radical change. And I needed it fast.

That night I called a man named Michael Kim. He had been recommended to me as one of the cleverest and most unconventional lawyers in New York. Born in South Korea, he then moved to the United States with his family when he was a boy. Later he served as a US Army airborne officer before attending Harvard undergrad, followed by Harvard Law. After law school, he'd done a five-year stint at the SDNY, where he'd earned the distinction of receiving more death threats than any other criminal prosecutor there.

One of the most famous threats against Michael had involved a defendant who'd hidden a razor blade in his rectum before a court appearance. The defendant had planned to pull it out and slash Michael's throat in front of the jury during closing arguments, but he was foiled. Michael now keeps a framed X-ray of this man's torso on the wall of his office. Whenever he has to berate one of his young associates for not giving their all, he lights up the X-ray, revealing the metal rectangle in this man's body, and says, "That. That is commitment."

Michael Kim. (© MICHAEL KIM)

I explained our situation, expecting the same type of confident law-yer patter I'd heard from so many others, but Michael was circumspect. "Having Judge Griesa is a real problem," he said. At least he was being honest about that. "I'll look it over, but I'm not sure there's much I can do."

However, the following afternoon Michael called back sounding more upbeat. "Bill, this isn't going to be easy, but I have a plan."

"What is it?" I asked apprehensively.

"You have to think about it like you have an arrow in your neck," he said. "It has to come out one way or another. It's not going to be pleasant. If we pull it too suddenly, it may hit an artery and you'll die. So we need to ease it out slowly and gingerly."

He then explained his strategy, and how he wanted to set a trap for BakerHostetler. It was totally counterintuitive. I loved it.

From that moment forward, Michael Kim was my lawyer in New York.

Four days later, Michael sent a short and courteous letter to Judge Griesa introducing himself as my new counsel. He told the judge that we would fully comply with every aspect of the subpoena, including sitting for the deposition on April 15. He ended his letter by promising that we would try to resolve all disputes with the other side without "troubling the Court." This was music to Judge Griesa's ears.

This might have looked like total capitulation, but Michael had identified a chink in our opponents' armor. They had simply asked for too much. In an attempt to get the sensitive information they *really* wanted, they'd buried it in requests for all sorts of other information they didn't care about. Michael's insight was that we could easily com-ply with parts of the subpoena and not put anyone at risk.

Ten days later, we submitted 328,525 pages of documents to Baker-Hostetler. These included Russian court files, Russian Central Bank data, and bank records. Much of this was material John Moscow and BakerHostetler had already seen, and some of it was publicly available.

Every few days from then on, we sent them a further dump of sim-ilarly innocuous documents that they had asked for.

The lawyers at BakerHostetler were not naïve. They could easily see what we were doing. But they were in a bind. They couldn't go back to the judge and say we weren't cooperating, because we were. Nor could they claim that we weren't giving them what was stated in the subpoena, because we were handing over exactly what they'd asked for. We were just giving it to them in an order of our choosing.

BakerHostetler could have obtained everything they wanted if they'd only been willing to delay the deposition, which Michael graciously offered to do. But from the moment the judge had granted the subpoena, the Russians were so keen to get me into the deposition room that they stuck with the April 15 date.

As the day drew closer, we hadn't handed over a single document jeopardizing anyone's safety.

Sitting for a deposition, though, was potentially even more dangerous than the document requests. I would be under oath and obliged to answer any and all questions. They could ask about my family, Vadim's or Ivan's relatives in Russia, our sources—anything. If I refused to answer, I could be held in contempt of court, which is a criminal offense under US law.

Two days before the deposition, I arrived in New York to prepare with Michael. The following morning, I went to his office on 3rd Avenue and East 49th Street for the first time. It was generic, modern, and functional. There was no marble, no modern art, no pretense at all.

We went to a conference room that had been set up for a mock deposition and got started. Michael played the role of a lawyer from BakerHostetler. He slid a document across the table.

"Are you familiar with this?" he asked.

I glanced at it. "Yes. It's the complaint I filed with the New York DA's Office."

Michael broke character, shaking his head. "No. They could put any stack of papers in front of you. When they give you something, you have to read it carefully page by page to make sure what they're presenting is exactly what you think it is."

"But that could take ten or twenty minutes," I protested.

"Whose twenty minutes are those?"

"What do you mean?" I asked.

"They have a total of seven hours to depose you. If they want to waste twenty minutes verifying a document, that's their choice—and it's their twenty minutes."

This guy *was* clever.

We carried on. A short while later, Michael interjected, "Isn't it true that you stole the two hundred and thirty million dollars?"

"Of course not! It was the Russian government that—"

Michael held up his hand, cutting me off. "Bill, you have to train yourself to believe that there are no human beings in the room, just mannequins. They can smile or shout or whisper. This isn't a conversation and you're not there to convince anyone of anything. You're just there to answer questions truthfully."

"So the answer is 'No,'" I said.

"Correct. Most importantly, if they ask a question you don't know the answer to, you just say, 'I don't know.' Don't try to help them. It doesn't matter if you look smart or stupid, there's no legal consequence. If you start speculating or having arguments, that will only get you into trouble."

We went through these and many more tips. By the end of the day, I was as ready as I would ever be.

The next morning, I met Michael at his office, and we walked the short distance to 30 Rockefeller Plaza, where the deposition would take place. We rode the elevator to the 45th floor and were led to a large conference room with a horseshoe-shaped table. We were the first to arrive. Michael indicated that I should sit at the top of the horseshoe, opposite a video camera at the far end of the room. Wires crisscrossed the table, and a laptop was open to my left displaying a livestream to some unknown location. A short while later, Paul Monteleoni and another SDNY prosecutor arrived and sat next to Michael.

Just after 9:00 a.m., Prevezon's legal team strutted in, confident as peacocks. The senior lawyers took their seats on their side of the table, while associates and paralegals carted in boxes of documents, lining them along the wall. The junior lawyers then disappeared to an overflow room where they'd watch the deposition on the video feed. There appeared to be nearly two dozen lawyers, from two different law firms. I estimated Prevezon would spend at least several hundred thousand dollars in legal fees on just this one day.

Oddly, John Moscow was nowhere in sight. The task of deposing me had been assigned to his colleague, Mark Cymrot.

The deposition began and I was sworn in. Before Cymrot started his questioning, Michael asked if anyone other than the lawyers in the adjacent room was watching the video feed. Cymrot squirmed and acknowledged that, yes, there were other "people looking in." He named Denis Katsyv and his lawyer, Natalia Veselnitskaya, both of whom were watching from Moscow, as well as Prevezon's Brooklyn-based real estate lawyer.

Michael was not satisfied. If this was being broadcast to Moscow, anyone could be watching. "Are you able to verify who's actually listening and who's not to a degree of certainty?" he asked.

Cymrot answered cagily, "I am not, sitting here, no."

I was certain officials in Moscow were watching. I pictured a team of men sitting around a conference table at Lubyanka—FSB headquarters—tucking into boxes of takeaway as they settled in to enjoy the spectacle.

Michael objected for the record, but there was no way to stop this, so we carried on.

The questions began.

Exactly as Michael had predicted, Cymrot handed over the complaint I'd filed with the New York DA's office. "Do you recognize this document?"

I picked it up, slowly flipping through and scanning every page. The room was completely silent as everyone waited. It didn't take 20 minutes, but it was still satisfying to know I was running down the clock.

When I finally confirmed it was the complaint I'd submitted, Cymrot went through the attached exhibits. "What is this document?" he asked, referring to a Russian bank statement.

Since I don't speak or read Russian, I said, "I don't know."

"You have no idea?"

"No."

"You gave it to the US attorney?"

"Yes."

"Did you explain it to the US attorney?"

"No."

"What did you tell the US attorney about this document?"

"Nothing."

I enjoyed giving these one-word answers.

"And you have no idea who created this document?"

"No."

Cymrot saw he was getting nowhere and moved on, eventually focusing on how we obtained evidence showing that Dmitry Klyuev had traveled to Cyprus with Interior Ministry officer Pavel Karpov. "Where did you get those travel records?" he demanded.

"We got them from an anonymous source in Moscow," I answered.

"And who's your anonymous source?"

Since Vadim handled all of our Russian sources, I didn't know any of their real names, how to get in touch with them, or where they lived or worked.

"I don't know." This was the type of question I was most scared of, since answering it could put someone in physical peril. But I really didn't know.

Cymrot was incredulous. "We don't know the name, we don't know the address, we don't know who it is, and we don't know where [Vadim Kleiner] got documents, and we don't know whether the documents are real, right?"

"I don't know."

Throughout that morning, I said some version of "I don't know" over a hundred times. I must have sounded like a complete idiot, but, as Michael had said, I wasn't there to impress anybody. I just kept reminding myself: *There are no human beings in the room, just mannequins.*

After about two hours of this back-and-forth, Cymrot started to fade. It didn't help that he was simultaneously being bombarded by messages on his laptop. I was sure his Russian clients and their overseers were expressing their frustrations to him in real time.

We broke for lunch just before one o'clock. Before leaving the building, I made my way to the restroom. As I walked down the hall, I was surprised to find John Moscow shuffling toward me. It turned out he *was* there, he was just watching in the overflow room.

This whole circus had probably been his idea, and it wasn't going well.

I smiled insincerely, extended my hand, and said, "Hey, John."

When we'd bumped into each other at the Cambridge Crime Conference back in 2010, he'd been all smiles. Now he put his head down, didn't acknowledge me, and kept on walking.

Michael and I went to a nearby sushi restaurant. I purposely ate a light lunch so I wouldn't get tired and let my guard down. Somehow, I had to find the strength to get through another five hours of this legal brinksmanship.

We returned to the deposition room and the questioning resumed. Cymrot had regained some of his confidence and moved on to another subject. He wanted to know which countries had ongoing investigations into Russian money laundering connected to the Magnitsky case.

Answering this question would be a lot trickier. I was personally involved in all of our law enforcement outreach, and I couldn't say "I don't know" because I *did* know. I would have to answer honestly, which would give the Russian government a blueprint of actions being taken against Russian money launderers. With this knowledge, the Kremlin could do any number of things to scupper investigations going on around the world.

Finally, they had me in a bind. I kept my cool, but on the inside I was panicking.

Just as I was about to answer, though, Paul Monteleoni intervened.

"I'm going to request that the witness not answer to the extent that that information is not already public," he said. He was asserting something called "law enforcement privilege," which meant that any information pertaining to live criminal investigations was off-limits. This stopped that line of questioning cold. Cymrot was annoyed, but there was nothing he could do, so he moved on to other subjects.

By late afternoon, his frustration was palpable. Associates scrambled in and out, searching for anything that might help pin me down. Cymrot's questions became more erratic, but nothing stuck.

Toward the end of the day, he said, "You were at the White House [on] February 14, 2014. Do you remember that?"

"No," I answered flatly. I'd only been inside the White House once in my life, accompanying my father when he received the National Medal of Science from President Clinton in 1999.

Cymrot perked up. He urgently whispered to an associate, who dashed out of the room and returned a couple of minutes later carrying a file box. The associate removed a document and passed it to Cymrot, who put it front of me. It was a White House visitors log. He showed me my name, including my middle initial, and repeated, "Did you have a meeting at the White House on February 14, 2014?"

Cymrot thought he'd finally caught me in a lie.

"No," I answered calmly. "I had a meeting at the Old Executive Office Building." This is a government building in the White House complex, but it isn't the White House.

The air went out of their side of the room. Cymrot said, "So I have to be very careful in asking my questions, is that right?"

"Yes."

The deposition petered out a short while later, ending twelve minutes before my seven hours were up. Michael politely offered for us to stay, but Cymrot was out of questions. As Michael and I took the elevator down to the lobby, he smiled and said, "Well done, Bill."

I got back to my hotel room completely spent. I passed on room service and ordered Chinese. As I ate Mongolian beef out of a cardboard container, I pictured Denis Katsyv and Natalia Veselnitskaya eviscerating John Moscow and Mark Cymrot for not delivering my head on a platter. The Russians had spent millions of dollars, and BakerHostetler countless hours, investigating, chasing, and litigating against me, but none if it had amounted to anything.

A few days later, BakerHostetler applied to the court to compel me to hand over the documents they *really* wanted and to sit for a *second* deposition. Reluctantly, Judge Griesa set a date for another hearing for the end of May so that he could make a decision.

Little did BakerHostetler know, this was the trap Michael had set. And they'd walked right into it.

The moment the May hearing got underway, Cymrot began ranting about how I wasn't complying with the court order. Every time he mentioned my name, Judge Griesa bristled. But Cymrot was intent on driving his points home, and he didn't relent.

Finally, Judge Griesa had had enough. "The government filed the case. Mr. Browder didn't file the case," he shouted. "[We've] spent enough time and effort on Mr. Browder."

That was the end of it. Judge Griesa suspended the subpoena, along with a further deposition, and told Cymrot to move on to other matters so the case could get moving.

Michael hadn't said a single word up to that point. He quickly asked the judge, "Since we're not a party here, may we be excused?" He didn't want to hang around for Judge Griesa to change his mind.

"Of course you may."

"Thank you."

Michael left. He hadn't filed a single motion, he hadn't submitted any long letters, and he had barely spoken in court. His strategy had been totally unconventional, but it had worked. It was perfect legal jiu-jitsu. He'd used our opponents' own weight to knock them over.

With that, Michael Kim had successfully extracted the arrow from my neck.

22

Vladimir Kara-Murza

SPRING 2015

After the deposition, I could now focus on trying to get justice for Boris Nemtsov. Because he'd been indispensable in passing the Magnitsky Act, it seemed fitting that the law he helped to create could now be used to punish the people who had ordered his killing.

I wasn't the only person who felt this way. Another important voice calling for Magnitsky sanctions was Vladimir Kara-Murza, the man who met Boris's ex-wife and daughter on the Bolshoy Moskvoretsky Bridge on the night Boris was killed.

Vladimir and Boris had been like family. Even though Vladimir, along with his wife, Evgenia, and three children, had a home in Fairfax, Virginia, he and Boris had spent thousands of hours in Russia campaigning, eating, vacationing, and drinking together. Boris was even godfather to Vladimir's middle child.

Vladimir was as committed to the Magnitsky Act as Boris had been—so much so that he'd been fired from his job as Washington bureau chief of RTVI, a Russian TV station, for supporting the Magnitsky Act in 2012. (When Vladimir started there, RTVI was independent, but by 2012 it had come under Kremlin control.)

I'd first met Vladimir in 2012, at the Canadian Parliament, where we both testified in favor of a Canadian Magnitsky Act. When Vladimir addressed the MPs in Ottawa, he switched effortlessly between French and English without a hint of a Russian accent. He had shed his accent through years of British schooling, first at high school in London and then at Cambridge University. He was so talented, charismatic, and articulate that whenever I heard him speak it felt like I was listening to a young Nelson Mandela or Václav Havel.

As it happened, Vladimir and I had an opportunity to make our case for Magnitsky sanctions against the people responsible for Boris's murder in Washington on April 30, 2015, a little more than two months after his assassination. We had both been invited to speak at a congressional memorial for Boris that would be held in room 2255 of the Rayburn House Office Building. Fittingly, this was where the Magnitsky Act had been conceived. It was the same room where, in 2010, I had first testified about Sergei's murder in front of the House Tom Lantos Human Rights Commission.

Rayburn 2255 was standing room only on the day of the memorial. The crowd ranged from staffers right up to senior lawmakers, including Steny Hoyer, the second-highest-ranking Democrat in the House; Eliot Engel, the ranking member of the House Foreign Affairs Committee; and Jim McGovern, the original sponsor of the Magnitsky Act in the House of Representatives.

This memorial was unlike any I'd been to. It was nothing like my mother's, which had taken place only a week before Boris was killed. Although her death had been tragic for our family, especially for my elderly father, who was now alone, losing her was part of the inevitable cycle of life. The speeches at her service were all about a life well lived. There was sadness, but also joy in remembering her.

But there is nothing inevitable about murder. The speeches at this service were different. There was certainly grief at Boris's memorial, but the prevailing emotion was rage. And nobody felt this more profoundly, or conveyed it more articulately, than Vladimir.

Vladimir—who with his balding head, furrowed brow, and trim beard resembled a young Lenin—never spoke above a moderate volume. He carefully listed Boris's best qualities—how he never betrayed his friends or principles, how he never put his personal interests above those of his country, and above all, how Boris had been thoroughly incorruptible. In a country whose foundation is corruption, this was his ultimate sin.

Toward the end of his address, Vladimir held up a sheet of paper with the names of eight people he said were responsible for inciting

Vladimir Kara-Murza at Boris Nemtsov's
congressional memorial, April 2015.
(© NATIONAL ENDOWMENT FOR DEMOCRACY)

Boris's murder and who he felt should be sanctioned under the US Magnitsky Act.

I spoke shortly after Vladimir, and also called for the use of the Magnitsky Act in Boris's case.

We found fertile ground for our message that day. In addition to the lawmakers present, there was one person there who was arguably more important than anyone else in Washington when it came to the Magnitsky Act: a congressional staff member named Kyle Parker. Kyle, a direct and no-nonsense Mainer in his mid-40s with a light brown beard, was a Russia expert who had literally written the law and knew every aspect of its implementation. The US government never added anyone to the Magnitsky List without consulting him first.

By 2015, Kyle, Vladimir, and I had all become close friends, united by our commitment to the Magnitsky Act and seeking justice in Russia.

But if the ground at the memorial was fertile, it was also treach-

Kyle Parker. (© HERMITAGE)

erous. The audience consisted primarily of Americans, but included a handful of Russians as well. Whenever there was an event on Capitol Hill involving Russia, the Russian embassy sent official representatives to observe and dispatch cables back to Moscow. But if one of these events had something to do with the Magnitsky Act, the Russians also sent clandestine operatives from their intelligence services.

It was one thing for me, a British national, to call for Magnitsky sanctions, but another thing for Vladimir, a Russian national, to do the same. Even though he kept a residence in the United States, he was mostly based in Russia. At the end of May, he would be returning to Moscow to continue his (and Boris's) anti-Putin advocacy work.

None of this intimidated Vladimir.

After the hearing, he returned to his home in Fairfax, where he spent several days with Evgenia and their kids. He then went on advocacy trips to New York and Berlin for Open Russia, the NGO he worked for that was funded by the Russian opposition figure and former oligarch, Mikhail Khodorkovsky.

On May 22, Vladimir boarded a flight to Moscow. From Moscow, he flew to Kazan, a provincial city 500 miles east of the Russian capital, to host a lecture featuring a prominent Russian historian who was openly critical of Putin. The venue was the State Museum of Fine Arts, a grand building brimming with gilt-framed oil paintings, only a few blocks from the Volga River. On the day of the event, however, the Russian Ministry of Culture instructed the museum to shut their doors to Vladimir and his colleagues.

Vladimir was accustomed to this sort of obstruction and quickly moved the event to a backup location—a conference hall at the Ibis Hotel. As the group walked over, Vladimir received an urgent call from the hotel manager informing him that this venue had suddenly become unavailable. The manager justified this last-minute change by claiming their "air-conditioning had leaked in the hall."

Vladimir scrambled, and found a space at the nearby Museum of Soviet Arcade Games, a quirky venue full of CCCP-branded foosball and video games. The audience—a still healthy 100-odd people—filed in. But as Vladimir started, the electricity went off and the police arrived, evacuating everyone. They claimed a bomb had been planted in the building (a story that, to no one's surprise, later turned out to be false).

With no other options, Vladimir took the remaining diehards to a nearby café, where the professor was finally able to speak. During the two-hour lecture, several suspicious-looking strangers were spotted with recording equipment, openly filming the attendees. Everyone knew these were FSB agents, but despite their presence, the talk continued and was a success.

The following evening, Vladimir boarded an Aeroflot flight back to Moscow, satisfied that he'd gotten the better of the FSB that week. He ate some bland in-flight food, landed around 10:30 p.m., and went straight to his apartment near the Boulevard Ring. He was in bed and asleep before midnight.

The next day, he met a small camera crew and filmed two interviews for a documentary he was making about Boris's life—one interview at an office building, the other in a room at the Park Hyatt Hotel. If FSB agents were following him in Moscow, they kept their distance. They certainly didn't make themselves known that evening, when he had an early dinner with his father.

The next morning, Vladimir ran some errands before dropping off his dry cleaning. He then had a buffet lunch with a fellow activist at a restaurant called *Bobry I Utki* ("Beavers and Ducks"). The only thing he consumed that didn't come from the buffet was a glass of cranberry juice, which was brought to him by a waiter. After lunch, he took the Metro to a meeting at the RIA Novosti building, a six-story cement block that had been built as the press center for the 1980 Olympics. This building is now the headquarters of Russia Today, or RT, the Kremlin's main international propaganda outlet.

Vladimir was there to meet with a former colleague to attempt to convince him to join Open Russia. The two men, plus one other colleague, gathered in a conference room. But as Vladimir reclined in his chair, his stomach turned and an acrid ball formed at the back of this throat. He was about to be sick.

He excused himself, hurried into a bathroom stall, dropped to his knees, and vomited for several minutes. When he thought he was done, another wave of nausea swept over him. It just kept coming. He'd never been so sick in his entire life.

When it finally subsided, it took all of his energy to stand and stagger back to the meeting, using the walls to keep from falling over.

He re-entered the conference room, tried to speak, and then collapsed. His colleagues quickly moved him to a sofa. He was moaning and coated in sweat. He'd lost all color, and his breathing was rapid. Terrified, they called an ambulance.

The EMTs arrived shortly thereafter, but had no idea what had caused this. They loaded him into their ambulance, put on the sirens, and sped through the streets of Moscow to City Clinical Hospital No. 23 (one of the closest medical facilities to RIA Novosti). When he was admitted, Vladimir's blood pressure had dropped to a critical 100/20. The doctors were certain he was having a heart attack, which meant that he couldn't be properly treated at this particular hospital. They stabilized him as best they could, put him in another ambulance, and transferred him to the Bakulev Scientific Center for Cardiovascular Surgery, where they began to prep him for an emergency heart operation.

Vladimir's father rushed to Bakulev as soon as he heard the news.

He was a well-connected journalist, and as he careened through the Moscow streets, he managed to reach one of Russia's top heart specialists, convincing him to come to the hospital as well. The specialist got there before Vladimir went into surgery. After reviewing Vladimir's chart, he called for an immediate halt to the procedure. In his opinion, there was nothing wrong with Vladimir's heart, and if they went ahead with the operation, he would more than likely die on the table. There was a heated exchange, but in the end, the specialist prevailed.

At 2:30 a.m., Vladimir completely lost consciousness, and his diagnosis was changed to poisoning by an "unknown" substance.

At 6:00 a.m., he was transferred to Pirogov Hospital on Leninsky Prospekt, one of Russia's most advanced medical facilities. When he arrived, his condition had deteriorated even further. His brain was swelling, and his lungs and kidneys were failing. He was placed in a coma, intubated, put on a ventilator, hooked up to dialysis for his kidneys and hemodialysis to clean his blood, and given medication to control his dangerously low blood pressure.

That day was May 27. Vladimir's condition was so grave that it looked as if it would be his last.

23

The Diplomatic Pouch

SPRING 2015

That afternoon in London, I was boarding a flight to Lisbon for a family vacation. As my wife and I ushered our younger kids down the jetway, my phone rang. It was Elena Servettaz, the same reporter who'd alerted me to Boris Nemtsov's murder. Fumbling with a pink princess backpack and a folded-up stroller, I managed to pick up on the fifth ring.

"Bill," she said urgently, "Vladimir Kara-Murza collapsed in Moscow!"

I stopped cold. "*What?*"

"He was at a meeting. He got really sick. He's in the hospital."

"Is he going to be okay?" I asked loudly.

"I-I don't know."

My wife, who was leading our family procession, shot me a concerned look. I resumed moving down the jetway, dropped off the stroller, and then boarded the plane. "Who was he meeting with?"

"I don't know."

"Which hospital?"

"I don't know that either. I'm trying to figure it all out."

I had to steady myself against one of the seats. "I'm boarding a plane right now. I'll call you as soon as I land."

I hung up and slipped the phone into my pocket. My wife quietly asked, "What's going on?"

"Vladimir's collapsed and is in a hospital in Moscow," I whispered.

"Kara-Murza?" she mouthed.

"Yes." I nodded.

The color drained from her face. "Oh my God."

"Yes," I repeated.

We got the kids settled and took our seats. I frantically called a few of our mutual friends, including Kyle in Washington, to tell them what had happened and see if they knew anything more. They didn't. The plane's door closed and we started taxiing. That was the longest three-hour flight of my life.

As soon as we landed, I texted Elena Servettaz. I called Kyle again. I texted Vadim and Ivan in London. I texted reporters in Moscow. Everyone was still in the dark. But since Vladimir had been Boris's closest confidant, it was hard not to come to the most sinister conclusion.

That night, my family and I had dinner at the hotel restaurant. My kids were thrilled to be on vacation and oblivious to what was going on, but my mind was somewhere else, and I was attached to my phone.

The next morning, we finally got some news. According to the Russian media, Vladimir was suffering from multiple organ failure brought on by "acute non-alcoholic intoxication."

"Acute non-alcoholic intoxication" was conveniently open to interpretation, but for me there was only one translation: Vladimir had been deliberately poisoned.

Later that day, however, Vladimir's father made a surprising statement. He speculated that his son's condition could have been caused by "allergies," or "a stressful life," or even a "lack of sleep." He said, "It could be anything: yesterday's chebureki,* banana, apple . . . but I don't think there was a crime."

For me, it was obvious there was a crime, but I understood what his father was trying to do. As a longtime opposition journalist, he was well acquainted with the depravities of the Putin regime and was probably downplaying what was surely an assassination attempt. He was doing what he thought was best to save his son's life by trying to placate his son's would-be assassins.

There was some logic to this strategy, but it didn't change the fact that Vladimir was being cared for at a Russian hospital. If the Putin

---

* A minced meat pie.

regime wanted to finish Vladimir off, his doctors could simply not provide proper care, or even worse, an FSB agent could enter the hospital and poison him again.

As long as Vladimir remained in Russia, he was seriously at risk. He needed to be evacuated as soon as possible.

If Vladimir's father wasn't going to organize his son's evacuation from Russia, I hoped Vladimir's wife, Evgenia, would.

I called her at their home in Fairfax. I'd only met her once, and barely knew her, but I couldn't let this get in the way of what I needed to say: "If we don't get Vladimir out of there right now, I think they might make another attempt on his life."

There was a pause on the other end, but then she responded, "I completely agree. I've already spoken to Mikhail Khodorkovsky. He's sending a medevac plane from Tel Aviv, along with an intensive care specialist. They should be at Vnukovo tomorrow," she said, referring to one of Moscow's three main airports.

She'd also booked herself on the next flight to Moscow. In addition to evacuating him, we agreed that she needed to secure biological samples to be tested in the West. We needed to know what he'd been poisoned with if we had any chance of finding an antidote. Neither of us trusted the Russians to do this.

Before hanging up, she added, "We need to call the British embassy as well."

"I don't follow."

"Vladimir has a British passport, as well as a Russian one. He got it while he was at Cambridge."

Throughout the time I'd known Vladimir, I'd somehow missed the fact that he was a British citizen.

This had the potential to change everything. When we were fighting to free Sergei from jail, we couldn't get any Western governments involved. The consistent response was, "That's a sad story, but what does it have to do with us?" Since Vladimir was British, his poisoning had everything to do with the United Kingdom.

As soon as I hung up with Evgenia, I called the UK embassy in Moscow and spoke to a British consular officer. After explaining the situation, I said, "We want to get blood samples tested outside of Russia. If we can secure them, can we use the diplomatic pouch for transport?"

"Of course. We're all very concerned about Mr. Kara-Murza. We'll do whatever we can to help."

After that, all I could do was wait for Evgenia to get the samples.

She landed at Moscow's Domodedovo Airport at 5:45 p.m. the following day, which was a Friday. After clearing customs, she was met by Vadim Prokhorov, Vladimir's lawyer, and his giant briefcase that he carried with him everywhere. After hastily greeting one another, they jumped in his car and drove straight to Pirogov Hospital.

She called me from the road. "Any word from the British?" she asked.

"Yes. They're ready to help. If you can obtain the samples, they've promised the diplomatic pouch to move them to London."

"Great. I'll do my best." I had to admit, she was holding herself together remarkably well under the circumstances.

At 8:00 p.m., Evgenia and Prokhorov entered the hospital and went directly to the front desk. A receptionist, who barely looked up from her phone, said flatly, "Visiting hours are over. No visitors over the weekend. Come back Monday."

"Excuse me," Evgenia said. "I've flown all the way from the US to see my husband, who's very sick. I need to see him now!"

"I'm sorry, that isn't possible. Please come back Monday," the receptionist repeated.

"By Monday he could be dead!"

The receptionist finally looked up from her phone. "The only person who has the authority to let you in over the weekend is the hospital director."

"Then I'd like to speak to him."

She rolled her eyes. "He also won't be back until Monday."

Furious, Evgenia and Prokhorov stalked back outside. It was a warm, summerlike night. The sun, which stayed up well past 9:00 p.m. at that time of year, hadn't fully set. They sat on a nearby bench while Prokhorov made a series of calls, trying to find anyone who could get the hospital director back on a Friday night.

One person he spoke with was Yevgenia Albats, the same editor of the influential opposition magazine *The New Times,* who had reported that someone had paid a $6 million bribe to the FSB to arrest Sergei back in 2008. Nobody in Moscow wanted to be on the wrong side of Albats. She made some calls, and an hour later a late-model sedan pulled into the hospital parking lot. Two men emerged, one stocky and bald with a trim salt-and-pepper beard, the other taller with close-cropped black hair and beady eyes. They approached Evgenia and Prokhorov. The beady-eyed one introduced himself as the hospital director. The other man remained silent. "Follow me," the director said, annoyed that his weekend had been interrupted.

They were led directly to his office. Evgenia and Prokhorov took seats opposite his desk, and the other man sat in a chair along the wall.

The director crossed his arms. "What can I do for you?"

"I want to know how my husband is doing."

"He is in the intensive care unit under Dr. Protsenko." The director indicated the other man with a curt nod. "Your husband has suffered multiple organ failure and I'm afraid his situation is very serious."

"How serious?"

The director looked down, not meeting her gaze. "In my opinion, he has a five percent chance of survival," he stated.

Evgenia began to shake. She took three deep breaths, and asked, "What caused this?"

"Either food poisoning or his medications," the director said flippantly.

"His *medications*?" The only things Vladimir took were Celexa, a common antidepressant, and an over-the-counter nasal spray for allergies. Evgenia knew there was no way these two medications could cause multiple organ failure. If they did, tens of millions of people who suffered from anxiety and hay fever would be dropping dead all over the world. "Have you checked him for poison?" she asked.

"Why would anyone want to poison your husband?"

"There are many reasons. He was Boris Nemtsov's deputy, and Boris was murdered only three months ago!"

The director shook his head. "Those are two entirely different things."

It took all of Evgenia's will to remain calm. "I'm going to move my husband tomorrow," she said. "There's a medevac plane waiting at Vnukovo."

"Mrs. Kara-Murza," the director said. "Your husband cannot be moved. If we moved him from one side of the room to the other, he probably wouldn't make it. There's no way he would survive a trip to the airport, let alone a flight."

"Then I'll have a second opinion. There's an Israeli doctor here from Tel Aviv. I want him to see Vladimir in the morning."

"Mrs. Kara-Murza," the director repeated, even more condescendingly. "Why would you need a second opinion?"

"Why would I need a second opinion?" Evgenia demanded, rising from her chair a little. "You just told me you haven't checked him for poison, when my husband shows all the signs of having been poisoned!"

The director scoffed. "Imagine a train. And that train has hit your husband. Do you really care about what kind of train it is? No. You care about saving your husband. That is what we are trying to do."

Finally losing her temper, she shouted, "And that's what *I'm* trying to do. I will have my second opinion, and we will do our own toxicology tests. I need his blood. Now!"

Russian doctors are never spoken to like this. "No foreign doctors in my hospital, and no blood," the director announced. "Unless you have power of attorney, you can't ask for any of these things." Unlike most other countries, in Russia, spouses have no automatic legal rights over incapacitated partners. He thought that was the end of it.

Evgenia let out a sigh. She didn't have power of attorney.

But Vadim Prokhorov perked up. As Vladimir's lawyer, he *did*.

He reached into his worn, overflowing briefcase and, like a magician pulling a rabbit out of a hat, put a power of attorney on the director's desk. This document only covered Vladimir's political work, not his medical issues, but Prokhorov wasn't going to point that out. And, in the heat of the moment, the director didn't think to check. He glanced at it, ashen-faced. Prokhorov, stuffing the document back in his satchel, said, "Please do what Mrs. Kara-Murza is asking you to do, and take her to her husband."

Defeated, the director turned to Dr. Protsenko, who had been quiet throughout. "Do as he says. Give her an hour—and the samples."

Without another word, Dr. Protsenko escorted Evgenia to the ICU, a large room with six beds. "Your husband is over there," he said, pointing. She went to Vladimir's side. He was behind a tangle of tubes, wires, and beeping machines. She could barely recognize him. He looked like some kind of robotic octopus.

Dr. Protsenko explained Vladimir's treatment plan, which sounded comprehensive, but he offered no reassurance. "I'm sorry, but as my colleague said, your husband's situation is very grave."

Evgenia pulled up a chair, sat next to Vladimir, and held his hand. Even though he was unconscious, she whispered that she was there now and wouldn't leave Moscow without him.

An hour later, a nurse came into the room, drew some blood, took clippings of Vladimir's hair and nails, placed these in sealed bags, and handed everything to Evgenia, along with a copy of his medical chart. "I'm sorry, but it's time for you to leave," the nurse said. "I was told you can come back tomorrow."

It was after 11:00 p.m. when Evgenia left the hospital. She climbed into Prokhorov's car and they drove to her parents' apartment. Once there, she placed the samples in the refrigerator and emailed Vladimir's medical charts to me.

The next morning, she returned to the hospital with the Israeli intensive care specialist. After examining Vladimir, he concurred with his Russian counterparts. Vladimir could not be moved. Evgenia had suspected this, but hearing it from a trustworthy source was thoroughly demoralizing.

She was now faced with an impossible dilemma—if she moved her husband he would certainly die, but if she kept him in Russia, he would probably die too.

The KGB Poison Factory

SPRING–SUMMER 2015

Vladimir being stuck in critical condition in a Russian hospital was a body blow. It felt like the situation following Sergei's arrest. Here was another person I cared about, in mortal danger thousands of miles away, whom I felt powerless to help.

Kyle Parker felt this way too. In addition to the work he and Vladimir had done together on the Magnitsky Act, their families were close. Their kids played together, they had barbecues in one another's backyards, and their wives were friends.

As soon as I received Vladimir's medical chart, I forwarded a copy to Kyle. We needed to become poison experts—and fast. We both knew about the infamous KGB Poison Factory, which for decades had developed novel, vicious, and mysterious ways of killing Russia's enemies. The poisons they developed were often tested on prisoners in the Russian gulag before being deployed in the field. Favorites included ricin, dioxin, thallium, hydrogen cyanide, polonium (which had been used in London to kill Alexander Litvinenko), and even rare venoms extracted from jellyfish. We had to determine whether any of these—or something else—had been used on Vladimir.

Kyle and I reached out to anyone we thought could help.

In America, Kyle sent Vladimir's chart to a leading toxicologist at the National Institutes of Health; to an intelligence officer who specialized in biowarfare; to a Kazakh defector who'd been involved in the Soviet Union's poisons program; and to his own sister, a top oncologist at Memorial Sloan Kettering Hospital in New York.

On our side of the Atlantic, my team and I identified every UK poison expert we could find. We emailed Porton Down, a renowned British medical research facility run by the military; the National Poisons Information Service; a forensic pathologist at the Home Office; the toxicology department at Guy's Hospital; and a former homicide detective at London's Metropolitan Police.

Kyle heard back from some of his contacts within hours. The first response came from his source in US intelligence. He suspected there were *two* poisons at work. The first was designed to create the appearance of severe food poisoning. While the doctors were dealing with that, the second was doing the real job of shutting down Vladimir's organs. Kyle's source had seen this tactic used by the Russians before. From the assassin's perspective, it was a tidy little operation. Plausible deniability was built in. Doctors who weren't part of the scheme could honestly say, "We couldn't find anything wrong. We did everything we could, but unfortunately, the patient died."

The second response came from Kyle's contact at the National Institutes of Health. She didn't provide such a lengthy analysis, but did state categorically that, based on Vladimir's white blood cell count, we could rule out a radiological agent.

This was helpful. Because of Alexander Litvinenko, the first thing Kyle and I had thought of was radiation poisoning. We were quickly learning that identifying a poison was like looking for a needle in a haystack. If we were going to discover it, we needed to rule things out.

Our British outreach wasn't as successful—nobody seemed to be checking email over the weekend. The only response we received came from the former homicide detective. He didn't offer any theories about what Vladimir had been poisoned with, but he did provide a set of gruesome instructions to preserve the "crime scene"—i.e., Vladimir's body—in the event of his death. This included "milking" blood from his femoral artery, removing a section of his liver, and retrieving a vial of his eyeball fluid.

Reading this made my stomach churn. Vladimir was my friend. I didn't want to think about eyeballs or livers. I wanted to see him again—walking and talking.

And then we heard from Kyle's sister.

"Kyle, I hate to say this, but it doesn't look like he's going to make it," she wrote. She'd seen many dying people in her work. "You really should tell the family they need to say their goodbyes."

Neither Kyle nor I was going to tell Evgenia this. She was sitting at Vladimir's side and knew his condition better than we did. But if the pressure to find out what he had been poisoned with had been high before, now it was screaming. At least we had the samples we could test in the West.

I called the British embassy in Moscow on the morning of Saturday, May 30. I was connected to a different official than the one I'd previously spoken to.

"We have Vladimir's samples," I said to him. "Should his wife bring them to you, or will you pick them up?"

"Oh, so sorry, sir," the official replied. "Has no one rung you about this yet?"

"No."

"We're no longer dealing with this at the embassy. The matter has been passed to the Global Response Centre at Whitehall. Someone from there should be in touch with you shortly." The Global Response Centre is a division of Britain's Foreign and Commonwealth Office responsible for helping British nationals in trouble abroad.

I was heartened to hear the government was taking this so seriously, and a short while later, I did receive an email from them.

Only it was completely unhelpful. They made no mention of the diplomatic pouch. All they offered were the phone numbers for the Moscow offices of DHL, FedEx, and several other courier companies, along with some tepid moral support.

DHL and FedEx? Were they kidding? Anyone could go online and get this information in thirty seconds.

I called the person at the Global Response Centre whose number was listed at the bottom of the email. "I'm confused," I said to him. "I was told that you'd help us transport the blood."

"I'm afraid we can't do that, sir."

"But the embassy in Moscow promised we could use the diplomatic pouch."

"I'm sorry, but we can't provide that type of assistance."

I explained to him that Vladimir, *a British citizen*, could die, but the man was unmoved. It took me several minutes to calm down after this call.

We're all led to believe that if you're a citizen of a powerful country like the United States or Great Britain, and something bad happens to you abroad, your government will bring its full weight and force to protect you.

But that wasn't happening here.

This threw a wrench in our plans. Over the previous 24 hours we'd been obsessing about poisons and diagnoses, not logistics.

Since we were starting from scratch, I called DHL, only to discover that they didn't ship biomedical samples from Moscow. FedEx did, but they said it would take at least 72 hours and we'd have to secure an export license from the Russian government.

Good luck with that. One of the main reasons we wanted to use the diplomatic pouch was specifically to avoid entanglements with the Russian government. Perhaps equally important, in the event of Vladimir's death, these samples might be the only evidence of his murder, and the diplomatic pouch would maintain the chain of custody. Throwing them in a FedEx bio bag would break that chain irrevocably.

The only thing I could think to do was to go above everyone's head, so I drafted an email and sent it to Britain's foreign secretary, the Right Honorable Philip Hammond, a man I'd never met.

Because he was a high-ranking minister, I didn't expect a response, but remarkably, he emailed me a personal letter the next day—Sunday. He said he'd been following the case closely and wanted to help, but when it came to the diplomatic pouch, his hands were tied. He cited the Vienna Convention on Diplomatic Relations, explaining that he was forbidden from using the diplomatic pouch for anything other than official communications. To show that he cared, however, he offered to have an embassy official escort our courier to the airport and accompany them up to border control. Unfortunately, that was as far as he could go.

I was thoroughly disappointed. The Russians didn't give a damn about the Vienna Convention. They used their diplomatic pouches to move drugs, poisons, and cash around the world. Why couldn't the British bend the rules to use theirs to save one of their own citizens?

(I later realized I couldn't have it both ways. This was what Boris, Vladimir, and I had been fighting for—and what Sergei had died believing in: that Russia should be a rules-based country where the Russian foreign minister would write a similar type of letter, and mean it.)

That day, we decided to hell with the chain of custody. If the British government wouldn't allow us to use the diplomatic pouch, we'd use our own resources to get the samples to London. When these troubles became known to Vladimir's friends in Moscow, one of them volunteered to fly to London with the samples smuggled in their luggage. After that, it happened very quickly. The volunteer walked the samples into our office the next day, Monday, just after lunch, five days after Vladimir's collapse. They went right into the refrigerator next to that afternoon's leftover takeaway.

Now all I needed to do was find a testing facility. I began working the phones, starting with Porton Down, the medical research facility. But before I could finish explaining the situation, the person said, "Sir, we only take referrals from the government."

"But this is urgent," I pleaded. "Is there no way you can make an exception?"

"I'm sorry, there's nothing we can do without government authorization."

I then called the National Poisons Information Service, another government agency, but was told we needed a referral from law enforcement. Even if we could get that, it would take days or weeks.

I made a dozen more calls that went nowhere. Finally, at the end of the day, I was referred to a concierge doctor who catered to hedge fund managers, investment bankers, and other wealthy Londoners. He didn't come cheap, but I was ready to pay anything.

This doctor was connected to a private lab on Harley Street, an area in central London with a concentration of high-end doctors and medical experts. He assured me that they had all the necessary contacts to get the samples tested at any UK government lab. He said it would take a day, two at the most, but that we would have some answers imminently.

When I called Evgenia to inform her that the blood tests were now on track in London, she interrupted to deliver some completely unexpected news. "Bill, Vladimir's kidneys have begun working again!"

"Seriously? That's fantastic!"

"It is. Dr. Protsenko has decided to bring him out of his coma. They're going to do it tomorrow."

Evgenia had had a rough start at Pirogov Hospital, but since then things had improved. Most importantly, it seemed that Dr. Protsenko was genuinely trying to save Vladimir's life.

As the doctor and his staff prepared for the procedure, Evgenia was terrified about what she might find when Vladimir woke up. Would he be paralyzed? Would he respond to her voice? Would he even regain consciousness? She couldn't contemplate what their life might be like if Vladimir's mind had been taken from him.

The procedure took the better part of the day. As the doctors slowly decreased the medication used to induce the coma, Evgenia, holding Vladimir's hand, intermittently repeated, "Volodya," the Russian diminutive for Vladimir.

Toward the end of the afternoon, he blinked. Evgenia stood and leaned over him. He blinked again. She shouted out, "It's me! It's Zhenia!"

He fumbled with her fingers and squeezed her hand weakly. "Oh, Volodya," she said, tears welling in her eyes.

He *was* there. Vladimir remained intubated and couldn't speak, so he moved his eyes around the room, asking questions with them. First he looked at the ceiling. "You're in Moscow, in the hospital," Evgenia explained. "Those are the lights." He pointed his eyes toward the window. "It's June first. It's like summer outside today." He strained to look at the man standing next to the bed. "That's Dr. Protsenko," Evgenia said. "He's been taking good care of you." She got out her phone and showed him pictures of their children. "They're all fine, Volodya. They miss you so much."

Later that afternoon, she called to share the good news. A visceral wave of relief passed over me. I had been sure Vladimir wasn't going to make it. I called my wife to let her know. I called Kyle. I hugged

Ivan and Vadim in the office, fighting back tears of my own as the horror of losing Vladimir started to recede.

Overnight, Vladimir made even more progress. He began breathing without a ventilator, and the next morning the doctors removed his breathing tube. Evgenia desperately wanted to hear his voice, but his throat was so raw that he could barely make any noise, so they continued to communicate through blinks, smiles, and hand squeezes.

That evening, Vadim, Ivan, and I went to a local Thai restaurant to celebrate. Just after ordering, my phone rang. It was Evgenia.

It was impossible to hear her over the din of the restaurant, so I moved outside. "Can you repeat that?" I asked.

"Vladimir just had an X-ray," she said, her voice sounding different than before. "They've found something. Some kind of black spot on his stomach."

"A black spot? What does that mean?" I asked, that familiar feeling of dread descending over me once again.

"Dr. Protsenko says it could be necrosis. They need to operate on him right away."

"Shit. I'm so sorry. Please call me as soon as it's over."

I went back inside, just as our appetizers arrived, and informed Vadim and Ivan. Our celebration was over. We barely touched our food and asked for the check. We each went home. I stayed up, sitting on my couch in the dark, waiting for Evgenia's call.

It came late that night. Vladimir's pathology report showed no necrosis—the black spot was nothing to worry about—but because of the anticoagulants the hospital had put him on, he was prone to internal bleeding, and the operation caused an unexpected hemorrhage, leading to a stroke. Following this, Dr. Protsenko placed him back into a coma.

My mother's stroke and subsequent paralysis had put her on a long and terrible road to her ultimate death and had entirely upended our family. Vladimir was only 33, and I didn't want to think about what this might mean for him, Evgenia, and their children.

I tossed and turned the entire night. The next morning, I called the concierge doctor, hoping to get Vladimir's test results. Getting them wouldn't help Vladimir with his stroke, but it was still important to know what he'd been poisoned with.

We'd handed over the samples on Monday, and the concierge doctor had promised results by Wednesday at the latest. It was now Thursday and we still had nothing. He didn't take my call, so I waited 15 minutes and tried again. Still unavailable. I kept calling throughout the morning to no avail.

At around 11:00 a.m. he sent me a long email. "I know this may not be what you wish to hear, Bill, but the samples are under the charge of Porton Down and other government agencies and there is no way of directly influencing their speed of work." He ended by saying, "I am on your side, Bill."

People who say things like "I am on your side" usually aren't. I was beginning to suspect that this man wasn't being truthful with me. I finally got him on the phone sometime after lunch, and that's when he came clean.

He told me that the samples had never actually been sent to the government. Attempting to shift the blame, he explained that the technicians at the private lab were so scared of what the samples might contain that they never removed them from the sealed biohazard package they'd arrived in.

We promptly repossessed the samples—*which hadn't even been refrigerated!* We scrambled to find a lab anywhere that could help, and were referred to a French lab near Strasbourg that agreed to expedite the testing. Mark Sabah, my colleague who had been with me in Monaco, jumped on the Eurostar and took the samples there, but by that point they were so badly degraded that when they were finally tested, they revealed nothing definitive.

I didn't have time to dwell on this, though, because the next day Vladimir would be eased out of his second coma.

The following morning, the same process was repeated. As before, Evgenia sat at Vladimir's side, whispering his name, waiting for any sign of awareness. But this time, when his eyes opened, he was much more disoriented. He didn't look at her or squeeze her hand, and he didn't try to make any sounds.

He was breathing on his own, however, so they removed his breathing tube. A few hours later he tried to speak, but his words made no sense. Some of the sounds he made didn't even qualify as words. From someone as erudite and articulate as Vladimir, this was overwhelming for Evgenia.

Vladimir stayed on the ICU for another week. And even though he couldn't speak properly, he soon became more alert and aware of what was going on around him. By mid-June he was well enough to be moved to the neurological wing. The stroke had been a bad one: he couldn't walk, could barely eat, and chewing and swallowing were difficult. He had a lot of work ahead of him if he was going to return to normal.

Unlike in the West, in Russia the burden for a patient's rehabilitation falls on the family's shoulders. Evgenia had to teach Vladimir how to do all of these things on her own, including speaking. Initially, his gibberish was punctuated by flashes of lucidity, but as she worked with him over the following weeks, the lucid moments increased and the gibberish declined. The physical damage was real, but the Vladimir we knew and loved was still there.

Nearly six weeks after being poisoned, Vladimir was well enough to be transported to the United States. On July 4, Evgenia wheeled him onto a medevac plane, and they flew to Washington. Vladimir was picked up at the airport by an ambulance and driven directly to the Inova Fairfax Medical Campus, where he was placed in the ICU. The American doctors performed all of the toxicology tests that the Russians should have done on day one—they were so careful that they even made Evgenia wear a hazmat suit when she visited—but because so much time had elapsed since Vladimir's collapse, there was nothing for them to find.

After three weeks of rehabilitation at a different facility, Vladimir was finally able to return to his home in Virginia. The effects of the poisoning would dog him for months, but he had survived.

That November, Vladimir took his first trip since the incident, traveling to London for the Sergei Magnitsky Human Rights Awards. Two hundred and fifty people from around the globe would gather in Westminster, at Central Methodist Hall, next to Parliament, to honor some of the world's bravest human rights activists. Boris Nemtsov would be honored posthumously. His daughter, Zhanna, would accept the award on his behalf.

The day before the ceremony, Vladimir came to our office. He hobbled off the elevator with a cane, his back and shoulders stooped. He was at least 30 pounds lighter than when I'd last seen him. But while he was physically reduced, I could tell from the glint in his eye that he was more determined than ever to carry on with his mission to get justice for Boris, Sergei, and the many other victims of the Putin regime.

In the end, the Western institutions that were supposed to have saved him—the British government, Porton Down, our concierge doctor, the Harley Street clinic—had all failed.

He'd been saved by someone we thought wouldn't—his Russian doctor. Although there were many in the Russian system who wanted Vladimir dead, he'd been lucky enough to encounter someone who was intent on doing his job, and had been faithful to his Hippocratic oath to do no harm.

Vladimir Kara-Murza, a good Russian, had come under the care of Dr. Denis Protsenko, another good Russian. And that had made all the difference.

25

The Seagull

FALL–WINTER 2015

It took a while for my nerves to settle after Vladimir's poisoning. Thankfully, during the summer, the Russians left me alone. But on October 5, about a month before the Magnitsky Awards, Michael Kim, whom I hadn't heard from in a while, called from New York.

"Sorry to be the bearer of bad news, Bill," he said, "but Baker-Hostetler is at it again." He'd just received notice that John Moscow and Mark Cymrot were going back to court to force me to sit for a second deposition. Apparently, this time they'd learned from their mistakes. Instead of overbroad questions and document requests, they'd narrowed the scope in such a way that Judge Griesa would probably accept what they were asking for. In Michael's view, there was no way out of it.

He was right. On November 9, Judge Griesa accepted their request without any fuss, and instructed us to agree on a deposition date before the trial began. The trial date was still in flux, but it was due to start around the New Year.

I couldn't understand why the Russians were doing this. The first deposition had been a total bust, and they'd failed to get the sensitive information they were so eager to get their hands on. It had also cost them a small fortune.

But then, their reasons became clear.

On November 17, one day after the Magnitsky Awards in London, Mark Cymrot filed a document with the court formally accusing me and Sergei of stealing the $230 million. He based this filing on an official document the Russian General Prosecutor's Office had recently sent to the US Department of Justice that made the same allegations.

The Russians had been developing this fiction domestically for years, but now they were formally exporting it to the West.

It was a crazy defense strategy. Prevezon had the dirty money in their accounts in New York, not me, and they were the ones who had to explain why it was there, not me. *They* were on trial—not me. Lobbing conspiracy theories at the court wasn't going to get them acquitted.

As crude as this strategy was, at least our opponents had put their cards on the table. This accusation showed that the second deposition wasn't about defending Prevezon, and now it wasn't even about them trying to get our confidential information. It was about making false accusations against me in an official court-like setting. The Russians could then release my second deposition on the Internet (as they had done with the first one) as part of their campaign to convince the world that Sergei and I were somehow the villains, not them.

The deposition was going to happen, but negotiating the date wasn't straightforward. Everyone had scheduling conflicts in the month of December. I would have to fly in from London; the US government would have to be there too, and their calendar was full; the holidays were coming up; and, as a kicker, Mark Cymrot's daughter was getting married right after Christmas, putting a handful of days off-limits.

Cymrot appeared to be under a lot of pressure from his Russian clients, and demanded that I show up for the deposition on December 7. But the government couldn't make that day, and since both sides had to be there, I didn't show up.

My nonattendance so enraged the Russians that Cymrot filed a motion that same day to find me in contempt of court. That was a major escalation. Contempt is a jailable offense. Even Judge Griesa, in his diminished capacity, saw how inappropriate this motion was and dismissed it peremptorily. He ordered everyone involved to calm down and agree on a date.

That ruling should have been the end of it, but then, two days later, the *Daily Beast* published a story about Denis Katsyv and Natalia Veselnitskaya.

The *Daily Beast* had obtained a document showing that Katsyv was demanding the US Department of Justice reimburse him for $50,000 of "expenses" for a recent trip to New York for his own deposition. This included $995-per-night rooms at the Plaza Hotel and a $793.29 dinner, where Katsyv, Veselnitskaya, and one other colleague had enjoyed a feast of 18 dishes, 8 grappas, and 2 expensive bottles of wine.

The article was titled "Russians Stick US with $50K Hotel Bar Bill." The Russians were so triggered by it that, two days after it came out, Cymrot filed *another* motion to find me in contempt, and this one was truly unhinged.

He claimed a grand conspiracy existed between me and the US government designed to destroy the reputation of the Katsyv family. Cymrot accused us of coordinating a press campaign against them; of colluding so I could avoid the deposition; and, most ludicrously, of scheming together to bring the whole case against Prevezon in the first place. He made it sound like the US government was my puppet and would do anything I asked, like I was some kind of all-powerful Bond villain.

At the end of his motion, and for good measure, Cymrot demanded the judge also sanction the Department of Justice for their conduct.

The motion read as if it had been drafted by an emotional Veselnitskaya who was melting down in Moscow, and had then been Google-translated into English. In Russia, private individuals regularly conspire with their government, so it made perfect sense that they would project this behavior onto me and the US justice system.

There was something frantic and almost desperate in these actions. It was as if BakerHostetler was no longer running the case and Veselnitskaya was ordering them to undertake more ridiculous steps, no matter how doomed they were.

Judge Griesa was having none of it. He swiftly rejected this motion too, stating, "There is simply no merit whatsoever in such applications." All he wanted was to set a deposition date, which, since no one could agree, he declared would be December 18. That *was* the end of it.

This would be right in the middle of my family's Christmas vacation in Aspen, but I wasn't going to argue. The one consolation was that Judge Griesa would allow me to do it over video, so I wouldn't have to go to New York.

Elena, the kids, and I left for Colorado on December 13, arriving in Aspen late that afternoon. We were wiped out by the time we got to the house. Elena threw together a quick dinner while the kids played outside in the snow. By the time we were done eating at 7:00 p.m.— 2:00 a.m. London time—none of us could keep our eyes open. After putting the kids to bed, Elena and I crawled under the covers and were asleep within moments.

In my jet-lagged stupor I'd forgotten to turn off my phone, and at 1:00 a.m. it started buzzing. I tried to ignore it, but it continued to buzz. When I realized I wouldn't be able to fall back asleep, I picked it up and saw missed calls from Moscow correspondents at the *New York Times*, the *Wall Street Journal*, and the Associated Press.

I propped myself up in bed and found multiple emails asking for comment on an article just posted in *Kommersant*, one of Moscow's main daily newspapers.

I clicked the link. It wasn't written by a journalist or columnist, but by Putin's chief law enforcement officer, General Prosecutor Yuri Chaika. This was the same official who'd traveled to Switzerland in 2011 to try to stop the Swiss money laundering case against the Stepanovs.

I read it—and then re-read it. It was a full and faithful recap of BakerHostetler's allegations against me and Sergei, but it went much further.

According to Chaika, whose name translates to "seagull," Western intelligence agencies had sent me to Russia in the 1990s with a mission to weaken and destroy the country. My first assignment had been to invest in Gazprom, Russia's natural gas monopoly, get a seat on its board, and gain access to all of the company's confidential information. I would then share this with my Western intelligence handlers, as well as American corporations, in order to undermine Russia's national interests.

Chaika stated proudly that this plot had been foiled, but that while I was engaged in this operation I also happened to cheat on my taxes, bankrupt several corporations, and steal $230 million from the Russian Treasury. According to him, I then spearheaded a years-long, international "false PR campaign" to shift the blame for this crime onto honest Russian officials and private citizens like the poor Katsyvs, all with the blessing of Western intelligence. Along the way, Chaika implied that I was involved in the murders of Valery Kurochkin, Oktai Gasanov, and Semyon Korobeinikov, the three deceased members of the Klyuev Organized Crime Group mentioned in chapter 8 of this book, "Blame the Dead."

In the midst of this sprawling operation, Sergei just happened to be arrested, fall ill, and ultimately die of "natural causes" in jail. Chaika claimed this "tragedy" came as a windfall for me and my intelligence colleagues, since it allowed us to use Sergei's death to launch our "next special operation to discredit Russia in the eyes of the world community."

This new endeavor consisted of paying Western journalists to write manipulative stories appealing to "people's inherent sense of compassion," which, ultimately, led to the passage of the Magnitsky Act in the United States.

Toward the end of the article, Chaika tied a neat bow around everything. Referring to the Prevezon case, which he had been following intently, he said I would be revealed as an "international fraudster, swindler, and criminal" who'd been fooling the world for years.

After reading the article a third time, I let my hand fall onto the covers and stared at the dark ceiling above. It was the wildest thing I'd ever read—and that was saying a lot.

I was surprised by the fantastical nature of the narrative, but it spoke to Chaika's desperation and the stakes involved. By Chaika's logic, if he could convince the world that I was a fraudster, then the Magnitsky Act was also a fraud and should therefore be repealed. In this one article, Chaika made clear what we had always suspected the Prevezon case to be about for the Russians. Their massive investment in New York legal services—an amount that, when it was all said and done, I estimated would *exceed* the amount that had been frozen—had nothing to do with them defending themselves against money laundering. It had everything to do with destroying me so that the Russian government could knock the foundation out from under the Magnitsky Act.

The stakes of the second deposition could not have been higher.

26

The Writ of Mandamus

WINTER 2015–2016

The day after the Chaika letter was published, we were joined in Aspen by some old friends, Eduardo and Lina Wurzmann, along with their three children. The Wurzmanns were from São Paulo, but we'd met them in Moscow in the late 1990s before all my troubles began. I've always found Brazilians to be some of the nicest people in the world, and among Brazilians the Wurzmanns were especially wonderful.

When Elena and I originally invited them to Colorado, we'd had no idea the Prevezon case would be consuming my life. With my deposition imminent, I wouldn't be able to spend much time skiing or hanging out with them, but it was still comforting to have such good friends around during a difficult time.

There was a small chance the deposition wouldn't happen, though. Michael Kim realized that BakerHostetler and their Russian clients had made a serious tactical error by accusing me of stealing the $230 million. Back at the disqualification hearing in 2014, Cymrot defended John Moscow and BakerHostetler by swearing to Judge Griesa that Prevezon was not "adverse" to Hermitage. Judge Griesa had bought it, making this claim the basis for not disqualifying them.

But, as Michael pointed out, this recent accusation by Prevezon and their lawyers was the *definition* of adversity. He suggested we try once again to have John Moscow and BakerHostetler kicked off the case.

For technical reasons, the disqualification motion would have to come from Hermitage, not me personally, which meant we had to hire yet another lawyer. Michael suggested someone named Jacob Buchdahl at the firm Sussman Godfrey. We hired him, he wrote the motion, and then filed it on December 15.

Because the trial was coming up in the New Year, everything moved very quickly, and the second disqualification hearing would take place three days later, the same day as my deposition.

We woke that Friday morning to nearly a foot of new snow. My whole family and our guests were excited about the ski day ahead, a day that, unfortunately, I would be unable to participate in.

I ate an early breakfast with the Wurzmanns, helped the kids get outfitted in the mudroom, and then retreated to the office, where I parked myself in front of the computer for what was sure to be a long and arduous day.

I called Michael in New York to test the video link to his office, where the deposition would be held. When the image appeared, he was alone in the conference room. At around 9:15 a.m. Mountain Time, two lawyers from the government showed up. They said hello, set up on one side of the table, and laid out a few folders and legal pads.

Then, at around 9:45 a.m., the BakerHostetler team arrived. As before, they came in force. There were at least half a dozen of them, some wheeling carts stacked with giant legal briefcases full of papers. It took them a full five minutes to settle in.

This deposition would not be conducted by Mark Cymrot, but by his understudy, Paul Levine. Cymrot couldn't be in two places at once, and at that moment he was at the Federal Courthouse on Pearl Street trying to prevent BakerHostetler from getting kicked off the case. That hearing was supposed to have finished by the time my deposition started, but it was still underway.

When the clock struck 10:15 a.m., the deposition officially began. Even from Aspen, I could feel the tension in the room in New York. Levine leaned forward, preparing to go on the attack. But Michael interjected softly (he always spoke softly), "Since there's a disqualification motion pending in front of the judge, it would be inappropriate to begin until the judge has ruled."

At first, Levine looked like he would put up a fight, but Michael's logic was airtight. There was nothing Levine could do. Since we couldn't proceed until the judge ruled, we just sat there awkwardly and waited.

The clock ticked away. Ten minutes, then twenty, then thirty. A little after 11:00 a.m., everyone's phone rang at once. Judge Griesa had just instructed the lawyers to put the deposition on hold until he issued his ruling.

The deposition had been derailed, at least for the day. As Baker-Hostetler noisily loaded up their carts, I gazed out the window at the foot of new powder. I called Michael on his cell phone and asked, "Can I go skiing now?"

I could still see him on the video feed. He smiled and said, "Enjoy."

I said goodbye, turned off the computer, and rushed downstairs to grab my equipment. I loaded everything into our Jeep and headed to Snowmass, the next big ski mountain over from Aspen, to meet Eduardo and the kids.

Snowmass is about a 20-minute drive from Aspen, and as I took the back road behind the airport, I was reminded of when I was in boarding school in Steamboat Springs, Colorado. Back then, whenever more than a foot of snow fell overnight, the headmaster would ring a giant bell, call off classes, and declare a "Powder Day" where everybody skied—students, teachers, and staff alike. There was no sweeter sound than him ringing that giant bell.

This is exactly what Michael had just done for me.

As I passed Owl Creek, I called Eduardo to share the good news. He was delighted. He asked me to meet them at the top of Elk Camp, an area of Snowmass that gets some of the best snow but that has intermediate runs winding through trees that are great for kids.

I parked the Jeep, got my stuff, and went straight to the lift. There was no starker contrast between sitting in my office being interrogated by proxies for the Russian government and sitting on a chairlift surveying the mountains in the cool, crisp air, with the anticipation of soon being knee-deep in light powder.

Eduardo and the kids were waiting for me at the top. My children were especially happy since I'd been so absent on the trip. We turned and started making our way down the Grey Wolf Trail. Eduardo and

I brought up the rear, keeping the kids in front of us. As we floated through smooth, arcing turns, I felt my phone vibrate. I pulled to the side to see who was calling. It was Jacob Buchdahl.

I was surprised to hear from him so quickly. Like watching a jury come back after only 30 minutes, certain they're carrying a guilty verdict, I dreaded what he was about to say.

"Hello?"

"Bill—are you enjoying your day?"

"I am. What's happened?"

"We won!"

"We *won*?"

"Yeah. Judge Griesa just disqualified John Moscow and Baker-Hostetler!"

I stood there, gazing into the distance, the Rocky Mountains all around me. It had taken years and monumental effort, but we had finally gotten these sleazy lawyers thrown off the case.

Oblivious to the legal whipsaws of my life, my kids, who were waiting on the side of the trail below me, were now shouting, "Come *on*, Daddy, come on!"

I told Jacob he was a hero, stuffed the phone in my pocket, and resumed the run. It was, and remains, one of the best ski days of my life.

I basked in the glow of this victory for the next few days, savoring the chance to feel like a normal person doing normal holiday things. We skied, went sledding, had snowball fights in the driveway, and wrapped presents to put under the tree. I knew this was just a hiatus—Prevezon would soon hire new lawyers and be back at it in the New Year—but I wasn't going to think about that right now.

But then, two days before Christmas, Jacob called again. This time, he wasn't so upbeat. He told me that Judge Griesa had scheduled an urgent conference call for all the lawyers that afternoon. "I think he's getting cold feet about his disqualification decision," Jacob said.

"You've got to be kidding."

Later that day, everyone dialed into Judge Griesa's chambers. In a bizarre twist, Natalia Veselnitskaya also joined the call. She had specifically come to New York to deal with this crisis, and Judge Griesa allowed her to address the court. This was highly unusual. Veselnitskaya wasn't a member of the New York Bar and didn't even speak English. Using a translator, she pleaded for the judge to reinstate Baker-Hostetler, explaining that it would be difficult for Prevezon to find new representation only a few weeks before trial.

The judge was sympathetic. He seemed especially impressed that she'd flown all the way from Moscow to make her case. The next day, on Christmas Eve, Judge Griesa suspended his disqualification decision. He wasn't changing his mind just yet, but he wanted the lawyers to make more written arguments before issuing a final ruling.

In a massive feat of compartmentalization, I pushed this aside. We woke early on Christmas morning and went down to the living room to gather around the tree. The children took turns opening presents. When they were finished, Elena and I exchanged gifts with Lina and Eduardo. It took all of my effort not to let this capricious judge in New York ruin my Christmas, but I managed.

A few days later, we said goodbye to the Wurzmanns, and then we returned to London on January 3.

Judge Griesa's decision arrived on January 8. In a convoluted written opinion, he *un*-disqualified John Moscow and BakerHostetler. He simply re-changed his mind—again.

We filed an appeal three days later, but Judge Grisea rejected it outright, declaring his un-disqualification final. All he cared about was starting the Prevezon trial and he didn't want me standing in the way.

When I called Michael Kim, he said, "We've pretty much run out of road, but there's still one thing we could try." He explained that the only thing that could force the court to reverse itself was something called a writ of mandamus. "They almost never succeed, but it's our only option."

"That sounds pretty tenuous," I said.

"It is. We have to go to the appeals court and convince them the judge has completely gone off the reservation, and hope they intervene. Normally, I'd never recommend it, but with Judge Griesa acting so erratically, it just might work."

As Michael had said, this was our only shot. I gave the lawyers the green light, and Jacob filed our writ of mandamus with the Second Circuit Court of Appeals in New York on January 13.

While the Second Circuit considered the writ, the Prevezon case was back on track. The trial would start on January 27. Papers flew back and forth in a flurry of activity. It was dizzying. I was going to have to fly to New York for a last-minute deposition and then go straight to trial, where I would sit for days as the first witness.

As I was preparing to travel to New York on January 25, I got an email from Jacob. It contained a one-page attachment from the Second Circuit, which read, "Upon due consideration, it is hereby ORDERED that Appellant's stay motion is GRANTED and the district court proceedings are STAYED for the duration of the appeal."

In non-legalese, this meant everything was halted. The lawyers had to put down their pens. The trial was on hold until the Second Circuit determined whether or not BakerHostetler should be disqualified.

This was remarkable. For an appeals court to stop a major money laundering case just days before trial showed how seriously it took the misconduct of John Moscow and BakerHostetler.

From that moment, everything on the docket went silent. The next filing came three months later, on April 29, 2016. It was a notification from the Southern District of New York court system. The Second Circuit was still considering the disqualification, but Judge Griesa, who had served on the federal bench since 1972, had been permanently removed from the Prevezon case.

– 27 –

The Cellist

Almost a year earlier, in mid-May 2015, as the St. Tropez sky lit with
the pale blue of dawn, 12 uniformed officers of the French National
Police assembled in the driveway of a luxury villa located on Route
Belle Isnarde. There were no sirens blaring, no lights flashing.

The lead officer rang the doorbell. A middle-aged blond woman
eventually answered, bleary-eyed with sleep. Surprised and speaking
French with a distinct Russian accent, she nervously asked why they
were there. The officer presented the woman with a search warrant.
They then filed into her home and spent the next 12 hours turning her
house upside down. At the end of the day, the woman was placed under
arrest, taken to a police station in Aix-en-Provence, and questioned.
The following day, she was transferred to Paris, where she was questioned again, this time by Judge Renaud Van Ruymbeke, the magistrate
in charge of a French money laundering investigation connected to the
Magnitsky case.

After this interrogation, Judge Van Ruymbeke charged the Russian
woman with money laundering, and simultaneously froze $9 million in
her accounts in France, Luxembourg, and Monaco. This was the fifth
freezing order in the Magnitsky case.*

The raid, arrest, and freezing order came as a direct result of one of
the criminal complaints we'd filed after gaining access to the Moldovan
file. This file wasn't just leading us to countries like the United States

---

* For legal reasons, the identity of this woman needs to remain confidential.

and France, but all over Europe and around the world, as it helped to reveal the entangled web of a vast money laundering network.

The way money laundering works is both complicated and simple.

It's complicated by design. Unlike 40 years ago, when a money launderer could show up at a bank carrying a suitcase full of cash and open an account, today, the most cash you can deposit or withdraw is $10,000—anything more and you're required to file a declaration with the relevant authorities.

As a result, money launderers no longer deal in cash. They conduct their operations using wire transfers. They create hundreds of accounts in dozens of banks in the names of countless shell companies and then wire the money so many times and in so many denominations that they hope nobody has the patience, resources, or vigilance to track it.

It's also simple by design. Money laundering consists of nothing more than transferring money, and every transfer leaves an indelible trail, just as John Moscow had pointed out back in 2008. In all Russian money laundering cases, the money starts in Russia; then goes through a handful of transit countries like Moldova, Cyprus, Lithuania, Latvia, and Estonia; before landing in destination countries like France, Switzerland, and the United States. When it reaches this final stage, the money is accumulated in banks or kept in real estate, or used to make extravagant purchases like yacht and private jet charters, jewelry, or fine art.

What Russian money launderers hadn't been counting on was people like the OCCRP or us, and specifically, they hadn't been counting on Vadim Kleiner. After receiving the Moldovan file, he prepared criminal complaints that we submitted to over a dozen countries. Most of these had led to investigations being opened, which often gave Vadim access to even more bank transfer data. Whenever he got this new information, he would enter it into his database, gradually revealing more about where the $230 million had gone.

What had started as a relatively incomplete collection of wire transfers, company names, and bank registration documents had metastasized into one of the most comprehensive databases on Russian money laundering anywhere.

By 2016, Vadim was the go-to person for any journalist who had a question about Russian money laundering.

At the end of March of that year I got a call from a British journalist named Luke Harding. Luke was a sandy-haired, Oxford-educated man in his late 40s who worked for the *Guardian* and had once been their Moscow correspondent. He had written numerous articles and books exposing Russian corruption. We also shared a special bond. Like me, Luke had been detained at Moscow's Sheremetyevo Airport, held overnight, and deported back to London. His visa had also been permanently revoked, and to this day he has never returned to Moscow.

He asked if he could come by our office to discuss a project he was working on. When I asked what it was, he said, "Sorry, I can't speak about it over the phone."

The expression "Just because you're paranoid doesn't mean they're not out to get you" definitely applied to Luke. When he lived in Moscow with his British wife and their two small children, the family was regularly harassed by the FSB. Government agents broke into their 10th-story apartment multiple times, changing screen savers on computers, setting clock radio alarms to go off in the middle of the night, and even breaking a lock installed on a window next to their youngest child's bed. No one got hurt by any of these actions, but they were designed to let Luke and his family know they were under constant surveillance and always vulnerable.

Luke came to our offices on March 22. As we gathered in the conference room, he asked me and Vadim to leave our phones on our desks. We agreed, and when we returned, he was slipping his own mobile into a Faraday bag, a small black satchel that blocks all phone signals. That way, if his phone had been hacked, no one could listen in.

I was used to his general precautions, but this seemed a bit much. "What's with all the cloak-and-dagger?" I asked.

"My colleagues and I are working on a very sensitive story," he said. "I'm not leaving anything to chance."

"Now that we're in the same room, what's this all about?" I asked.

"Sorry, I made a commitment to my source that I wouldn't say anything until the story was out. But if it's all right with you, I'd like to run some names through your database to see if they're linked to the Magnitsky case in any way."

Even though this would be a one-way flow of information, these types of conversations often furthered our mission, so I told him we'd be happy to oblige.

He started by asking, "Have you guys ever come across a BVI shell company called Sonnette Overseas?"

Vadim typed into his laptop. After a moment, he said, "No."

"How about International Media Overseas, or Sandalwood Continental Limited?"

Vadim repeated the exercise. "Sorry, nothing."

"Have you ever heard of a Russian named Sergei Roldugin?"

Vadim closed his eyes, thought it over, and said, "Nope. Should I have?"

"Not necessarily. He's a minor celebrity—a cellist in St. Petersburg—but I was curious whether his name ever popped up in your system?"

Vadim checked. "I'm afraid he's not there."

Somewhat dejected, Luke changed the subject, and we talked about Vladimir Kara-Murza's poisoning, Prevezon, and other recent Russian developments. As we finished up, Luke said, "Keep your eyes on the *Guardian*. When this comes out, I think you'll be very interested."

Indeed we were. On April 3, the *Guardian* published an article titled, "Revealed: the $2bn offshore trail that leads to Vladimir Putin." Luke was part of a consortium of 370 journalists from 80 countries that broke a story called the Panama Papers. Central to it was a data leak containing over 11 million documents held by the Panamanian law firm Mossack Fonseca. The files revealed financial details of hundreds of thousands of offshore companies and accounts belonging to wealthy people from around the world.

There are many reasons why someone would set up an offshore company. Sometimes they do it for anonymity or personal safety reasons, sometimes to make it easier to invest in multiple countries, but sometimes, offshore companies are created for more nefarious purposes.

The leak even revealed that I owned a few offshore companies that had been set up by Mossack Fonseca. Unlike some of the other companies in the leak, however, mine had been set up for legitimate estate-planning purposes, and were fully disclosed to Western tax and regulatory authorities.

Journalists weren't interested in these kinds of companies, they were interested in the secret ones belonging to government officials and politicians enriching themselves through corruption.

The articles that came out on April 3 were divided by country, and each country had a star. In Russia, that star was Sergei Roldugin.

Luke reported that Roldugin wasn't just a cellist, but also Putin's best friend going back to the 1970s. Even though Roldugin professed to drive a used car and play a secondhand cello, he controlled companies that had accumulated billions of dollars of assets since 2000, effectively making him the richest musician in the world.

This was absurd. A quick Google search reveals that the richest musicians are Jay-Z, Sir Paul McCartney, and Sir Andrew Lloyd Webber, who are each worth around $1.25 billion. Yo-Yo Ma is probably the world's wealthiest cellist, and he's worth "only" about $25 million.

The *Guardian* wasn't the only outlet reporting on Roldugin. The OCCRP and the Moscow opposition newspaper, *Novaya Gazeta*, also put out large exposés that day describing some of the schemes used by Roldugin. The collective portrait they painted was shocking.

In one scheme, an oligarch allegedly paid tens of millions of dol-

Sergei Roldugin.

(© ALEXANDER DEMIANCHUK/ TASS/GETTY IMAGES)

lars to one of Roldugin's offshore companies for "investment advisory services." It was difficult to explain why a billionaire with access to firms like Goldman Sachs, JPMorgan, and Credit Suisse would want to pay an offshore company owned by an obscure Russian cellist this much money for investment advice.

Another report claimed that a different oligarch had "sold" an "asset" worth well over $100 million to a different Roldugin company for $2.

In a third scheme, it was reported that a Roldugin company received a line of credit for more than $500 million from an offshore affiliate of a Russian state bank. Roldugin's company allegedly didn't provide any collateral or security for this massive credit line.

All told, over $2 billion had flowed through Roldugin's companies.

Why had these important Russian individuals and institutions handed over piles of money to offshore companies owned by a cellist?

Roldugin could never provide any reasonable explanation. But the answer, in my opinion, is that this cellist was serving as a nominee for his longtime friend, Vladimir Putin.

This financial arrangement highlighted one of Putin's primary dilemmas. As anyone who follows Russia knows, Putin loves money. But because he's president, he can only earn his official salary (which is around $300,000 a year), and he can't hold any assets beyond those he accumulated before he was in government. If he did, anyone who got hold of a copy of a bank statement or a property registry with his name on it could use it as leverage to blackmail him. Putin is well aware of this, because he's used this tactic on many occasions against his own enemies.

Therefore, Putin needed others to hold his money so that no paper trail led back to him. For this, he needed people he could trust. In any mafia-like organization, these people are rare birds. There is no commodity more valuable than trust.

Roldugin was one such person for Putin. From the moment the two had met on the streets of Leningrad in their 20s, they were like brothers. Roldugin introduced Putin to his wife; he was the godfather to Putin's firstborn daughter; and through the decades they had remained the closest of friends.

President Vladimir Putin (left) gives a humanitarian award to
Sergei Roldugin (right), Kremlin, Moscow, September 2016.
(© MIKHAIL SVETLOV/GETTY IMAGES NEWS/GETTY IMAGES)

Since Putin had assumed power, journalists and Western governments had known that he was a very rich man, but had had no way to
piece together where he kept his money. Thanks to the Panama Papers,
they now had at least one small part of that picture.

For us, this news was potentially even more dramatic. If we could
somehow link *any* of the $230 million to Putin through Roldugin, it
would be a game-changer.

Vadim ran every Roldugin company mentioned in these April 3
articles through our system. But nothing hit.

However, these first articles just scratched the surface. Other journalists continued to mine the Panama Papers, and two days later, an
obscure Lithuanian website, 15min.lt, wrote another story about Roldugin. It reported that in May 2008 (just six months after the $230 mil-
lion fraud), one of the companies linked to Roldugin had received
$800,000 from an account at a Lithuanian bank. This account belonged
to a shell company called Delco Networks.

Vadim searched our database again. Delco *was* in our system. He found transactions showing that the $800,000 was connected to the $230 million tax refund. After leaving Russia, the money had passed through a series of banks in Moldova, Estonia, and, ultimately, Lithuania.

We could now link the crime that Sergei Magnitsky had exposed and been killed over to Roldugin. And from Roldugin, we could link it to Russian president Vladimir Putin.

This explained everything.

When Sergei was killed, Putin could have had the perpetrators prosecuted, but he didn't. When the international community demanded justice for Sergei, Putin exonerated everyone involved. When the Magnitsky Act passed in 2012, Putin retaliated by banning the adoption of Russian orphans by American families. Before the law passed, Putin's government had even arranged for Dmitry Klyuev, a convicted mobster, along with his lawyer, Andrei Pavlov, both private citizens, to attend the Parliamentary Assembly of the OSCE in Monaco to lobby against the Magnitsky Act, as if they were some sort of special government envoys.

Why had Putin gone to such lengths to protect a group of crooked officials and organized criminals?

Because, quite simply, he was protecting himself.

Out of $230 million, $800,000 is a pittance. But sums like these add up. It's like charging $5 for a toll. For one car, it's nothing, but after a million cars, you've collected a fortune.

Mossack Fonseca was merely one of hundreds of offshore trust companies. If these other companies' books were similarly exposed, I was sure we would find other trustees of Vladimir Putin who had received other tranches of the $230 million. And this was just one crime among thousands and thousands of crimes that had taken place in Russia since Putin took power.

We were looking at the tip of an enormous iceberg.

The Magnitsky Act says that Russian human rights violators will have their assets frozen in the West. It also says that beneficiaries of the $230 million crime will be sanctioned. That Putin was a human rights violator was not in dispute, but now he ticked both boxes.

The Magnitsky Act put all of his wealth and power at risk. That made him a very angry man.

His crusade against the Magnitsky Act wasn't just philosophical, it was personal.

We had genuinely hit Vladimir Putin's Achilles' heel.

28

Dezinformatsiya

SPRING 2016

Three days before the Panama Papers story broke, a group of five US congressmen, accompanied by two military escorts and several congressional staff members, arrived in Moscow.

They convened at the Ritz-Carlton Hotel on Tverskaya Ulitsa, Moscow's main thoroughfare, where, after dropping their bags and freshening up, they were met in the lobby by an American embassy control officer who ushered them into three black Chevy Suburbans. Still exhausted from their long flights, the Americans made the half-mile trip to the Federation Council, Russia's upper legislative chamber.

The trip had been organized by Republican congressman Dana Rohrabacher from Orange County, California. Early in his career, Rohrabacher had been a speechwriter for the anti-Soviet crusader Ronald Reagan, but now he was notorious on Capitol Hill for being Putin's favorite congressman. No one in Washington knew what had caused this metamorphosis, but it was long complete. In 2012, Rohrabacher burnished his pro-Putin bona fides by being one of only a handful of lawmakers to vote against the Magnitsky Act.

When the American delegation arrived at their destination, they were taken to a conference room and greeted by Russian senator Konstantin Kosachev, head of the Federation Council's Foreign Affairs Committee, along with a handful of his colleagues. The meeting was largely pro forma, touching on issues like US-Russia relations, the war in Ukraine, and trade.

It lasted for about an hour. As the meeting wrapped up, Kosachev quietly passed a note to Rohrabacher's staffer, Paul Behrends.

Kosachev requested that Rohrabacher and Behrends remain in the room for a private meeting without any other Americans present. Rohrabacher agreed. As the rest of the delegation descended to the lobby, Rohrabacher and Behrends stayed behind with Kosachev. As soon as they were alone, another official joined them—Viktor Grin.

Grin was no ordinary official. He was deputy general prosecutor of Russia and one of Yuri Chaika's closest lieutenants. Significantly, he was the man who'd initiated the posthumous accusations against Sergei, which had led to Sergei being the first dead man to be prosecuted in the history of Russia. For this, Grin had been sanctioned by the US government under the Magnitsky Act in December 2014.

Rohrabacher had previously been warned by FBI counterintelligence that he was being targeted by Russian agents as a potential asset. He should have walked out of the room the moment Grin walked in.

But he didn't.

This meeting was not pro forma. Grin handed Rohrabacher a two-page English-language document marked "Confidential." We don't know what else happened in that meeting, but after 15 minutes they parted ways.

Rohrabacher and Behrends then rejoined the American delegation, and they all climbed back into their Chevy Suburbans and drove to Spaso House, the ornate American ambassador's residence in Central Moscow, for an official reception honoring their visit.

The following day was filled with more meetings—including another rendezvous between Rohrabacher and a different sanctioned Russian official, Vladimir Yakunin, the former head of Russian Railways. Again, no other Americans were present.

The entire US delegation then boarded a LOT Polish Airlines flight to Warsaw. Over the next week, they traveled to the Czech Republic, Hungary, and Austria, before returning to Washington on April 12.

Three days after their return, and unrelated to their trip, the Global Magnitsky Act was added to the House Foreign Affairs Committee's agenda for debate. The Global Magnitsky Act, an extension of the original Magnitsky Act, would enable the US government to impose asset freezes and travel bans on human rights violators and kleptocrats from *anywhere* in the world, not just Russia. It had already passed the Senate by unanimous consent. Coming before the House Foreign Affairs Committee was the last hurdle before heading to a floor vote in the House of Representatives, where it was all but certain to pass.

The Global Magnitsky Act would significantly expand Sergei's legacy. Whenever the United States sanctioned a bad guy anywhere in the world, it would be a reminder not just of Sergei's sacrifice, but also of Russia's role in his murder. It was very important to us that it become law.

About a week after Rohrabacher returned to Washington, however, I received an urgent call from Kyle Parker. He was now working as the senior advisor on Europe and Russia to Rep. Eliot Engel, the ranking member of the House Foreign Affairs Committee. "Magnitsky has just been pulled from the agenda!" he exclaimed.

"What? How?" I asked.

"It's Rohrabacher. He's back from Russia and just met with Royce"—the committee chairman—"and somehow it got removed."

"Why would Royce do that?"

"Apparently, Rohrabacher brought something with him, some kind of document."

"Shit. Can you get a copy?"

"I think so. Give me a day." Because of Kyle's job, anything having to do with Russia in Congress came across his desk.

The next day, Kyle sent over a two-page, single-spaced, unsigned document with no letterhead, which was what Rohrabacher had received from Viktor Grin and was now passing around Washington. It was a rehash of Yuri Chaika's *Kommersant* piece and suggested, in a form of subtle extortion, that if the Magnitsky Act were eliminated, US-Russia relations could improve dramatically. This "improvement" could theoretically include lifting Putin's adoption ban.

When I asked Kyle why Chairman Royce, who was well known for his tough stance on Russia, had given any credence to this document, Kyle said, "Rohrabacher's also peddling a movie supporting this thing."

Kyle was able to get a link and password for the film, which he shared later that evening. The film was called *The Magnitsky Act: Behind the Scenes*. It was written and directed by Andrei Nekrasov, the same floppy-haired intellectual who had interviewed me at the Finrosforum in Helsinki back in 2010 where I first met Boris Nemtsov.

Since then, Nekrasov had interviewed me three more times. The first two had gone well, but the third went off the rails when, midway through, Nekrasov began spouting FSB talking points, like the idea that Maj. Pavel Karpov was innocent, or that Sergei hadn't testified against him or his colleague Lt. Col. Artem Kuznetsov. I cut the interview short. I'd never thought anything would come of these interviews, but apparently something had. I clicked the link and settled in.

The film began as a B-movie dramatization of the Magnitsky story in which I featured heavily as the narrator. But about a third of the way through, the tone shifted, when Nekrasov stepped into the spotlight and became a character in his own film—that of the heroic investigator.

He claimed that the Magnitsky story the West had come to accept was untrue. Over the course of the film, his depiction of me morphed from human rights crusader to nefarious financier who'd fabricated the entire thing in order to cover up my own "financial crimes" in Russia. He was all too happy to use his anti-Putin reputation to lend credibility to his "new findings," which—it cannot be overstated—were identical to those of the Russian government, just presented in a slicker, more digestible package.

The film was riddled with lies and misrepresentations. He followed the familiar Russian drumbeat, claiming that Sergei wasn't a whistleblower; that Sergei and I stole the $230 million; and that Sergei wasn't murdered. In Nekrasov's telling, on the last night of Sergei's life, Sergei hadn't been beaten by eight riot guards, but instead the bruises and lesions on his wrists, hands, and ankles were self-inflicted.

I'd heard other versions of these assertions from the Russian government so many times that it was difficult to be shocked. But one thing that *did* shock me was how Nekrasov treated Sergei's mother.

Before we were aware that Nekrasov had gone to the dark side, he had asked for an interview with Natalia Magnitskaya, and we'd vouched for him. Because of this, when he conducted the interview at our office in London, Natalia believed she was talking to a sympathetic friend about her son's death. When they reached the subject of what had caused Sergei's death, she said what any mother would say: "It would be harder to think he was killed than that he died of an illness."

But Nekrasov was no friend. He twisted her interview, making it sound as if she believed that Sergei hadn't been murdered. To drive this home, at the end of the segment, Nekrasov disingenuously stated in a voice-over—a voice-over she could not respond to—"According to Magnitsky's mother, doctor's negligence, not murder, was the cause of her son's death."

This characterization couldn't have been further from the truth. Since Sergei's death, Natalia had taken every opportunity to accuse the Russian authorities of murdering her son.

I was certain that when Natalia saw this film, she would be traumatized all over again. I was furious at Nekrasov, but also at myself for allowing her to be put in a situation like this.

Regardless of how I felt about it, Nekrasov's film was effective propaganda. And this made it dangerous. A viewer who didn't know the facts of the Magnitsky case could easily come away with the impression that there was something wrong with the story I'd been telling since Sergei's death.

This was precisely the point. Nekrasov's movie was classic Russian *dezinformatsiya*. It didn't have to prove anything. All it had to do was plant a seed of doubt. If this film gained any traction, then the Magnitsky justice campaign could be put in jeopardy. This was the intention of our adversaries—and now Nekrasov seemed to be counted among them.

Making matters worse, his movie wasn't just floating around Washington. That same day, I received a call from a staff member at the European Parliament warning me that Heidi Hautala, my friend and ally who had initiated the European Magnitsky campaign and who had introduced me to Boris Nemtsov, would be hosting a screening of Nekrasov's film at the European Parliament.

Rohrabacher's actions in Washington were at least consistent, but Heidi? She had been the most pro-Magnitsky member of the European

Andrei Nekrasov and Heidi Hautala.
(© ITAR-TASS NEWS AGENCY / ALAMY STOCK PHOTO)

Parliament. The only explanation I could come up with was that some-how the FSB had gotten to Nekrasov, who was her boyfriend, and out of love or duty, Heidi was doing this for him.

Whatever her reasons, this was another shocking betrayal.

I reached out to Heidi directly, but it was no use. She wasn't going to stop the screening.

Worse than this was that right around this time Nekrasov announced that his film would air on major television stations in France, Germany, Norway, and Finland in the following weeks, reaching a potential au-dience of millions.

My first thought was to make our own video rebutting Nekrasov's lies. But because this was all happening so quickly, we didn't have time.

Desperate, I called one of Europe's most feared libel lawyers, Al-isdair Pepper, at the law firm Carter-Ruck in London. I wasn't crazy about becoming a libel plaintiff. All of our success in the justice campaign came from being able to speak the unvarnished truth, making me a committed believer in free speech.*

I knew that using libel lawyers was never a good look, particularly when it came from a wealthy financier, but the lies Nekrasov was telling about me and Sergei, and the way he had misrepresented Sergei's mother and manipulated her feelings, were too outrageous. Yes, I had to defend myself, but more importantly, I had to defend *them*.

Alisdair watched the movie, identified Nekrasov's numerous lies, and drafted an eight-page letter with evidence and exhibits refuting them. He then sent his letter to every organization involved in the production and distribution of the film. (It had been funded with grants and payments from multiple European organizations that had no interest in being part of a Russian propaganda campaign.) He demanded each to "disassociate yourself from the film and have nothing further to do with it." Failing this, he promised we would sue everyone involved for significant damages.

The letter worked. The screening at the European Parliament was abruptly canceled just half an hour before it was scheduled to start. Nekrasov, who was in Brussels for his film's European premiere, couldn't believe it. Nor could the Russians accompanying him—a group that included five Russian state television camera crews; Andrei Pavlov; Maj. Pavel Karpov; a Russian-American lobbyist named Rinat Akhmetshin; and—Natalia Veselnitskaya.

Her presence was curious. This film had nothing to do with Prevezon or the Katsyvs. She claimed to be there as a representative of an NGO called the Human Rights Accountability Global Initiative (HRAGI), which was a mysterious organization we had never heard of.

---

* I'd also been on the other side of multiple libel claims—and the worst had happened to come from Maj. Pavel Karpov. Following our YouTube video about his ill-gotten gains, Karpov sued me in London in August 2012 for defamation. Even though he didn't live in the UK and only earned about $15,000 a year, he was somehow able to hire high-flying British libel lawyers who charged up to $1,500 per hour. We were in court for over a year. Ultimately, the judge threw out the case as an abuse of process, and ordered Karpov to pay our legal fees, amounting to $900,000. He never has, and has since been subject to a UK arrest warrant for contempt of court.

When Kyle Googled HRAGI, all he found was a bare-bones website featuring a collection of stock photos of generic-looking, happy families. HRAGI's stated purpose was overturning Putin's adoption ban—code for repealing the Magnitsky Act in the United States.

Kyle did some more digging, and found that HRAGI had been registered in Delaware only two months earlier. It had been set up with the help of BakerHostetler and wasn't much more than a shell NGO with a DC postbox at 1050 Connecticut Avenue NW, just a few blocks north of the White House. (We later learned that HRAGI had been partially funded by Denis Katsyv.)

Nekrasov, Veselnitskaya, and the Russians left Brussels humiliated. Following their defeat, the German and French television stations removed the film from their scheduled programming, and shortly thereafter, the Norwegians and Finns quietly shelved it too.

We'd won this round in Europe, but things weren't so straightforward in Washington. Since Nekrasov's film wasn't being shown publicly in the United States, we had nobody to send Alisdair's letters to. If the film had caused Chairman Royce to remove the Global Magnitsky Act from his committee's agenda, then, somehow, I had to convince him to ignore it.

I called his office, but couldn't pierce the thick layer of staff surrounding him. The best I could do was to get one of his junior people on the phone. I warned the staffer that Royce's committee was the target of an active Russian disinformation campaign. He listened politely, promising to bring it up with the chairman. I'd experienced enough of these types of conversations to know that when a young staffer promises to bring it up with their boss, they have no intention of mentioning it to anybody.

If I couldn't get to Royce directly, I'd try getting to him indirectly. I decided to go to the *National Review*, a conservative magazine I was sure Chairman Royce read.

I pitched them the story of how Royce, whose signature issue was countering Russian disinformation, had just fallen victim to exactly that. They liked it. The story came out four days later. The article, "Russian Propaganda Mysteriously Stalls a Human-Rights Act in Congress," went through the entire chronology of Rohrabacher's trip to Moscow and the spiking of the bill. It concluded, "As long as the Global Magnitsky Act remains stuck in committee on specious grounds, Russia's information offensive is winning."

One week later, Global Magnitsky was back on the agenda.

Apparently, Royce got the message.

29

Strike Magnitsky

SPRING 2016

The Global Magnitsky Act hearing would take place on May 18. I couldn't be in Washington that day because I had to be in Rome to testify at a Council of Europe hearing about Russia's abuse of Interpol. By then, I'd been subjected to five Russian Interpol notices—I was the de facto poster child for Interpol abuse.

Since we'd successfully countered Rohrabacher's intrigue on the committee, I wasn't too worried about missing the hearing in the United States. I expected it all to go smoothly.

I arrived in Italy on the evening of May 17 and checked into the Hassler, an iconic hotel just next to the Spanish Steps. Normally, I'm so tightly scheduled that I barely have the chance to enjoy my surroundings. But I had a bit of time after dinner, and Rome is so irresistible, that I took a stroll around the neighborhood. As I stepped into the wide ellipse of the Piazza del Popolo, I was interrupted by a call from Kyle in Washington.

"Bill, something's up with the committee. There's a team of people on Capitol Hill lobbying to get Global Magnitsky taken off the agenda again."

"Who?"

"One's an ex-congressman from Oakland named Ron Dellums. Another is Akhmetshin, that guy who was in Brussels with Veselnitskaya." He paused. "The third is Mark Cymrot."

"Fuck, these guys just don't stop."

"No, they don't."

This wasn't good news, especially about this new person, Akhmet-shin. Since he'd popped up at the European Parliament, we'd looked into his background. He seemed to be making a conscious effort to remain enigmatic, as there were no readily available pictures of him online. Nonetheless, we were able to piece together that he had grown up in the Soviet Union, had spent time working for Russian military intelligence, and eventually had emigrated to Washington, where he became an American citizen and started lobbying for various foreign interests.

As for Ron Dellums, we later learned he had been paid roughly $5,000 to make a quick, 24-hour trip from Oakland to DC to open doors. Dellums—an 80-year-old former representative who'd been out of Congress since 1998—was probably told he was there to help Russian orphans. He'd likely never heard of the Magnitsky Act, and surely didn't understand the role he was playing in this Russian operation.

One person who must have understood was Mark Cymrot. It turned out he had been moonlighting as a lobbyist briefing staffers on the House Foreign Affairs Committee with information recycled from the Prevezon case about all of my "misdeeds" in Russia.

Once Kyle told me all this, I was no longer able to enjoy my walk around Rome, and went back to the Hassler. As soon as I got to my room, I learned that Dana Rohrabacher had also jumped back into the fray. That day, Rohrabacher sent a letter to every member of the House Foreign Affairs Committee, parroting Cymrot's story and telling them how he planned to submit an amendment to strike "Magnitsky" from the law's title.

Having the name "Magnitsky" on the law was significant not just for us and Sergei's family, but also, and for different reasons, for Vladimir Putin. When it came to the Magnitsky Act, Putin wanted two things: the repeal of the original law, and for Sergei Magnitsky's name never to be uttered again.

By then it was already 5:00 p.m. in Washington, and there wasn't much I could do about Rohrabacher all the way from Rome. I just had to hope that this latest intervention wouldn't have any effect on his colleagues on the committee.

I went to bed and woke the next morning at 6:30 a.m. I attended a breakfast meeting, and then made my way to the Italian Parliament, where the Interpol hearing was taking place. It was hard for me to focus on Interpol with all the intrigue in Washington. But when it was my turn to speak, I put Rohrabacher out of my mind and did my best.

After my speech, I had a buffet lunch and stuck around for as long as I could to talk to European lawmakers. But I had a flight to catch that afternoon, and besides, I desperately wanted to follow events in Washington.

I went back to my hotel, grabbed my bag, and headed straight to Fiumicino Airport, where I intended to watch the House Foreign Affairs Committee hearing on my laptop before flying back to London.

After passing through security, I found a quiet seat near the gate and logged into the committee's livestream. The hearing had just gotten underway, and Global Magnitsky was last on the agenda. I sat there tapping my foot. The meeting droned on as they discussed other subjects; I hoped they'd get to Global Magnitsky before I was in the air.

Finally, at 4:30 p.m., just as British Airways announced they were beginning to board, Chairman Royce introduced the bill, urging all members to vote for it. I wasn't going to miss this by getting on the plane, so I stayed put.

Royce asked if there were any comments. A few members voiced their support, and then Dana Rohrabacher got his turn.

He introduced his amendment to remove Sergei's name, and then launched into a vicious personal attack, describing me as an oligarch who'd stolen billions from Russia. Mixing up components of the Russian smear campaign, he accused me of evading $230 million of Russian taxes (never mind these were the taxes we *had* paid and that were subsequently stolen). He even suggested the Russians were perfectly justified when they tortured Sergei. According to Rohrabacher, they'd needed to extract information from him so they could figure out where I'd stashed my "stolen billions."

I had no idea if Rohrabacher was an actual Russian asset, but if he was, his handlers must have been facepalming. He couldn't even keep the basic contours of their carefully constructed cover-up straight.

Rep. Dana Rohrabacher.
(© TOM WILLIAMS/ CQ-ROLL CALL, INC./GETTY IMAGES)

Despite his blunders, it was painful for me to listen to him. I marveled at the disconnect between his words and his appearance. Rohrabacher was close to 70, often wore a sweater vest like Mr. Rogers, and looked like a jolly uncle out of a Norman Rockwell painting. He couldn't have appeared more harmless, but there he was, using his position as a US congressman to assist the Russian government in their cover-up of a political murder.

The next person to speak was Rep. Eliot Engel, who said, "There is a good reason we put [Magnitsky's] name on a law years ago, and we should reject any attempt to revise history or sweep it under the rug. We should not be apologists for Putin."

That was more encouraging, but just then, British Airways announced boarding was complete and they were about to close the door. I'd been so engrossed that I'd almost missed the flight. I leapt up, ran to the gate agent, presented my boarding pass, and made it just in time.

Once on the plane, I found my seat, stashed my laptop, and strapped in. As the plane taxied, I tried to connect to the committee hearing on my phone, but the flight attendant noticed and scolded me, so I switched it off. British Airways didn't have WiFi on its European flights, so I was just going to have to wait until we landed to find out what happened.

As soon as the wheels touched the tarmac at Heathrow, I turned on my phone and tried to call Kyle, but it went straight to voicemail. I tried Vadim, but he didn't pick up either. When I got off the plane, I found the nearest seat, took out my laptop, and went back onto the House Foreign Affairs Committee website. The hearing was over, but they'd posted a recording. I scrolled to where I'd left off and resumed listening.

It wasn't just Engel who rejected Rohrabacher's amendment. Rep. Gerald Connolly from Virginia said, "I felt listening to [Rohrabacher] like I was watching RT," Russia's international propaganda outlet.

Rep. David Cicilline from Rhode Island said, "To allow the Russian government any modicum of influence over this legislation, including its name, would be shameful and would dishonor the work of Mr. Magnitsky."

Several others, Republicans and Democrats, chimed in with similar sentiments.

Rohrabacher was allowed to speak again, and he made a last-ditch effort to muddy the waters, but it didn't work.

When the vote was called, Rohrabacher lost 46–1. He had been slaughtered. Our current problems in Washington were over.

30

Whac-A-Mole

SPRING 2016

Only they weren't.

Ten days later, I received an email from Paul Behrends, the congressional staff member who'd accompanied Dana Rohrabacher to Moscow. Behrends wanted to know if I was available to come to Washington in early June to appear as a witness at the House Subcommittee on Europe and Eurasia, which Rohrabacher chaired.

In normal circumstances, being invited to testify at a congressional hearing would be a big opportunity, but since this was coming from Rohrabacher, it was obviously a trap. When I told Kyle about the invitation, he quickly confirmed that it was. Rohrabacher's plan was to use his subcommittee as a venue to screen Nekrasov's film and then put me on the spot afterward.

Why was Rohrabacher carrying so much water for the Russians? From his secret meetings in Moscow to all of his machinations with Global Magnitsky—and now this. It wasn't normal behavior.

Thankfully, this time I didn't have to make any end runs around Chairman Royce. When he got wind of Rohrabacher's plans, he swiftly used his authority to cancel the subcommittee hearing. In its place, Royce announced a general hearing on US-Russia relations before the full House Foreign Affairs Committee, where no films would be shown.

Dealing with the Russians and their American enablers felt like playing a game of Whac-A-Mole. Every time they got beaten down in one place, they popped up somewhere else.

And sure enough, in early June, Nekrasov announced the US premiere of his movie at the Newseum, a museum dedicated to free speech and the First Amendment located only a few blocks from the US Capitol. To give the movie an air of legitimacy, he had somehow convinced Seymour Hersh, the famous investigative journalist who'd exposed the My Lai Massacre in Vietnam, to introduce the film and moderate the post-screening discussion.

Now that the movie was being shown in a public setting in the United States, Alisdair Pepper *could* get involved, and I instructed him to send one of his threatening letters to the Newseum.

Sergei's mother, who was still traumatized by Nekrasov's mistreatment, also wrote to them, pleading that they do the decent thing and not "show a fallacious film which makes a mockery of Sergei's life and death."

These letters went out on June 9, 2016.

That same day, our lawyer, Jacob Buchdahl, was finally getting his chance to argue for the disqualification of John Moscow and Baker-Hostetler in front of the Second Circuit Court of Appeals in New York. Our adversaries had hired former US attorney general Michael Mukasey to argue their side. Natalia Veselnitskaya was so invested in the outcome that she had flown in from Russia to sit in the courtroom and watch the proceedings.

In Europe that evening, Elena and I were headed to Belgium for an event in honor of Queen Elizabeth's 90th birthday at the residence of Sir Adrian Bradshaw, NATO's deputy supreme allied commander in Europe. Sir Adrian promised that a number of important officials would be there who might be helpful in furthering the European Magnitsky campaign.

That afternoon, after getting updates from both Alisdair and Jacob—neither had any news yet—Elena and I boarded the Eurostar at St. Pancras in London. We arrived at Midi Station in Brussels two hours later. After checking into our hotel and changing into our evening wear, we took a car to Mons, half an hour west of the city center. Although we were in Belgium, this would be a thoroughly British affair. As we stepped out of the car, we found a military band, complete with Scottish bagpipers in kilts, lining the driveway. We were met by

Sir Adrian and his wife, who escorted us into the party and introduced us to some of the other guests.

Midway through the band's rendition of "God Save the Queen," my phone buzzed.

It was Alisdair. I excused myself to take the call. He'd just heard from the Newseum's president, Jeffrey Herbst.

"Bill, they're not backing down," Alisdair said. "In fact, they've dug in their heels. They have no intention of canceling the screening."

"Should we write another letter ratcheting up the pressure?" I asked.

"I wouldn't advise it. This is a museum dedicated to free speech. I don't think this is the hill you want to die on, Bill."

He was right. The Russians were my enemies, not the Newseum.

I had to hand it to Nekrasov. It was a stroke of genius to choose the one venue in Washington that would defend his right to show a Russian propaganda film under the auspices of freedom of speech. In retrospect, threatening a libel suit against a museum dedicated to the First Amendment might not have been such a clever idea.

I tried to shake this off and returned to Elena. We mingled some more, I exchanged business cards with a few European officials, and we left by 11:00 p.m.

As we were driven back to the hotel, Jacob Buchdahl called to give an update on what had happened in court that day. It had gone extremely well for us. Jacob said the other side tried to argue away the disqualification with technicalities, but their arguments fell on deaf ears. "The judges weren't having any of it," Jacob said. "I think we have a real winner. It'll take a few months for a ruling, but I'm feeling very confident."

At least that was some good news to end a long day.

As the car cruised through the darkened woods of the Belgian countryside, Elena fell asleep on my shoulder. I scrolled through a backlog of emails. Buried among them was a Google Alert for a *New York Times* article. I clicked the link and skimmed it. It was a curtain-raiser for Nekrasov's screening. Surprisingly, it laid out his main anti-Magnitsky arguments as if they had some merit.

I must have made a noise because Elena stirred. Looking at me drowsily, she asked, "What's going on?"

"The *New York Times* is promoting Nekrasov's film," I said.

She perked up. "What? How did that happen?"

"I have no idea."

This shouldn't have happened. The *New York Times* is the most reputable newspaper in the United States, and is known for having a rigorous process that prevents the paper from falling victim to any kind of disinformation. Besides, by that point, the Russians had lost all credibility with the Western press in relation to the Magnitsky case. They'd told so many verifiable lies, and made so many misstatements and exaggerations, that nobody believed a word they said.

I had to find out how they'd managed to pull this off.

When we returned to our room, Elena ordered room service and made some tea while I got on the phone.

I called several journalists in Washington and pressed them. Everyone acknowledged there was something going on in relation to me, but, under the rubric of protecting sources, no one would tell me who was behind it.

It was late at night, but I decided to reach out to some reporters in London. Most didn't pick up, but one did, and he didn't seem to be infected by this journalistic *omertà*. He said, "It's Glenn Simpson," like it was the most obvious thing in the world.

Glenn Simpson had worked at the *Wall Street Journal*, covering Russian organized crime out of their Brussels bureau in the early 2000s. I'd met Glenn several times back when I was running the Hermitage Fund, trying to expose corruption at some of the companies we invested in. He was tall, unkempt, and vaguely bearlike. In 2011, he had given up journalism to set up an investigation firm in Washington called Fusion GPS.

"I thought Glenn was one of the good guys," I said.

"Perhaps he was, but now he does opposition research for anyone willing to pay," the journalist said, referring to the types of investigations done by firms that dig up dirt on political candidates and public figures. "He's been bragging for weeks that he tracked you down in Aspen to serve you with that subpoena."

It took me a moment to process this. *"Glenn Simpson was the one who put my family at risk by sharing information with the Russians?"*

"Yes. I'm sorry you weren't aware. This is kind of a poorly kept industry secret."

I thanked him and hung up. If Simpson was working for my adversaries, that meant Katsyv and Veselnitskaya were paying him. All paths seemed to lead back to this obscure Russian lawyer. Veselnitskaya had hired John Moscow and BakerHostetler; she'd coordinated with Rinat Akhmetshin to set up HRAGI; she'd been at the aborted film screening in Brussels with Nekrasov; she'd engaged a team of Washington lobbyists to advocate against the Global Magnitsky Act; and now she'd brought on Glenn Simpson to run a smear campaign against me.

Simpson's involvement changed everything. He'd been running Fusion GPS for five years and was widely regarded as a well-connected and effective smear campaigner, having left a trail of ruined reputations of politicians and businesspeople from around the world. The Russians had made dozens of unsuccessful, ham-fisted attempts to destroy my credibility—but this guy was the real deal who knew what he was doing.

The game of Whac-A-Mole had just become a lot more intense. If Simpson was going to be working the media following the film screening, then Vadim and I needed to be in Washington to run damage control.

The two of us boarded a Virgin Atlantic flight from Heathrow to Dulles on June 12, the day before the screening. We checked into the Grand Hyatt and prepared for a full slate of meetings the following day with members of Congress, government officials, and journalists. Our hope was to inoculate anybody who might be susceptible to Veselnitskaya's disinformation campaign.

She and her team seemed to be just as busy. As I rolled out of bed the next morning, I learned that Rohrabacher's office had been working late into the night, emailing screening invitations to every single member of Congress.

Veselnitskaya's team had also been reaching out to the media. Most mainstream Washington reporters had received invitations to the screening from someone named Chris Cooper, another *Wall Street*

Journal alum who, like Simpson, had left journalism for greener pastures.

This flurry of invitations to the Washington establishment was worrying. Throughout the day, Vadim and I crisscrossed the capital trying to head off Veselnitskaya.

Our last meeting was with Deputy Assistant Secretary of State Robert Berschinski, one of the key officials responsible for sanctioning people under the Magnitsky Act. When I pulled out our presentation, he told me it wasn't necessary. He knew exactly what the Russians were up to. From his perspective, this was one of the most out-in-the-open, well-resourced, and sophisticated foreign intelligence operations on US soil he'd ever seen.

I was heartened that someone so senior in the US government was fully briefed on the situation, but quickly learned he couldn't do anything. "Unfortunately, we don't conduct counterintelligence operations," he explained, "that's the FBI's job." He promised to send some of his staff to the screening and get them to write a report, which would make its way into an interagency memo, but that, along with his sympathy, was all he could offer.

Everyone assumes that if a senior official at the State Department is aware of this type of operation, then the US intelligence community will actively be working to thwart it. It wasn't as if the FBI didn't know about the Russian disinformation campaign. Robert Berschinski may or may not have alerted them, but Kyle certainly had—*in May*—and now, a month later, they had still done nothing.

The reality is that the US government is so mammoth, siloed, and bureaucratic that in order for anything to happen, someone extremely important has to intervene and declare, "This is unacceptable. Stop it, now."

That wasn't happening here.

Vadim and I left the State Department somewhat dejected. We returned to the Grand Hyatt, where we found a table in the atrium and set up our laptops and phones to monitor events at the Newseum. Kyle would be there and had offered to text us updates throughout the evening. The last thing I was going to do was show up at the screening. I wouldn't give Veselnitskaya and her people the opportunity to create the spectacle they so longed for.

The event took place in one of the Newseum's nicest rooms, on a high floor with a balcony overlooking Capitol Hill. There was a reception before the screening, with hors d'oeuvres and cocktails, and as people filtered in, they were drawn onto the terrace to enjoy a balmy summer evening.

The Russians and their Western enablers were well represented. Veselnitskaya, Akhmetshin, and Nekrasov were there, as were Glenn Simpson, Chris Cooper, and a crowd of assistants and underlings. There was also a phalanx of Russian state television reporters and camera crews scattered around the room to document every development.

However, they weren't the only Russians there. Around a dozen uninvited Russian dissidents had arrived too. A reception desk had been set up to check people's invitations, but since the event wasn't full, and because Nekrasov had raised such a stink about his right to free speech, they could hardly be turned away.

My biggest fear—that politicians and their aides would show up en masse—didn't materialize. Not a single member of Congress came, not even Rohrabacher. With the exception of Kyle and one other friendly staffer, the only people there connected to Congress were Paul Behrends and a small contingent from Rohrabacher's office.

As the sun set, someone from Nekrasov's team moved through the crowd, announcing that the film was about to begin. Kyle wandered in from the balcony and, before finding a seat, grabbed a bag of popcorn and a box of Whoppers that were being handed out, as if this were a normal movie theater.

Kyle took a seat next to one of Robert Berschinski's aides from the State Department. As they chatted, a plump, auburn-haired, expensively dressed woman in her 40s sat next to Kyle. When he turned to say hello, he was completely stunned. It was Natalia Veselnitskaya. He recognized her, but, apparently, she had no idea who he was. He didn't bother introducing himself. The arrangement could not have been more ironic. Here was the man who had literally written the Magnitsky Act sitting shoulder to shoulder with the person whose mission was to destroy it.

The shades were drawn and the lights went down. Seymour Hersh, who was in his late 70s, took the stage. He looked like a typical jaded reporter, with a gray jacket and thick glasses. Reading from notes, he introduced Nekrasov and promised that the film would go "a long way to deconstructing a myth."

The film began. For the next two hours and five minutes, the audience sat quietly and took it all in. The film was more or less the same version Kyle and I had seen, except that Nekrasov had added a segment at the end that attempted to exonerate Putin's cellist friend, Sergei Roldugin, from any links to the stolen $230 million. When the credits rolled, the lights went back up and Nekrasov moved toward the stage.

But instead of applause, the room erupted with boos and jeers.

One person shouted, "Shame! Shame!" Another yelled, "*You* should be put on the Magnitsky Act!" Loud conversations in Russian broke out. Nekrasov stood next to Hersh on the small stage, lights shining in their faces. Hersh tried to calm the room, saying, "We've all watched some journalism. It's called journalism."

A man and a woman, both with Russian accents and sitting in different parts of the audience, shouted in unison, "It's not journalism! It's propaganda!"

Hersh managed to quiet the audience enough to begin the Q&A. The first question came from Drew Sullivan, a cofounder of the OCCRP who'd done some of the key work on the Moldovan file and the Panama Papers. There was no one in that room who knew more about money laundering in connection to the Magnitsky case than Drew.

This was a very unlucky break for Nekrasov. It was Drew who had managed the investigation linking Roldugin to the $230 million fraud, and he wasted no time setting the record straight. He explained that if Nekrasov had only bothered to come to the OCCRP, as any competent journalist would have done, then Drew would have shared with him the documents showing these links.

Nekrasov must have realized how tenuous his position was. He was acting as a de facto defense lawyer for Putin. He had presented himself as a truth-finder, but now that he was debating a real-life truth-finder, he looked weak and ignorant. Growing more flustered and aggressive, Nekrasov tried to explain that these issues were "complicated" and that following money was like trying to find a drop of water in a swimming pool.

To which Sullivan coolly said, "Yeah, it's called money laundering."

Nekrasov, realizing he couldn't win this argument, abruptly moved to the next question.

But his luck didn't improve with the second questioner, or with the third. The fourth was a former colleague of Nekrasov's, a Russian man named Alex Goldfarb. And his comments were devastating.

Goldfarb stood and calmly introduced himself as a longtime friend of Nekrasov's who had produced two of his anti-Putin films. His voice dripping with disappointment, Goldfarb said, "It's personal and emotional for me, because this film is a one-hundred-and-eighty turnaround from what Andrei was before."

Nekrasov crossed his arms as Goldfarb spent a full six minutes forensically destroying the foundations of Nekrasov's movie. Before sitting, Goldfarb said directly to Nekrasov, "I think it should be mentioned that Mr. Putin's regime, which clearly is a beneficiary of this film, is a murderous dictatorship. I want you to repeat this now as you have many times before."

But Nekrasov wouldn't.

That said it all.

I slept very well that night.

When the reviews came in, they weren't kind. The next day, the *American Interest*, a Washington-based political magazine, published a review under the headline "Russia's Big Lie." Then came the *Washington Post* with an editorial titled "Russian Agitprop Lands in Washington." Following this, the *Daily Beast* published "How an Anti-Putin Filmmaker Became a Kremlin Stooge." Put together, these articles tore apart Nekrasov mercilessly. There wasn't a single positive story about the film in the Western press.

Nekrasov, Veselnitskaya, Simpson, and the Russians certainly got a spectacle—just not the one they'd bargained for.

31

FARA

SUMMER 2016

If Veselnitskaya was humbled by this setback or the debacle at the Second Circuit a few days earlier, she certainly didn't show it. The day after Nekrasov's screening, she appeared in the front row of the public gallery at Chairman Royce's US-Russia hearing at the House Foreign Affairs Committee. Two rows behind her was Andrei Nekrasov.

Natalia Veselnitskaya (second row, left of center) and former US ambassador to Russia, Mike McFaul (front, center). Andrei Nekrasov is in the fourth row just over Veselnitskaya's shoulder. Washington, June 2016.

(© KYLE PARKER)

Vadim and I were there too. We'd picked an inconspicuous spot on the side of the room, hoping to avoid both of these people. It was the first time either of us had seen Veselnitskaya in person. She was over-dressed and looked so harmless that it was hard to imagine she'd been the source of so much trouble.

As the hearing got underway, Kyle, who sat on the dais behind the committee members, texted to alert us that Rinat Akhmetshin had just entered the room. Since we had no pictures of Akhmetshin, Vadim leaned forward and casually snapped some with his BlackBerry. These would prove to be very useful in the future.

The hearing was as anodyne as Royce had intended. It certainly wasn't what Veselnitskaya and the Russians had hoped for. There was no movie. Neither Sergei nor I was mentioned even once.

As the room emptied, someone outside the room warned that a Russian film crew was waiting to ambush me in the hallway. I texted Kyle, asking if there was another way out. He said that Vadim and I should meet him at the front of the room. As the crowd exited toward the back, we pushed in the opposite direction. When we reached the dais, Kyle escorted us through a members-only anteroom and then to an empty hallway. He was concerned there might be other Russians waiting outside on the street, so he took us down an elevator reserved for members of Congress to a maze-like sub-basement under the Ray-burn House Office Building. Eventually we emerged into the light of day on C Street SW. There were no Russians in sight.

Vadim and I said goodbye to Kyle and hailed a cab. As we rode through Washington, I still couldn't believe what was happening. I was literally dodging Russians in US government buildings on Capitol Hill. What made this all the more outrageous was that these Russians weren't working alone. They were being assisted by a cadre of sophis-ticated Western enablers. This angered me more than anything.

It's one thing for Russians to act the way they do. Their society is so harsh and unforgiving that in order to get through life, most people are either getting screwed or screwing someone else—and often both. There are few rewards for doing what is right. It takes exceptional individuals like Sergei Magnitsky, Boris Nemtsov, and Vladimir Kara-Murza not to descend reflexively into nihilism, dishonesty, and corruption.

In the West, and especially in America, it's different. There's no question we have our own issues, but Americans like John Moscow, Mark Cymrot, Chris Cooper, and Glenn Simpson have led charmed lives. They went to the best universities, associated with the highest-caliber people, lived in comfortable homes, and operated in a society that at least aspires to honor good conduct and ethical behavior.

Everyone is entitled to a legal defense, but this wasn't about the law—it was an active Russian disinformation campaign. For these people to use their considerable knowledge, contacts, and skills to assist Putin's cronies in exchange for nothing more than money was even more contemptible than the actions of the Russians themselves. Many Russians can't help what they do. But Americans like these *can*, and they act with full cognizance.

That afternoon I met Juleanna Glover for coffee in the Grand Hyatt's atrium. When I expressed my outrage about these people, she responded, "Bill, it looks like they're in violation of FARA. If they are, they're completely exposed."

She was referring to the Foreign Agents Registration Act, which says that anyone trying to influence US policy on behalf of a foreign government is legally required to register with the Department of Justice. It was enacted in 1938 to help prevent Hitler's agents in the United States from spreading Nazi propaganda in the run-up to World War II. Now we faced Putin's agents in the United States spreading Russian propaganda, apparently without a worry in the world.

Juleanna, Kyle, and I had been discussing FARA for a while, but I had my doubts about its usefulness. During World War II and for about 20 years afterwards, the law was vigorously enforced, but since 1967 there had only been five criminal convictions for FARA violations.

But Juleanna, who knew the world of Washington lobbyists better than anyone, said, "You don't understand, Bill. FARA is a *criminal* statute. These people get upset if the spread at a cocktail party isn't up to scratch. The remotest possibility of ending up in prison puts the fear of God in them."

If we really were going to try FARA, then Kyle suggested a man we all knew named Thomas Firestone, who was an expert on both FARA and the Magnitsky case. Thomas had been the resident legal advisor at the US embassy in Moscow when Sergei was arrested, and had written the cables back to Washington detailing Sergei's torture, mistreatment, and murder. His factual reports cut through the Russian cover-up, giving the US government the confidence it needed to pass the Magnitsky Act and sanction the people involved. Thomas truly was one of the unsung heroes in the Magnitsky story.

Following up on Kyle's suggestion, Vadim and I visited Thomas at his law firm's office (he'd since left government). When we briefed him on Veselnitskaya's disinformation campaign and the Westerners involved, he asked us for names. Vadim rattled them off while Thomas jotted them down on a yellow legal pad. He then turned to his computer and logged in to the Department of Justice's FARA database to check if any of them had registered.

None had.

Looking up from his computer, he said, "I'd like to introduce you to Heather Hunt, head of FARA at the counterespionage unit at the DOJ." He wrote to her that afternoon.

Vadim and I returned to London on Saturday, and by Monday we were on a conference call with Heather. We walked her through our story, but like any good prosecutor, she wanted hard evidence, which we promised to provide in writing.

We spent the next two weeks laying out all of the events that had taken place that spring. Taken separately, everything that had happened could be described as unconnected. Mark Cymrot claimed he was representing Prevezon, not the Russian government. Glenn Simpson insisted he was working for John Moscow, not the Russian government. Ron Dellums had been hired by HRAGI, not the Russian government. And Andrei Nekrasov asserted he was an independent journalist, not a paid propagandist for the Russian government.

Taken together, however, it was hard not to see the obvious connections. There was a strong reason to suspect that this was an operation using cutouts for the benefit of the Russian government, being run by Natalia Veselnitskaya.

We filed our complaint with Heather on July 15, 2016, accusing Cymrot, Simpson, Cooper, Akhmetshin, and three other Americans of violating the Foreign Agents Registration Act.

Several weeks later, Heather invited me to Washington to brief her team. There was a whole procedure to visit the building known as "Main Justice" on Pennsylvania Avenue. I'd had to go through a pre-screening, which required a copy of my passport in advance, and when I showed up, I had to move through a bank of metal detectors and wait for an official escort.

Since I'd be visiting the counterespionage unit, I assumed I would be taken to some soundproof room in the basement. But instead, I was led just past reception on the ground floor to a standard conference room that looked straight out onto the sidewalk. Anyone walking by could peer in.

I was greeted by two of Heather's staff, who informed me that she wouldn't be attending. Not two minutes into the meeting, we found ourselves at an awkward impasse. I was expecting them to pepper me with detailed questions, while they appeared to know virtually nothing about the case. It seemed as though they hadn't even read the complaint. I had to start at square one, giving these two the same briefing I'd given Heather over the phone weeks before.

They took notes, and when I finished, I asked, "So what do you think? Are you guys going to act on this?"

In a bit of a non sequitur, one of them gave the standard law enforcement reply, "We can neither confirm nor deny whether there's an ongoing investigation."

I'd seen firsthand what an ongoing investigation at the Department of Justice looks like. In the Prevezon case, Paul Monteleoni or his colleagues had contacted us nearly every day for six months before filing against Prevezon. I was certain these FARA guys were doing nothing.

Perhaps they needed a little push. If the Russian operation was prominently reported, I was sure the FARA people would get off their asses. I pitched the story to the *New York Times*, the *Washington Post*, the *Wall Street Journal*, CNN, *Business Insider*, and several other outlets. But none of them bit.

This made no sense. Throughout the summer of 2016, I fielded constant calls from journalists asking for any information about Russian interference in Washington. Donald Trump had recently become the Republican nominee for president, and he had not been shy about his affection for Putin. In addition to Trump's own murky business in Moscow, there were multiple people on his campaign team who had unexplained connections to Russia. It was all the media could talk about.

Our FARA situation might not have been connected to Trump, but it was a concrete story about Russian interference in Washington. When I challenged these journalists on why they weren't interested, they said things like "It's not a story unless there's an actual investigation," or "These are all obscure characters who no one cares about."

To me, these excuses didn't ring true, and I felt like there was something else going on. I decided to circle back to the British journalist who'd first alerted me to Simpson to see if he knew anything.

"Your problem's Glenn again," he said. "Bill, how do you not know this?"

"I must be talking to the wrong people," I said.

"Yes, well . . . Glenn's made himself into the central node of information-trading on Russia and Trump. He and his team have collected loads of information on Trump, and these news organizations are practically prostrate in front of him, hoping he'll throw them a bone. No one will touch him. Full stop. Which means no one will touch your story, either."

As much as I hated to admit it, I'd hit a dead end. The Department of Justice wasn't going to investigate, and aside from a tiny and virtually unread piece in one of *Politico*'s daily online newsletters, our FARA story didn't see the light of day. I was just going to have to leave it at that.

We did get one huge win that autumn, though. In mid-October, as I was picking up my youngest son, Noah, from school, an email came in from Jacob Buchdahl in New York.

The Second Circuit had announced their disqualification ruling.

We'd won. Decisively.

I opened the attachment. The panel of three judges didn't mince words. They said the circumstances of our case "truly are extraordinary" and acknowledged that I was in real danger from the Russian government. They said I had every right to expect my confidences to be protected by my former lawyers. For these reasons, they instructed the district court to "enter an order disqualifying [John] Moscow and BakerHostetler."

I stopped in the middle of the sidewalk as Noah continued to skip along ahead of me. I couldn't help but smile. I was finished with John Moscow and BakerHostetler once and for all.

32

The Dossier

FALL 2016

On November 8, 2016, Vadim and I were on the Eurostar to Paris. We were traveling there to meet with Judge Van Ruymbeke, the French magistrate who had overseen the freezing order of the assets belonging to the Russian woman arrested in St. Tropez in 2015.

Since the arrest, he had significantly expanded his investigation. However, as excited as I was about this meeting, a dark cloud loomed over everything—the US presidential election, which was taking place that same day.

According to every reputable poll, Donald Trump had only a slim chance of winning. But if he pulled it off, it would be disastrous for me. Throughout his campaign, he'd unashamedly praised Putin and predicted how "nicely" they would get along. Since Trump was a self-proclaimed dealmaker, and Putin had been trying to get his hands on me for years, it wasn't hard for me to picture some shady, back-room deal where I would be handed over to the Russians.

No one could figure out why Trump was so pro-Putin. It wasn't a stance that would win him more votes. Most Americans have a negative view of Russia and especially of Putin. Nor would Trump get more support from the Republican establishment, which for decades had been more hawkish toward Russia than the Democrats.

On the surface, it appeared that Trump was acting irrationally, but what I've learned over the years as an investor is that almost everyone behaves rationally. If someone does something that appears irrational, it just means you don't have all the information.

Throughout the election campaign, everyone speculated about what this information was. I wasn't privy to any inside knowledge about Trump's contacts with Russia, but in mid-September I heard a strange rumor that wasn't widely known.

It came from a man named Cody Shearer, a political operative with links to the Clintons. Cody had gotten my number through his brother, Derek, a former US ambassador to Finland and an acquaintance of mine. I had no idea how Cody made a living, but in the few times we'd spoken, he hadn't been shy about discussing mysterious Russian FSB "sources," "high-level" operatives in US intelligence, and other clandestine contacts of his throughout Europe. He was a colorful character.

"Bill," he said in a gravelly voice, "I've heard some really disturbing stuff out of Moscow. I've been calling around to see if it checks out."

"What is it?" I asked.

"An FSB source told me the Russians have been collecting videos of Trump with women since '87. There's a ton of these things. And they're not pretty."

Cody's call came about a month before the Pussygate scandal broke,* but even at that point I was pretty sure that no one cared about Trump's sex life. He'd had three wives, multiple girlfriends, and a reputation for chasing anything that moved. Everyone knew what they were getting with Trump. "So what?" I asked Cody.

"You don't understand. The tapes aren't just sex. They involve some really perverted shit."

"Have you seen them?" I asked.

"No," he admitted.

"Then how do you know they even exist? The FSB is constantly spreading disinformation."

"Everything my source has told me in the past has been solid."

I hardly knew Cody. And what he was saying was outrageous. Be-

---

* On October 7, 2016, a tape was released that featured Donald Trump saying, among other things, "And when you're a star, they let you do it. You can do anything. Grab 'em by the pussy. You can do anything." Everyone thought that would be the end of his presidential campaign. It wasn't.

sides, he was associated with the Clintons—he had every reason to be peddling a story like this. I wanted no part of it. "I'm sorry," I said. "I haven't heard anything."

Despite my skepticism, as Election Day drew nearer, I couldn't get Cody's rumor out of my head. If Trump managed to win and there was even the remotest chance this story was just a little bit true, then Putin would theoretically be able to blackmail the President of the United States. This would make Trump a real-life Manchurian Candidate. What this meant for Putin's enemies in the West was anyone's guess.

This was all I could think about as I rode the Eurostar to Paris on November 8. The *New York Times* had given Trump only a 15 percent chance of winning, but that didn't stop me from checking Twitter compulsively for any news about which way the wind was blowing.

Like many people living in the UK, I had a bad feeling. Five months earlier, the Brexit vote had taken place, and I'd gotten it completely wrong. Everyone I knew, as well as the pollsters, were certain British voters would choose for the UK to remain in the European Union. But we had all failed to grasp just how much some people in the middle of England hated Brussels, and how much more they hated the idea of losing jobs to immigrants.

It felt like something similar might be happening in America. Maybe Trump would be the US equivalent of Brexit.

Vadim and I arrived at Gare du Nord in Paris at 6:00 p.m., checked into our hotel, and went out for dinner. I was so distracted that I couldn't concentrate on our meeting preparation. After dinner, I returned to my room and checked the news. Nothing. Because of the time difference, there wouldn't be any poll updates until the middle of the night. I forced myself to sleep, but by 5:00 a.m. I couldn't take it any longer.

I picked up my phone and saw that Trump had just won Florida. *Shit*. A few minutes later, it was North Carolina.

I turned on the TV. Filling with dread, I watched as Trump won more states. At 7:35 a.m., he won Pennsylvania, and an hour later, it was Wisconsin. That was it. Trump was president-elect of the United States of America.

The unthinkable had just happened.

Within moments, I received an email from my brother, Tom. "Don't come to America," he warned. "It's not safe for you here." Similar messages poured in throughout the morning as I forced myself to get ready for our meeting with the French judge.

As Vadim and I walked into the judge's offices near L'Opéra, I was completely preoccupied. I let Vadim take the lead at our meeting. When it was over, we went outside and grabbed a taxi. On the way to Gare du Nord, I made calls to friends in the United States. Everyone had the same message: "You're fucked."

I feared they were right, but maybe my friends and I were being too emotional. I decided to talk to some cooler heads in the Republican establishment. First, I called my friend Ken Hersh, a Stanford business school classmate and old poker buddy who was now head of the George W. Bush Presidential Center in Dallas. "Trump's not a real Republican. Never has been," he told me. "I wish I could give you some comfort, Bill, but I can't. I have no idea what this guy's going to do once he's in office."

I then called former attorney general John Ashcroft, who used to be Juleanna's boss, and who had been an advisor to Trump during the campaign. Perhaps he knew more than Ken. Unfortunately, he was equally uncertain about Trump's intentions.

I tried to calm myself on the train ride home. America was still a rule-of-law country, and people like me couldn't just be picked up off the street. But that could all change under Trump. As I thought about it, I realized my only real option was to wait it out and see how bad things might get. If America's institutions weren't going to hold, I could just take the extreme step of not setting foot in the United States while Trump was president.

The Magnitsky Act, however, was a different matter. The law I'd worked so hard to pass was suddenly exposed. Trump would have a difficult time repealing it, since this required an act of Congress, but he could easily refuse to add new names to the Magnitsky List, or even worse, remove people from it.

The outgoing Obama administration had similar fears. Following Trump's victory but before his inauguration, they added five more names to the Magnitsky List, including Andrei Pavlov. He had been one of our highest value targets right from the start. He'd played a central role in almost everything that had happened, from orchestrating the collusive court judgments that had been used in the $230 million fraud, to showing up in Monaco at Dmitry Klyuev's side, to threatening Alexander Perepilichnyy. But because he wasn't a Russian government official or a colorful ex-con, he had managed to slip under the radar. No longer.

The outgoing administration also pushed the Global Magnitsky Act over the finish line, and President Obama signed it into law on December 23. This defeated Putin's efforts to derail it or to remove Sergei's name from it.

More broadly, the US government announced a new raft of sanctions and expelled dozens of Russian diplomats in response to Russia's interference in the US election. Whenever Washington does something like this, Moscow reciprocates. You sanction some of ours? We sanction some of yours. You expel some of our diplomats? We send an equivalent number of yours packing.

Only this didn't happen. The Russians seemed to know something that the rest of us didn't. This was when I really began to worry that Cody might have been right. Maybe Putin *did* have something on Trump, and come January 20, 2017, the American president would effectively be under Putin's control.

As the inauguration drew closer, this almost unimaginable notion became less far-fetched. There had been constant chatter around Washington about the existence of a damning dossier explaining how Trump was connected to the Russians. By the beginning of January, this dossier was actually in the hands of the FBI, certain members of Congress, and nearly every major US news organization. The press had reported on its existence, but no outlet took the step of publishing it, since they hadn't been able to verify it. Still, people took it seriously. Remarkably, the FBI had even briefed both President Obama and President-Elect Trump on it.

Then, late on the night of January 10, as I lay in bed checking the news, BuzzFeed broke ranks with the rest of the media and published the dossier in its entirety. I clicked on the PDF link and started reading. It was a 35-page document compiled by a former British intelligence officer, claiming that the Russian security services possessed video *kompromat* of Trump watching prostitutes perform "golden showers" in the presidential suite of the Moscow Ritz-Carlton. It also alleged that Trump and his associates would receive a 19 percent stake in Russia's largest oil company, Rosneft, (a stake worth about $13 billion at the time) in exchange for lifting US sanctions. It suggested that the Kremlin had been cultivating Trump as an asset for decades. And these were just the highlights. It was jaw-dropping.

The dossier had everything—sex, money, spies, conspiracy. Most shockingly, it seemed to corroborate Cody's improbable story.

To say that the dossier put me in a good mood was an understatement. Even if only 10 percent of it was true, it appeared to have the power to stop Trump from taking the oath of office.

But the next day, after dropping my daughter Jessica at a birthday party in Hampstead, I got a call from the British journalist who'd first told me about Glenn Simpson.

I smiled. "The dossier is the greatest thing, isn't it?"

"It's interesting, if true," he said.

"You think it's *not* true?" I asked.

"I have my doubts. You know who stands behind it, don't you?"

"Chris Steele," I said, referring to the former British MI6 officer who'd been identified as the author.

"No. I mean who stands behind *him*. It's Glenn Simpson."

"*Glenn Simpson!*" I stopped cold. "Are you fucking kidding?"

"I'm not."

I felt like I'd been punched in the gut. If Simpson was involved, then I had to assume that the dossier was compromised. Simpson had gladly spread the Russian government's spin about me and Sergei in exchange for money in the anti-Magnitsky campaign. What would prevent him from doing something similar regarding Trump in exchange for a whole lot more money?

Nothing.

But what made the whole thing even more damning was that *Simpson had been handling the dossier at the exact same time he was working for Veselnitskaya and the Russians.*

This was highly significant. We knew for sure that Putin wanted

Trump, and not Hillary Clinton, to be president. We also knew that the allegations in the dossier had the potential to cost Trump the presidency, whether they were true or not. It was also highly likely that the Russians knew about this dossier as it was being prepared.

The easiest way for the Russians to diminish the potency of this dossier would be to deliberately insert disinformation into it. The upshot was that a bunch of "facts" would find their way into the dossier which, over time, could be disproved. This would then enable the Russians and, not incidentally, Trump himself to claim that everything in the dossier was false, even if something in it turned out to be true. They and all of their mouthpieces could then point at it and scream, "FAKE NEWS!" And they wouldn't be wrong.

(This is exactly what Trump did on January 10, 2017, when he tweeted "FAKE NEWS - TOTAL POLITICAL WITCH HUNT!")

This created a perilous situation for those opposed to Trump. The resistance to Trump desperately wanted to believe this dossier—as I briefly and foolishly had—but if one of the legs of this resistance rested on this compromised dossier, then that resistance would falter and ultimately fail.

As with everything else that had been thrown at Trump, he weathered the storm and was inaugurated nine days later. As I watched him give his address from the Capitol Building, it looked like Trump's most partisan detractors had been prescient: Putin now had his man in the White House.

It was going to be a long, and potentially dangerous, four years.

33

The Khlebnikov File

WINTER-SPRING 2017

The danger associated with Trump came from two sources. The first was that he could do a direct deal with Putin to hand me or one of my colleagues over to the Russians. But beyond that, having Trump in the White House would embolden Putin, and dictators like him, to do whatever they wanted without fear of consequence or condemnation.

One of the first people in our orbit to face this new and dangerous environment was the Magnitsky family lawyer, Nikolai Gorokhov.

Nikolai had been working for the Magnitskys in Russia since 2011. He was a former prosecutor and acutely aware of the danger this placed him in, but Nikolai was cut from the same cloth as Sergei. He felt it was his duty to hold Sergei's murderers to account.

To fully appreciate how dangerous the world had just become, we have to go back to 2015, when Nikolai became a key witness for the US government in the case against Prevezon.

At that time, the SDNY had a significant obstacle in the case. To win, they needed hard evidence proving the stolen money had moved from Russia, through a network of international banks, and into New York. We'd supplied them with reams of Russian bank records from our money laundering database, but Paul Monteleoni and his team considered this to be intelligence, not evidence, and it wouldn't be admissible in court.

Normally, US prosecutors use mutual legal assistance requests (MLAs) to obtain this kind of evidence from their counterparts in other countries. And that's exactly what happened here. The SDNY had formally asked half a dozen countries, including Estonia, Latvia, and Cyprus, to share their banking information, and they'd all cooperated. There was only one exception: Russia.

Without the Russian evidence, the US wouldn't be able to complete the money trail, and the case would collapse. Which is precisely why the Russians didn't hand it over.

But then Nikolai showed up. He realized that the Russian authorities in charge of the cover-up had made a crucial error when they formally named Sergei as one of the people who had stolen the $230 million. You might recall that after trying to blame the crime on a cadre of dead men, the Russian authorities decided to add a living ex-convict, Vyacheslav Khlebnikov, who would plead guilty in order to make the case appear more legitimate. But what they seemed to forget was that the moment Khlebnikov named Sergei as his "co-conspirator," Nikolai, as the Magnitsky family lawyer, gained the legal right to see the case file.

Nikolai applied for access to it, which was shot down. He applied again. This was also shot down. He applied *again*. Shot down. Nikolai knew that corruption in the Russian legal system was endemic, but not always perfectly executed. So he kept at it. Finally, on his 12th try, he got a judge who mechanically followed the law and, at long last, granted Nikolai's request.

Nikolai, a naturally reserved man, didn't betray his excitement. He quietly thanked the judge and then went to the clerk to retrieve the file. When he received it, he found one of the largest case files he'd ever seen: 94 volumes at roughly 300 pages each.

As he thumbed through the file, he realized the Russian authorities had made another crucial error. In an attempt to make the case appear credible, they included data showing the real bank transfers that had taken place within Russia. If this information was made public, it would exonerate Sergei and expose the real perpetrators of the crime (not to mention, reveal the inner mechanics of the Russian money laundering system).

Nikolai needed to make a copy of every single page.

Facing the magnitude of this task, he ordered a digital Pentax camera from the United States and bought a special tripod that would allow him to point the lens straight down onto a tabletop. The camera didn't have a remote, so Nikolai, who was something of a tinkerer, designed one himself. After testing the setup at home, he returned to the court-house day after day and spent eight hours every day taking a high-resolution photograph of each page. He expected someone to come in at any moment and tell him to stop, so he worked as quickly as he could. After three weeks, he had copied the entire file. The total haul was roughly 27,000 images on seven SD cards.

These contained the exact banking information that the Russian government should have provided to the SDNY when the Americans made their mutual legal assistance request. When Paul Monteleoni heard about Nikolai's file, he asked Nikolai if he would be willing to share it.

Nikolai had been fighting for Sergei and his family for years with little to show for it. He realized the SDNY's case might be one of the few chances the Magnitsky family would have to see any real justice, so he agreed to help.

But Nikolai couldn't just email the files to Paul and be done with it. To establish the chain of custody, he had to go through a rigorous legal process. Paul brought Nikolai to London, where Nikolai met with agents from the Department of Homeland Security (DHS) at the US embassy. These agents questioned him, made official copies of the SD cards, and had him sign an affidavit verifying the origin of the files.

Paul then told Nikolai he would need to come to New York to sit for a deposition. This meant he would have to subject himself to the scrutiny of Prevezon's defense team, which at that time was still John Moscow, Mark Cymrot, and BakerHostetler.

If an average Russian was asked to testify on behalf of the US government against alleged Russian money launderers, they would run away as fast as they could. But Nikolai wasn't an average Russian.

He agreed.

To protect Nikolai, the SDNY redacted his name from all court records, sealed every docket item mentioning him, and referred to him only as "witness-1." They also demanded that BakerHostetler, Denis Katsyv, and Natalia Veselnitskaya sign a strict confidentiality agreement. All of this may have looked good on paper, but given our adversaries' past conduct, it seemed extremely unlikely they would stick to the deal. The possible consequences if they didn't were anyone's guess.

Recognizing this risk, Paul proposed bringing Nikolai and his family to New York, where they would stay under US government protection until the deposition was completed. Even though the actual deposition would only take seven hours, the legal wrangling leading up to it could take weeks, or even months (as it had with me), and during that time Paul didn't want Nikolai or his family sitting in Moscow, in harm's way.

Nikolai's wife, Julia, and 13-year-old daughter, Diana, came ahead of him, arriving in August 2015. They were met by Svetlána Angert, a Russian-speaking DHS agent, and placed in an apartment overlooking the Hudson River in Hoboken, New Jersey. When Nikolai arrived two weeks later, the family was moved to a government safe house on Manhattan's Upper West Side.

Once together in New York, the Gorokhovs felt secure. While Nikolai spent his days with the SDNY, Diana went to the local middle school, MS 256, where she absorbed English like a sponge. One of the agents looking after them, Aleksander Schwartzman, was a black belt in aikido, and enrolled Diana in a local dojo. Meanwhile, Julia, who had never been to the United States, wandered the city wide-eyed, taking pictures and treating their stay like an extended holiday.

Nikolai and Julia Gorokhov, New York, 2015.
(© NIKOLAI GOROKHOV)

But their bliss was interrupted in September following a call from Julia's mother. While making a routine check on the Gorokhovs' empty Moscow apartment, she discovered that it had been broken into. It didn't appear as if anything had been taken, but someone had certainly been there. Everything was covered in a thin layer of dust, except for Nikolai's computer screen and keyboard, which had been wiped clean. Whoever had been there also made themselves tea, leaving two half-filled cups on the living room table. This was a standard calling card of the FSB.

It was impossible for Nikolai and Julia not to worry after that, but Nikolai resolved to stick to the plan.

On October 1, two months after his arrival in New York, Nikolai was deposed. He had to square off against John Moscow. Veselnitskaya watched the livestream from Russia. As soon as it started, John Moscow demanded to know where Nikolai and his family were staying in New York.

Nikolai refused to answer.

John Moscow then asked who was staying with him, and if he had a full-time security detail. Again, Nikolai refused to answer.

John Moscow then asked when he planned to return to Russia.

Nikolai didn't answer this, either.

They went back and forth like this for hours, Nikolai constantly parrying John Moscow's questions. This thuggishness might have worked on a less steely person, but it didn't faze Nikolai, who dealt with far scarier people in Russia every day.

John Moscow's questions took up most of the day, and the US government got its turn with Nikolai the next morning. Paul asked the questions that would satisfy the court about the chain of custody for Nikolai's evidence. When it was over, Paul had what he needed, and BakerHostetler had been given the opportunity to challenge Nikolai.

At this point, if anything were to happen to Nikolai, it wouldn't prevent his evidence from being presented in court. He understood that somebody could still punish him for assisting the US government, but this wouldn't alter the trial's outcome.

The United States was a foreign land for the Gorokhovs, and they wanted to return home. At the end of October, and with the gratitude of the US government, they flew back to Moscow.

Once there, Nikolai resumed his work, Julia went back to her job, and Diana returned to her school. Slowly, their lives returned to normal. In time, the trip to New York felt more and more like a dream.

*   *   *

Whatever risk Nikolai faced, it was compounded in early 2017, when he made another important discovery in the case. That was when he came into possession of a tranche of emails showing that Andrei Pavlov had been colluding with the Russian Interior Ministry to cover up the authorities' involvement in the $230 million crime. Nikolai felt that if these emails came to light, they would undermine one of the foundational pillars of the Russian government's false narrative—that the police were not involved in any way.

Nikolai was scheduled to present these emails to a Russian judge on March 22, 2017.

But he never made it to court that day.

On the afternoon of March 21, Julia got a panicked call from their daughter. "Mama," Diana said, her voice shaking, "Papa fell from the roof!" The Gorokhovs lived on the top floor of a five-story apartment building in Moscow, meaning that Nikolai would have fallen 50 feet to the ground.

Julia knew that Nikolai was working on the roof that day, hoisting up a Jacuzzi and some building materials as part of a bathroom renovation. Nikolai would have been operating a winch he regularly used to haul things up. It had always been safe before.

Julia tried to get more information out of Diana, but she was so distraught that she could barely speak. Julia hung up and called 112, the Russian equivalent of 911, asking if they knew anything about a man falling from a building. Although Moscow is a huge metropolis, with roughly the same population as New York City, the dispatcher said, "Yes, we have a person who fits that description. He's been airlifted to the Botkin Hospital."

When Julia called the hospital, they confirmed that Nikolai was indeed there. But they wouldn't tell her anything more.

Julia rushed out of her office and took the Metro straight to the hospital. When she arrived, she ran to the reception desk and, breathless, asked to see her husband.

Like Evgenia Kara-Murza before her, Julia Gorokhov was stone-walled. All they would tell her was that Nikolai was in the ER. She was instructed to sit in the waiting area, off to the side of reception. From there she couldn't see the corridor linking the ER to the bank of elevators going up to the main hospital and wouldn't know when Nikolai was being moved, so she decided to sit on the floor in the hallway and wait.

Four hours later, orderlies pushed Nikolai out of the ER on a gurney. Julia leapt up. Nikolai's eyes were open—at least, his right eye was. His left eye was swollen and covered in bandages, and the whole left side of his head was bruised and lacerated.

She called out his name, but all he did was moan. She implored the orderlies to stop and let her talk to him, but they ignored her and pushed him into an elevator, holding up their arms to indicate she couldn't follow.

Unsure of what to do, Julia remained at the hospital for two more hours, begging the nurses and receptionists for more information. All they would tell her was that Nikolai had been taken to the ICU and that to see him she needed to come back the next day during visiting hours. At around 10:00 p.m., a family friend picked her up and drove her back to the Gorokhovs' apartment. Once home, she barely slept.

Around dawn, as she was finally drifting off, she was jerked awake by a phone call. It was a man she barely knew named Ilya. It took her a moment to place him. He was an acquaintance of Nikolai's from college whom she'd met in passing a few times over the years.

After reminding her of who he was, he said, "You probably expected something like this, didn't you?" His tone was harsh and unsympathetic.

"Like what?" Julia asked.

"Not this call, but what happened to Nikolai. . . . How is Nikolai, by the way?" he asked, almost as an afterthought.

"Not well. He's in intensive care."

"Are you planning on filing a criminal complaint?"

This was probably the last thing on Julia's mind at that moment. "I-I don't know," she said.

"I would advise you not to. Anything can happen while he's in the hospital."

This sounded like a threat. All she could think to say was, "Thank you. I have to go now." She hung up.

Struggling to put Ilya out of her mind, she got out of bed, made tea, and helped Diana get off to school. A few hours later, Julia returned to the hospital.

When she arrived at reception, she was again told, "You can't see the patient."

"Why not?" she demanded.

"He's unconscious."

"So?"

"I'm sorry, but you can't see him," the receptionist repeated.

Julia thought, *What kind of hospital doesn't allow a wife to see her injured husband?* She paced the waiting area, hoping that either Nikolai would regain consciousness or that the doctors would change their minds. Neither happened. She left, distraught, just after visiting hours ended at 3:00 p.m.

That evening, she got a call from a colleague of Nikolai's named Alexander, asking how Nikolai was and if she needed anything. After updating him, she told him about the disturbing call from Ilya and his insistence that she not file a complaint.

"He's wrong," Alexander pronounced emphatically. "To protect Nikolai, we *must* file a complaint."

The next morning, Alexander came to their apartment and helped her draft a complaint describing the incident. Julia finished by writing that she believed Nikolai's fall was a deliberate attempt on his life in retaliation for his work on the Magnitsky case.

She and Alexander then hand-delivered the complaint to the local branch of the Interior Ministry. She passed it to the duty officer, who gave it a cursory glance and started laughing. "You can't be serious," he said. "Your husband isn't important. Who would want to kill him?"

They spent 15 minutes trying to explain what was going on, but the officer was completely uninterested. Julia left the complaint with them anyway.

When she arrived at the hospital that afternoon, she was finally allowed to see Nikolai. The ICU was a large ward on an upper floor, full of patients, some screaming, each cordoned from one another by nothing more than a flimsy curtain and their own misery. When Julia got to Nikolai's bed, he was conscious. But when he spoke, he didn't make any sense. He kept repeating, "Why are you here?" without acknowledging who she was, and, "How are the others?" She had no idea which "others" he meant.

She was relieved he was alive, but terrified that his head injuries had caused permanent brain damage. She still hadn't seen his medical report, and the doctors had told her next to nothing, but it was hard to imagine that her 53-year-old husband could emerge from a 50-foot fall with his full faculties intact. She sat by his bedside for as long as visiting hours allowed, and went home under a cloud of uncertainty.

That cloud darkened as soon as she arrived back at their apartment building, where she was approached by two uniformed police officers, one of them filming her with a handheld video camera. It quickly became apparent that they weren't there to investigate Nikolai's fall at all. Instead, they demanded, "When will you withdraw your complaint?"

She looked down and without uttering a word went upstairs.

The next morning, she awoke and spotted a police car stationed outside their building. She called her mother and asked her to escort Diana, who was 15, to school. She wanted an adult to be present in case the officers approached her daughter.

The same police car was still there when Julia left for the hospital that afternoon. She was again met by the two officers, one with his video camera, barking, "Are you sticking to your story?" She continued to ignore them.

Thankfully, there were no police waiting at the hospital, and when she got to the ICU, she found Nikolai conscious. He had improved remarkably overnight. He was now fully aware of who she was, but still struggled to comprehend why he was there. Elated, Julia grabbed his hand. He tried to smile, but his injuries made it too painful. He asked if

Diana was all right, and wondered about us in London. Julia was happy to report that Diana was shaken but fine, and that we were just grateful he'd survived.

That day, Julia finally got his medical report. Nikolai had suffered a shattered lower jaw, eleven broken ribs, internal bleeding, a fractured skull, a severe concussion, and a badly damaged left eye and orbital socket. But his arms and legs were fine. His heart and lungs and other vital organs were intact. Recovery would require months of painful convalescence and maxillofacial surgery, and his vision would be permanently impaired, but compared to the alternative, his condition could only be described as a miracle.

He and Julia spoke until visiting hours ended. Although Nikolai couldn't recall the moment of his fall, he remembered most of what led up to it. The Jacuzzi, which he'd purchased secondhand online, had been delivered by three men working for a moving company he'd contacted earlier that week. He'd also arranged for them to pick up and deliver several bundles of drywall. Since the Gorokhovs lived on the top floor, it was easier to bring everything up to the roof with the winch than up the stairs. Nikolai had been on the roof with one of the men working the winch, while the other two men were on the ground. They brought up the drywall first, then attached the Jacuzzi. That was as far as his memory went.

The next thing Nikolai knew, he was in the ICU three days later. Somehow, the Jacuzzi, Nikolai, and the winch had all plummeted to the ground. Nikolai had landed in the tub on his left side, and his head had bounced violently on the pavement, leaving behind a large pool of blood.

Despite his injuries, Nikolai's recovery progressed quickly. Ten days after his fall, he was able to walk out of the hospital on his own. When he and Julia reached their building, they were confronted by the same two officers who'd been hounding her every day since the incident. Nikolai was incensed, but too weak to challenge them, so he and Julia ignored the officers and pushed past.

Nikolai convalesced at home over the following days. During that time, the police persisted in harassing him and his family. They served all three of them, including Diana, with summonses, threatening Julia with criminal prosecution for filing a false complaint and demanding that Nikolai sign a statement swearing that the whole thing had been an accident. They badgered Nikolai and Julia by constantly calling their mobile phones—unlisted numbers that they'd never provided to the police. They even tracked down Diana on VKontakte (Russia's version of Facebook), messaging her to contact the police right away.

None of this had the desired effect. Julia didn't withdraw her complaint, Nikolai wouldn't sign any false statements, and Diana wasn't talking to anybody.

The Gorokhovs weren't going to go along with the police, but that didn't stop the police from officially pronouncing that the incident was no more than an unfortunate accident involving a Jacuzzi that was too heavy and a winch that had failed.

Based on the evidence, Nikolai was sure that wasn't the case. The Jacuzzi had *not* been too heavy. The winch had a capacity of over 1,000 pounds and the tub weighed less than 300 pounds. The winch had already been used that day to bring up three much heavier loads of drywall. Moreover, photos of the winch showed that its counterweights had been tampered with, making it unstable.

Perhaps the most glaring giveaway was the report filed by the responding officers. They questioned only two of the three movers. It was as if the third man didn't exist (and to this day, no one knows his identity). The two men they did question both lied. They said no one had gone up to the roof with Nikolai, which wasn't true. They also claimed that they'd carried the drywall up the stairs, and had only used the winch on the Jacuzzi. Also untrue.

And then there was the threatening call from Ilya.

None of it added up. On April 7, only a couple weeks after the incident, Nikolai filed a more exhaustive and expanded criminal complaint of his own. Unsurprisingly, the authorities refused to investigate, and stuck to their story.

If someone had been responsible for pushing Nikolai off the roof, as we all suspected, we would never find out who that was.

But at least Nikolai, unlike Sergei, was still alive.

– 34 –

Senator Grassley

SUMMER 2017

About a month later, with Nikolai on the mend, I was heading to the United States for a very important trip.

The Prevezon case was finally going to trial. After four years and a massive investment of time and energy, the Russians were going to have to defend themselves in court.

I was slotted to be the government's main witness. I would spend the beginning of the trial setting out the facts of the $230 million fraud and telling the court what had happened to Sergei. The government needed this for context so their subsequent arguments about money laundering would make sense to the jury. After sitting for the government, I would then be subjected to what was sure to be a grueling, multi-day cross-examination by Prevezon's new American lawyers. In all, the trial was expected to last a month, and Paul Monteleoni told me to be prepared to sit on the stand for a full week.

Six days before trial, the SDNY won a significant victory. The judge who had replaced Judge Griesa ruled that Nikolai's evidence would be admissible.

This was a crucial development. If this evidence hadn't been allowed, the government wouldn't have been able to draw an uninterrupted line from the $230 million crime in Russia to assets to New York, and they almost certainly would have lost the case.

Prevezon had done everything they could to prevent this evidence from being admitted. But now that it had been, they weren't left with much. Their remaining defense strategy would most likely be a scorched earth attack against me. They would recklessly malign me, accuse me of committing the crime Prevezon had benefitted from, and generally make me out to be a self-interested mastermind and crook. Since there's no such thing as libel in court, they could do this without fear of any consequence. If they pulled it off, they might be able to confuse financially unsophisticated jurors, who would throw up their hands and say, "We just don't know who did what, and therefore we can't find Prevezon guilty."

Before heading to New York, I made a stop in Washington. The month before, we'd had an unexpected break with our FARA complaint. A staff member for Sen. Charles Grassley had read the small *Politico* story about our complaint and brought it up with his boss. Since then, Senator Grassley, the chairman of the Senate Judiciary Committee, one of Washington's most powerful congressional committees, had become interested.

For many years, Senator Grassley had been looking into the issue of non-enforcement of FARA. Our complaint was not only timely and specific, but emblematic of this problem. I'd had several conference calls with his legislative counsel, Patrick Davis, describing all the people involved in the anti-Magnitsky disinformation campaign, as well as our disappointing experience with the FARA division at the Department of Justice.

Senator Grassley decided to take up the cause and wrote to the DOJ, demanding to know what they planned to do with our complaint. He'd given them two weeks to respond, and by early May, nearly a month later, he'd still heard nothing.

I was used to being ignored by law enforcement, but I doubted this was true for someone like Senator Grassley. He agreed to meet with me on Thursday, May 11, to discuss how to hold the DOJ's feet to the fire.

I landed in Washington on the evening of May 10, feeling unusually tired. Things were piling up. When the Prevezon trial was over, I would need to sleep for at least a week. But for now I had to run like hell and hold myself together.

By the time I reached the Willard InterContinental Hotel that night, I felt a heavy cold coming on.

I woke the next morning feeling worse. I was due to meet Senator Grassley in the afternoon, which I couldn't miss, so I took some Sudafed, soldiered through my schedule, and made it to his office at 3:00 p.m. Patrick Davis greeted me. After going over the status of things with the DOJ, Senator Grassley joined us in the conference room. He was an 84-year-old Iowa Republican who'd been in the Senate for 36 years. This was the first time I'd met him, and I found him to be pleasant and sympathetic.

We discussed what could be done when he received the inevitable "We can neither confirm nor deny" response from the DOJ that we both knew was coming. He vowed that when he got that letter, he would haul them in front of the Judiciary Committee to force answers out of them. In that scenario, he asked if I would also be willing to testify.

I said, "Of course."

When I got back to the Willard that evening, I had a full-blown cold. I collapsed into bed without eating dinner and was asleep by 7:30 p.m.

The next morning, I woke wracked with chills, my T-shirt soaked through. This was no ordinary cold. I called the front desk and had them bring me a thermometer. Sure enough, I had a fever. The hotel sent a doctor to the room, and he gave me a flu test. Positive. He told me to take some Tylenol, drink lots of fluids, and stay in bed. I canceled all my meetings and slept the whole day.

By evening, my fever had spiked to 103.5. I could barely make it across the room to the toilet. How the hell was I going to get to New York? And even if I could get to New York, how would I be able to sit in a witness box for a whole week? Unfortunately, I couldn't just call in sick. This was a major trial in a US Federal Court. There were dozens of lawyers, multiple witnesses, a jury, the judge—everything had been scheduled and choreographed in advance, and I was slated to play a big role.

The notion of letting down the Magnitsky family, Nikolai, my team, and the government after four years was unthinkable. That night, I drank some NyQuil, curled up in bed, and prayed that my fever would break by morning.

It didn't.

I woke early, the sun still not up, feeling miserable. I had a splitting headache and another drenched T-shirt. In my pre-dawn delirium I resigned myself to letting Paul know that there was no way I could make it on Monday. It would be physically impossible for me to appear in court.

I picked up my phone to draft an email, but before I could, I spotted a message from Paul that had come in at 2:35 a.m.

I opened it. While I'd been asleep, Denis Katsyv had agreed to pay $5.9 million to the US government to settle the case. I was so sick that I didn't know what to think. But in the moment, I was overcome by absolute physical relief. I put my phone on Do Not Disturb and fell back asleep for several hours.

When I woke, I got out of bed, made some tea, and called Ivan and Vadim. We agreed it was disappointing that Prevezon would never be found guilty in a US court, but it was still a solid outcome. The government's investigation had unearthed an additional $1 million flowing to Prevezon from the $230 million fraud, which, when added to our original discovery of $857,764, meant they had received nearly $1.9 million. This settlement was three times that amount.

In my mind, innocent people don't pay $5.9 million to make their problems go away, and this was on top of the $15 million or so I estimated Prevezon had paid in legal fees. That was a steep price to avoid explaining the provenance of an alleged $1.9 million of dirty money.

My fever finally broke on Tuesday. I felt strong enough to do some work and contacted Patrick at Senator Grassley's office to inform him of the Prevezon settlement. He already knew. It had taken them by surprise as well, but it was unconnected to the FARA issue and they were still full steam ahead. He also informed me they'd just heard from the DOJ. Sure enough, Senator Grassley *had* received the exact "We can neither confirm nor deny" letter we'd expected.

Patrick asked if I'd be available to testify at a Senate Judiciary Committee hearing on July 16. I'd be in Colorado with my family then, but I told him I'd be there for sure.

I returned to London in a much better mood. I wasn't sick anymore, I wouldn't have to deal with Prevezon's lawyers, our FARA complaint was bearing unexpected fruit, and there was even some forward momentum on an entirely different front—it looked more and more likely that Canada would pass its own version of a Magnitsky Act within the next few months.

Topping it off, NBC was about to release a long and, I hoped, hard-hitting exposé on everything surrounding the Magnitsky case. I didn't know when it would air, but I hoped it would at least come out before the Judiciary Committee hearing.

About a month later, on July 7, as Elena and I were packing for Colorado, the story aired on MSNBC. The reporter, Richard Engel, didn't just go into Sergei's story and the $230 million fraud, but also talked about Vladimir Kara-Murza's poisoning, Boris Nemtsov's assassination, and Nikolai Gorokhov's rooftop "accident." It was fantastic.

Elena and I got up at dawn the next morning, herded the kids into a van, moved through Heathrow, and eventually settled onto our United flight from London to Chicago, where we would make a connection to Aspen. Even though I was traveling with young children, I was able to relax for the first time in a long while.

Elena let me sleep for nearly the entire flight.

35

Trump Tower

SUMMER 2017

We landed at Chicago O'Hare in the early afternoon after an eight-hour flight. I was well rested, but the kids were tired, hungry, and cranky. Elena and I knew that if we didn't get some food into them, our four young children would mutiny, presenting us with overlapping meltdowns before our next flight. Elena occupied the kids as best she could while I scouted the terminal for a restaurant everyone could agree on. I found a sushi place called Wicker Park Seafood at the far end of Terminal 1. I went back, grabbed everybody, and brought them to the restaurant, where we got a table and ordered.

The food arrived quickly. As soon as the kids tucked into their California rolls and shrimp tempura, their moods improved. Crisis averted.

Midway through the meal, my phone rang. It was a reporter from the *New York Times* named Jo Becker, a two-time Pulitzer Prize winner whom I'd met once before in London.

Since the inauguration, the Trump-Russia scandal had only gotten bigger and more breathtaking. Just the night before, Trump had had an impromptu meeting with Putin at the G20 Summit in Hamburg, Germany. I assumed Jo was calling about this, but she immediately went in a completely different direction. "Do you know anything about a lawyer named Natalia Veselnitskaya?" she asked.

I could hardly believe it. "Do I ever!" I said.

I stepped away from the table and found a quiet row of seats near a large window overlooking the tarmac. Jo knew a lot about Veselnitskaya already, and had many in-depth questions. To make things easier, I forwarded her our presentation on Veselnitskaya's disinformation campaign—the same presentation I'd unsuccessfully pitched to a dozen journalists the previous autumn—and took her through it page by page.

When we were finished, I asked, "What're you going to do with this?"

"You'll see," she said cryptically. "It should be out later today."

I returned to lunch, overcome with anticipation. This was the first journalist I'd spoken to who'd shown any interest in Veselnitskaya, and Jo was a top reporter at the *New York Times*, no less. As I finished eating, I continuously refreshed the *Times* app on my phone, but nothing came up. By the time we boarded our next flight, a small United Express jet with broken WiFi, I still didn't know exactly what the *Times* was going to report.

As soon as the plane touched down a few hours later, I powered up my phone and checked. There it was. "Trump Team Met With Lawyer Linked to Kremlin During Campaign."

The story was a bombshell. It revealed that Natalia Veselnitskaya had met with Trump's son, Donald Trump, Jr.; his son-in-law, Jared Kushner; and his campaign manager, Paul Manafort, on June 9, 2016, in Trump Tower to discuss the Magnitsky Act. Since the Trump-Russia scandal had begun, this was the first verified contact between a Russian and Trump's inner circle during the run-up to the election.

I walked through the airport stunned, absently "helping" Elena corral our kids. The fact that the Magnitsky Act was at the center of one of the biggest political scandals in US history was disorienting. What was equally unbelievable was that the Russian government, through Veselnitskaya, had been able to get an audience with the son of the next president of the United States.

As we waited for our luggage in baggage claim, my youngest daughter, Hannah, tugged at my arm and asked, "Daddy, can we go swimming tomorrow?" I mumbled something noncommittal, unable to stop scrolling through the article over and over. I kept getting stuck on that date—June 9, 2016.

Why was it so familiar?

I checked my calendar. *That was the same day of the final disqual-*

ification hearing against BakerHostetler at the Second Circuit! The one Veselnitskaya had attended. Glenn Simpson had been there too. Veselnitskaya must have gone straight from court to Trump Tower. I couldn't believe it.

When we arrived at the house, I tried to help Elena get the kids settled, but my phone was blowing up. Emails, texts, and phone calls were coming through from every corner of the globe. Dozens of outlets converged on me: I'd been quoted in Jo's article and was one of the few people in the West who had firsthand knowledge of this mysterious Russian lawyer.

It looked like swimming with Hannah was going to have to wait.

I went to a quiet corner of the house to answer messages and book TV interviews for the next day. Between the jet lag and the adrenaline, I only managed a few hours of sleep that night. Early the next morning, I drove to the Aspen Institute. Fortunately, Aspen is the one of the few places between Salt Lake City and Denver with a functioning TV studio. It's usually used to shoot interviews for the Institute, and is a bare-bones operation. They have a single cameraman named Jason who works out of a cramped, foam-covered basement room. He probably just did it for a paycheck so he could live near the mountains and go skiing in the winter. That week, though, it was back-to-back-to-back, and Jason and I spent every waking moment together.

From that small room I introduced the world to Natalia Veselnitskaya, Russian lawyer and Kremlin operative. I explained the Magnitsky Act and why repealing it was Putin's top foreign policy objective. I also said that once Trump was the presumptive Republican nominee, Putin had seen an opening and dispatched Veselnitskaya to the United States to help achieve his objectives.

Every journalist wanted to know what I thought had actually happened at the Trump Tower meeting. Even though I wasn't there physically, I was a hundred percent sure that my name had come up and that Veselnitskaya was asking for the repeal of the Magnitsky Act in the event that Trump won. I had no idea what she'd offered in return. But what I could say for certain was that she was part of a sophisticated Russian intelligence operation, and that, with such a big ask, they wouldn't have sent her to Trump Tower empty-handed.

The only people who could answer these questions definitively were the people who'd been there. In the aftermath of the *New York Times* story, Veselnitskaya went to ground, but Donald Trump, Jr., wasn't so scarce.

Initially, Trump Jr. tried to play down the whole thing, claiming it was nothing more than a "short introductory meeting" mostly about "adoption." He didn't expand on this, but as we all know, "adoption" meant the Magnitsky Act and nothing else.

After unrelenting media pressure to say more, Trump Jr. released an email chain showing how the meeting had come about in an attempt to tamp down the controversy. It did just the opposite.

The emails were between Trump Jr. and a British music promoter named Rob Goldstone, who worked for the son of a powerful Russian oligarch close to the Katsyvs. Goldstone told Trump Jr. that the "Crown prosecutor of Russia"—an inaccurate description of General Prosecutor Yuri Chaika—had offered to send a "Russian government attorney" to "provide the Trump campaign with some official documents and information that would incriminate Hillary and her dealings with Russia and be very useful to your father."

Trump Jr. responded, "If it's what you say I love it."

We now knew what was being offered in return.

This was now a scandal, and it was explosive. Putting aside all of its major political implications, it was the perfect backdrop for the upcoming Senate Judiciary Committee hearing on July 16. Even though the hearing was nominally about FARA, because my testimony would focus on Veselnitskaya's activities in Washington, it was sure to be a major hit.

Then the hearing got an even bigger boost when the Senate Judiciary Committee invited Donald Trump, Jr., Glenn Simpson, and Paul Manafort to testify as well. Adding them to the mix would bring the entire world to the hearing room.

Before the Trump Tower meeting came to light, I'd planned to drop my middle daughter, Veronica, at sleepaway camp in New Jersey and then go to Washington. But now that Trump Jr., Simpson, and Manafort had been added to the witness list, the hearing had been postponed to July 26, meaning I'd have to make two trips back east.

On July 14, the day Veronica and I were due to fly to Newark, I woke early, still recovering from jet lag and a ragged sleep schedule from the previous week. Trying not to disturb Elena, I reached for my phone and quietly scrolled through my emails and the news. Nothing explosive had happened overnight.

But then, a little after 7:00 a.m., NBC posted a story with the headline, "Former Soviet Counterintelligence Officer at Meeting With Donald Trump Jr. and Russian Lawyer."

It turned out that Veselnitskaya had not been alone.

For some reason, the reporter, Ken Dilanian, was careful not to name this "former Soviet counterintelligence officer," * but it was obvious to me who this was. I linked the article and tweeted, "Curious NBC doesn't name the 'Former Intelligence Officer.' The only known associate of Veselnitskaya who fits that profile is Akhmetshin."

An hour later, the Associated Press confirmed that, indeed, Rinat Akhmetshin had also been at the Trump Tower meeting. My phone blew up yet again. As Veronica and I went over her camp packing list one last time, I was constantly interrupted by reporters wanting to know more about Akhmetshin.

We were scheduled to fly to Newark via Denver that afternoon. After we checked Veronica's bags and went through security, a journalist working on the story called and asked, "Have you ever met Akhmetshin? This guy's a real mystery. I can't find a picture of him anywhere."

"I don't know him," I answered. "But he did sit a couple of seats from me at a congressional hearing last year. A colleague of mine actually snapped some pictures of him."

"Amazing! If you could possibly send me those, it'd make my day."

I called Vadim. He sent the images directly to the journalist, who quickly published his story along with the pictures. The photo credit, in very small print underneath, read, "Hermitage Capital."

When Veronica and I landed in Denver 45 minutes later, I had mes-

---

* At the height of Veselnitskaya's disinformation campaign the year before, Dilanian had tried to write a story for NBC that appeared to have been fed to him by Veselnitskaya and Akhmetshin repeating the false Russian narrative about me and Sergei. Fortunately, after we supplied Dilanian's bosses at NBC with the facts of the case, they vetoed his story.

Rinat Akhmetshin, Washington, June 2016.
(© HERMITAGE)

sages from more than a dozen photo editors, all begging for permission to publish the same pictures. I agreed, and looked forward to the next day's news.

We checked into a hotel in New York that night, had Chinese food for dinner, and got in bed early. The next morning, we went down to the hotel café for breakfast. There was a small table with the morning papers at the entrance, and the first one I spotted was the tabloid *New York Post*. The top of the front page was taken up by Vadim's picture of Akhmetshin, along with the headline, "Trump Spooked—Former Russian 'Spy' Also Attended Meeting with Jr."

The same picture made it into more than a dozen publications around America that day.

I'd been booked to do an interview that morning with Fareed Zakaria at CNN, and when it was finished, Veronica and I hit the road. As we drove, we entered an area with poor phone reception, giving Veronica and me the chance to chat without any interruptions. This lasted right up to the camp's gates near the Delaware River, where we arrived just before the registration cutoff.

While I was on the road with Veronica, the US press corps had finally woken up to our FARA complaint. By the time I returned to Aspen the next day, multiple journalists were looking into Chris Cooper, Andrei Nekrasov, Dana Rohrabacher, and even his right-hand man, Paul Behrends. The stories that came out about Behrends were so damning that he was promptly fired from his staff position on the House Foreign Affairs Committee.

Then, on July 19, just one week before the hearing, President Trump put himself in the middle of everything in an extended on-the-record interview with the *New York Times*. In typical Trump fashion, it was all over the place, but toward the end of the interview, he said something very revealing.

During the gala dinner on the last night of the G20 Summit in Germany, Trump abandoned his assigned seat next to the wife of the Japanese prime minister to join his own wife, Melania, who happened to be seated next to Vladimir Putin. Trump, accompanied by no staff or translators, spoke to Putin for about an hour. When the *Times* asked what they discussed, Trump said, "Actually, it was very interesting, we talked about adoption."

Trump Jr. would make the exact same claim about his meeting with Veselnitskaya the next day. None of this was coincidental. At the end of July, it was reported that President Trump had dictated Trump Jr.'s initial statement to the press as the president flew home from Germany on Air Force One.

Most people barely noticed this admission, but it was extraordinary. President Trump and his son both knew that "adoption" was an innocuous-sounding code for the Magnitsky Act, and now both men were trying very hard to make the Trump Tower meeting sound a lot less sinister than it had been.

My upcoming testimony at the Senate Judiciary Committee would be my opportunity to tie everything together. It would show that the Magnitsky Act was not only the driving force behind Putin's official policy toward the West, but was also behind his audacious intervention in the US political process.

It truly would be the chance of a lifetime.

36

Senate Judiciary Committee

SUMMER 2017

I spent the week leading up to the Senate hearing writing and rewriting my testimony. It was the most important document I'd ever produced, and it had to be perfect.

Usually, witnesses read prepared remarks from a piece of paper, but I had no intention of doing that. When I testified, I would look the lawmakers in the eye and tell my story from the heart.

Delivering this opening statement could take no longer than seven minutes. After reading it out loud a number of times, I recited it from memory, pacing the office while I timed myself with my phone. I went back to the computer to cut sections and make tweaks, and recited it again. Repeat, repeat, repeat. For that whole week, I lived and breathed this testimony.

On the night before leaving Colorado, I submitted the text to Patrick Davis at the Senate Judiciary Committee. It was as good as it was going to get.

I arrived in Washington the next afternoon and checked back into the Willard. As soon as I was settled, I recited my speech one last time. Just under seven minutes. I ordered a light dinner from room service, called Elena, and got ready for bed. I climbed under the covers pretty early. In the morning, I would be testifying alongside Donald Trump, Jr., Glenn Simpson, and Paul Manafort. I needed to be rested and have my wits about me.

Before turning in for the night, I checked my email. A message had just come in from Patrick. "Bill, due to the volume of press interest, the hearing location has been moved to Hart 216, which is a much bigger hearing room."

This thing was going to be huge.

I had my suit and tie on the next morning by 7:00 a.m. I checked the news as I rode the elevator downstairs. Trump had just tweeted a major policy shift: he was banning transgender Americans from serving in the military. It was still early in the Trump presidency, and we were learning that whenever Trump was unhappy with the day's news cycle, he would tweet something outrageous, knowing the media would drop everything and scramble toward the new shiny object. I hoped the press wouldn't do that today.

I met Juleanna, who would accompany me to the hearing, in the hotel restaurant. If the situation got hairy, especially with Glenn Simpson, then she would be there to whisper some helpful advice.

After a quick breakfast we made our way to the lobby to meet my security team. Normally I don't have security in Washington, but I was about to air a whole lot of dirty Russian laundry on national television, and anything could happen. The two men assigned to me had recently returned from military contracting jobs in Iraq. They were like Hollywood caricatures of bodyguards: each about six-foot-four, well over 250 pounds, bald, goateed, and wearing ill-fitting suits and comfortable shoes that they could run—or kick ass—in. Since we were going to a government building, neither was armed, but their presence was still intimidating.

The four of us left the hotel, climbed into a blacked-out SUV, and made the short drive to the Hart Senate Office Building.

As we exited the elevator on the second floor, we found several hundred people snaking through the corridor toward Hart 216. I had no idea how big the hearing room was, but there was no way even half of these people would fit inside.

If Trump had been hoping to wag the dog with his transgender ban, it hadn't worked.

Since I was a witness, we didn't have to stand in line. We pressed to the front. As we passed through the double doors of the hearing room, a scrum of television cameras and newspaper photographers descended on us. Just then, Patrick Davis appeared, grabbed my arm, and led us from the commotion to an anteroom behind the dais. Patrick pointed to a pair of empty seats in the corner and excused himself to speak with Senator Grassley.

The room bustled with staff members making last-minute calls and sending emails. There was a lot of coming and going. Something unexpected seemed to be happening.

Patrick returned a few minutes later. "Trump Jr., Manafort, and Simpson aren't showing up," he said. "Trump Jr. and Simpson have negotiated closed-door testimonies, and it looks like we're going to have to subpoena Manafort. You'll be on your own after the panel of DOJ guys."

This came as somewhat of a relief for me. Trump Jr. and Manafort had attracted the world's attention to this hearing, but if they'd actually shown up, they would have sucked all the oxygen out of the room. Now the senators could focus on my story without any sensational distractions. (I also didn't have to worry about Glenn Simpson spouting more Russian disinformation.)

A few minutes before 10:00 a.m., we re-entered the hearing room. All I saw were flashes and all I heard was the whirring *rat-a-tat-tat* of camera shutters opening and closing. I became suddenly hyper-self-conscious. I didn't want to make any strange expressions that would be captured for posterity.

Every seat in the room was taken. Reporters were jammed shoulder to shoulder around the press table, their laptops open and ready. A dozen pool photographers sat on the floor between the witness table and the dais where the senators were seated.

The DOJ officials were arrayed at the witness table. My security guards were told to stand along the wall while Juleanna and I were shown to a pair of reserved seats in the second row. Cameras still clicked everywhere. Out of habit, I reached for my phone, but decided not to check it. I didn't want any messages to be picked up by a random photographer.

Senator Grassley pounded his gavel. The hearing began. The senator explained that Trump Jr., Simpson, and Manafort wouldn't be appearing that day. The collective disappointment was palpable.

After 20 minutes of formalities, the DOJ officials were sworn in. Each man read his statement, barely glancing up from the pages in front of him. None of them wanted to discuss their failures in enforcing

Senate Judiciary Committee hearing, July 26, 2017.

(© C-SPAN)

FARA, so they filled their time with jargon and tedious shoptalk, knowing that no one would remember a single thing they said. It seemed to
work. As they spoke, the senators busied themselves by looking at their
phones and whispering to aides.

Fifteen minutes later, the senators' questions began. The officials'
answers were no more inspired than their prepared statements. Everyone had shown up for fireworks, but this panel was turning out to be a
complete dud.

This monotony went from being merely boring to something more
damaging when Senator Grassley interrupted the hearing to announce
that the Democrats had just invoked something called the "two hour
rule." Juleanna leaned over and quietly explained this was a procedure that would limit the hearing to exactly two hours and not a minute longer.

"Why would they do that?" I whispered.

She shrugged. "It probably has nothing to do with you. Most likely
it's some kind of unrelated political retaliation."

Whatever the reason, every minute these DOJ guys droned on was now one less minute for me to speak.

As the hearing progressed, it increasingly appeared as though I wasn't going to be able to testify at all.

I looked to Juleanna. "Could this really be happening?"

"Don't worry. Grassley will find a way."

She was right. A few minutes later, Senator Grassley announced they would reconvene the hearing at 9:00 a.m. the following morning. My testimony would be the only item on the agenda.

It normally took months for me to schedule 10 minutes with a single senator. But now I was going to get a full two hours with a group of the most important lawmakers in the United States.

*   *   *

I woke very early the next morning, ready to go.

The previous evening, I'd been invited to do an interview on CNN, and I arrived at their studio behind Union Station at 6:30 a.m. Ahead of me on the show was Anthony Scaramucci, President Trump's newest communications director, who, overnight, had gone on a tirade in an interview with the *New Yorker*. He'd called Trump's then chief of staff, Reince Priebus, a "fucking paranoid schizophrenic," and when the reporter suggested Anthony was being media-hungry, he replied, "I'm not Steve Bannon, I'm not trying to suck my own cock."

I'd known Anthony Scaramucci, a slick and voluble New Yorker, for a long time. I liked him too. After *Red Notice* was published, whenever I bumped into him, he'd cup his hands in front of his crotch like he was holding something heavy and say, "Dude, you got some brass fucking balls on you taking on Putin!" Profanity was part of his charm, but even under Trump, his comments to the *New Yorker* had probably gone too far.

That morning, as I sat in CNN's greenroom, Anthony called in to the show. He was trying to defend himself, but the host, Chris Cuomo, wasn't having any of it. The interview was heated and went on for nearly 30 minutes. These morning shows are scheduled to the second, and this type of overrun practically never happens.

When Anthony was finally done, I got ready to go on set. I still had plenty of time before the hearing. But during the commercial break, a flustered producer rushed into the greenroom and said, "I'm so sorry, Mr. Browder, but we don't have any more time for you. The previous guest went on for too long."

"I'm getting bumped by the Mooch?" I asked, laughing.

She nodded. "I really apologize."

With two hours to kill before the hearing, my bodyguards and I went to a diner near the Capitol, where I treated them to breakfast. Over scrambled eggs and toast, they told me war stories about IEDs and fighting insurgents in Iraq. It was a good distraction.

After breakfast, we walked over to the Hart Senate Office Building. I knew that without Trump Jr. or Manafort the crowd would thin, but I wasn't prepared for what I found. When we exited the elevator, the hall was completely empty. There was no line, no phalanx of reporters, no extra staff. In the hearing room, there was a single pool photographer sitting cross-legged on the floor in front of the witness table, and the only TV cameras were from C-SPAN, whose mission is to film every committee proceeding no matter how mundane. The only reporter at the press table was a man I'd never seen. He wore a red-and-blue Hawaiian shirt under a navy sport jacket.

I was disappointed, but what could I do? I would just focus on the senators and act as if the room were full.

I took the only chair at the witness table, my two bodyguards flanking me in the front row.

At just before 9:00 a.m., Senator Grassley descended from the dais to say hello and thank me for agreeing to stay an extra day. I gestured at the nearly empty room. "Since no one else is speaking, do I need to stick to seven minutes?" I asked.

Senator Grassley put a hand on my shoulder and in an avuncular tone said, "Nope, you take all the time you need, Bill."

I was sworn in. I had no papers, no notepad, no pen, and no one was there to help me (Juleanna was on a plane to California for a prior obligation). But I wasn't nervous. Without the time constraint, I took 11 minutes and told the story for all it was worth.

Senate Judiciary Committee hearing, July 27, 2017.
(© DREW ANGERER/GETTY IMAGES NEWS/GETTY IMAGES)

Most Senate hearings are about showmanship. Senators make speeches and then ask questions that further their partisan agenda, and there was a little of that here. The Republicans were keen to discredit Glenn Simpson and have me say that the Trump dossier was a complete fiction. And the Democrats wanted me to state that the Trump Tower meeting was evidence of a conspiracy between the Russians and the Trump campaign.

I did neither. I stayed laser-focused on playing it straight down the middle. I couldn't afford for this hearing to become partisan. I needed Republicans and Democrats to continue to work together to fight off Putin as he tried to derail the Magnitsky Act.

Fortunately, as the hearing progressed, the partisanship fell away. There was genuine desire among all the senators to understand how Russia worked and why Putin behaved the way he did.

For an hour and 45 minutes, I unpacked Putin's motivations. I drew a line from the $230 million fraud to Putin's proxy, the cellist Sergei Roldugin. I explained that this wasn't a one-off, but one of thousands of crimes Putin had benefitted from, allowing him to accumulate an estimated $200 billion fortune. I pointed out that nearly all of this wealth was held at financial institutions in the West and at risk of being frozen under the Magnitsky Act. For these reasons, the law was an existential threat to him and his senior officials.

Four of the nine senators were former prosecutors, and they brought all of their prosecutorial skills to bear with their questions. By the time I was done answering, an epiphany had emerged among the lawmakers in the room. For the first time, it all made sense: one of the main reasons Putin had interfered in the US election was because of the Magnitsky Act.

After the hearing finished, I stood in front of the witness table chatting with Patrick Davis. As we spoke, a senior staffer for California Sen. Dianne Feinstein, the ranking member on the Senate Judiciary Committee, approached and asked if I could join Senator Feinstein in the anteroom for a word. I followed the staffer and met Senator Feinstein. She thanked me for staying an extra day and said that this was one of the most powerful testimonies she'd heard in her 25 years as a US senator.

It turned out that even though the hearing room was empty, tens of thousands of people had been watching, and I got a lot out of it: a mountain of new Twitter followers, a viral C-SPAN video (such things do exist), a blizzard of press coverage, *Red Notice* back on the *New York Times* bestseller list, and, crucially, ironclad support for the Magnitsky Act.

During the Q&A, Senator Cornyn, a Texas Republican, and Senator Feinstein had each stated flatly that there was no way the Magnitsky Act would ever be repealed. Senator Whitehouse, a Rhode Island Democrat, had gone even further by suggesting an amendment to the law making it impossible for any president to remove people from the Magnitsky List without the express consent of Congress (an amendment that hasn't been made at the time of writing, but one I would fully support).

But more important than all of this was the exposure. If one-tenth of 1 percent of Americans had heard of Sergei and the Magnitsky Act before the Senate Judiciary Committee hearing, by the time all the media died down, that number had grown exponentially. A good part of the American public—and surely, Vladimir Putin himself—had gotten the message.

The Magnitsky Act was here to stay.

37

Global Entry

FALL 2017

The Russians reacted to my testimony in typical fashion. A few days after the hearing, Deputy General Prosecutor Viktor Grin, the same sanctioned official who'd met with Rep. Dana Rohrabacher in Moscow in the spring of 2016, announced they were again putting me on trial in absentia. The charges were fraud, false bankruptcy, and, that good old standby the Putin regime regularly uses against its enemies, tax evasion. My codefendant this time was my colleague Ivan. Neither of us would dignify this trial by even sending lawyers to represent us, but the Russians were still intent on making their point.

If these actions were meant to somehow intimidate me, they didn't. I continued my work on the Magnitsky campaign, and a few months later, on October 4, the Canadian House of Commons voted 277–0 to pass their own version of the Magnitsky Act. It passed the Canadian Senate unanimously on October 17, and was signed into law the next day.

The Canadian Magnitsky Act was a major milestone. It wasn't so much that Russians bought villas in Toronto or kept their money in Montréal banks, but rather that other countries would follow Canada's lead. Many nations are either too proud or too anti-American to follow the United States, but there's no such thing as being anti-Canadian. I knew this move would open the floodgates, and that a cascade of other countries would soon adopt Magnitsky Acts of their own.

Apparently, Putin knew this too.

On the afternoon of October 19, as I was planning a celebratory trip to Ottawa for me and the Magnitsky family, I received an automated email from US Customs and Border Patrol (CBP). It read, "There's been a recent change to the status of your application. Please log on to the Trusted Traveler website for more information."

This was odd. I wasn't flying to Canada through the United States, and I hadn't applied for anything from CBP. I thought it was spam or some kind of phishing attempt. Although the email address, no-reply@cbp.dhs.gov, appeared legitimate, that meant nothing. Several years earlier, on April Fool's Day, I'd received an email from events@whitehouse.gov inviting me to a weekend retreat with President Obama. I was initially excited and flattered, until I spotted several typos and realized it was a prank. When I confronted my then 15-year-old son, David, he smiled mischievously and explained that it was very easy to make an email look like it had come from the White House, or anywhere else for that matter.

I ignored this CBP email for about half an hour, but it ate at me. I had to see what it was all about.

I never click links in unsolicited emails, so I typed in the address. A real US government website popped up. After going through their verification process, I received a surprising message: "Your Global Entry Status has been revoked." Global Entry is a US government program that allows members to skip immigration lines at most US airports.

Like anyone else, I'd prefer not to stand in line, but that wasn't the key issue. Maybe something more sinister was going on. It seemed unlikely, but there was so much focus on Trump, Putin, and a possible conspiracy between them that I couldn't help but wonder if they had made some dirty backroom deal involving me.

But how could I find out? I couldn't just call up the US embassy in London and ask if I was on some new Trump-Putin no-fly list. Most likely they wouldn't know, and if they did, they wouldn't tell me.

The first logical step was to see if my US visa had been revoked as well, or if this was just a problem with Global Entry. British and European citizens travel to the United States on something called an ESTA. It's kind of like a "visa-lite." You apply for it online, pay $12, and unless you're a terrorist or some other type of bad guy, it's approved straightaway and lasts two years. I logged onto the ESTA website to check my visa status, but it didn't tell me anything.

The easiest way to see if it still worked would be to buy a refundable ticket and check in online. If the airline issued me a boarding pass, my ESTA was intact. But when I tried this, I got a canned message from United Airlines telling me they couldn't issue me a boarding pass and that I had to resolve the problem in person at the airport.

I took the Tube to Paddington Station and boarded the Heathrow Express. The whole trip took less than an hour. I went to the nearest check-in desk and waited in a short line. When it was my turn, I greeted the gate agent and handed over my passport. He typed my information into his computer. Nothing. He retyped the information. Still nothing. I asked if something was wrong. He didn't know. He then brought over a supervisor. She also was rebuffed by the computer.

She then called someone who I assumed was a CBP official stationed at Heathrow. The supervisor told me to come to her station and stand to the side. She'd let me know as soon as my problem was resolved.

A little while later, she glanced in my direction. The sour expression on her face told me everything. "I'm sorry, Mr. Browder," she said, "but your ESTA is no longer valid."

"Why? What happened?"

"They wouldn't tell me."

"What should I do?"

"I suppose you should contact the American embassy. I'm sorry again. But there's nothing we can do for you here."

I stepped away from the desk. I knew the Russians were somehow behind this. But how were they getting the United States to do their bidding? If this really was a conspiracy between Trump and Putin, I was in big trouble.

On the train back to London, I grasped for any reasonable explanation that didn't involve Trump and Putin. The only thing that kept coming back to me was that maybe, just maybe, this had something to do with Interpol, and not some unfathomable conspiracy.

Back at the office, I logged onto Interpol's website to see if I was on their Wanted List. I wasn't. This didn't give me much comfort, though.

Interpol's public Wanted List only covers a small fraction of their database. Most people who are in it have no idea until they're stopped at a border and find themselves being led away in handcuffs.

I could have solved this mystery in a second if I could only have peeked at Interpol's full list, but for a civilian, that was impossible. Only law enforcement had access to it.

However, because of the many money laundering investigations we'd initiated, I knew a lot of police officials and prosecutors. I spoke to several, but they each told me some version of "Bill, you know I can't tell you that." A few were quite disappointed that I even asked.

I continued working through my list of contacts. I hoped I wasn't burning too many bridges, but I really needed to know. Finally, I got someone I'd only met once. I expected him to rebuff me like the rest, but instead he said cheerily, "Sure, let me check," as if it was nothing. I heard keystrokes in the background. After half a minute, he said, "Yes. There appears to be something on the system."

"From where?" I already knew the answer.

"Russia."

"When was it issued?" I asked.

"Last Tuesday."

That was October 17, the same day the Canadian Senate passed the Magnitsky Act. This latest Interpol warrant was a direct retaliation.

With this new information, I called Patrick Davis at Senator Grassley's office to see if he could find out if my ESTA issue was somehow linked to this Interpol notice. He contacted DHS and reported back that, indeed, the ESTA system syncs with Interpol's. Anyone who is wanted by Interpol automatically loses their ESTA.

A human being hadn't been behind me losing my ESTA. No one in the United States had intentionally targeted me. I felt foolish for thinking it was a conspiracy at all. Of course, the US president, no matter who that was, wouldn't be coordinating with Putin.

Nevertheless, the ordeal was deeply ironic. Since Sergei's murder, one of my main purposes in life has been to get corrupt Russian officials banned from traveling to countries like the United States—but instead here was Putin effectively using Interpol to ban me from traveling to America.

Fortunately, this travel ban would be brief. The news went public on Sunday evening on my friend Jay Nordlinger's blog at the *National Review*, under the title, "Why Is Bill Browder Banned from America?" The response was loud and swift. People everywhere had the same knee-jerk reaction that I'd had, and went to the same dark place. Did we now live in a world where Putin's enemies could be barred from entering the United States because Trump was president?

The next morning, Senators McCain and Cardin issued a joint press release calling for my visa to be reinstated. "Mr. Browder's work has helped to remove corrupt actors from our financial system. . . . It would be unfortunate if the U.S. decided to bar him based on a decision by those same Russian officials who have been targeted by [the Magnitsky Act]."

Within two hours, the Department of Homeland Security had reinstated my ESTA.

Two days later, Interpol deleted the arrest warrant from their system, and ordered all 192 member states to remove any mention of me from their national databases.

This defeat was humiliating for Putin, but one thing he could control was his own country's court system. On December 29, 2017, the Tverskoy District Court in Moscow found Ivan and me guilty of our latest "crimes." Ivan was sentenced to eight years, and I was given another nine, both in absentia.

I now faced 18 years in a Russian prison camp if I were ever extradited to Moscow.

38

Danske Bank

WINTER–SUMMER 2018

In mid-February, I took my family on a Swiss ski vacation to a resort called Crans Montana, two hours from Geneva. We had a wonderful week together, but at the end, we had to split up. Elena and the kids needed to be home on Sunday evening in order to return to school—and I had business in Geneva.

On Sunday afternoon, I took my family to the airport, gave everybody a hug, and told them I'd see them the following evening.

The next day, I gave a speech about the Magnitsky Act at the Geneva Human Rights Summit, which took place on the premises of the United Nations.

The Magnitsky justice campaign was riding high. Only a month after the passage of the Canadian Magnitsky Act, on the eighth anniversary of Sergei's murder, the Lithuanian Parliament had passed their own Magnitsky Act. Then, in early February 2018, the Latvians did the same. I was confident that, very soon, more countries would be adopting Magnitsky Acts of their own.

After speaking, I stuck around for a while to meet with various politicians and human rights activists, and then went to the airport at around 5:00 p.m. for an evening flight to London.

After checking in, I bought some Swiss chocolates for my family and proceeded to border control. My latest issue with Interpol had been fully resolved, so I wasn't anticipating any trouble.

But when I handed over my passport, the officer put it into his machine, leaned over his screen, and squinted. He didn't hand my passport back, but instead picked up his phone. Since he was behind a partition, I couldn't hear what he was saying.

I stood there awkwardly. People behind me began shuffling to the other line. Then he turned on his microphone and started asking me questions in English.

"How long have you been in Switzerland?"

"Seven days," I answered.

"What were you doing here?"

"I went skiing with my family and then had business at the UN."

He looked over my shoulder. "Where is your family?"

"They went home yesterday."

"Home is the UK?"

"Yes."

He slid me a piece of blank paper and a pen. "Please write your home address in the United Kingdom."

"Why do you need that?"

"I ask the questions, Mr. Browder."

I'd been in Switzerland dozens of times and had never been asked a single question when leaving the country. I didn't like where this was headed. Where I lived in the UK was no business of the Swiss.

Nevertheless, this man was compelling me to answer. I scribbled down my home address and gave him the paper.

"What future travel plans do you have?"

This was completely off-base. I gave him a vague answer about having no immediate plans, which was true, because I had no bookings, but not entirely true, since I did have several commitments around Europe in the coming weeks.

He switched off his microphone and picked up the phone. Once again, I couldn't hear anything. He was an officer of the law standing behind a sheet of glass moving his mouth, talking about me.

I texted Elena. "I think there's trouble. They're not letting me through the border in Geneva."

"Interpol?"

"I don't know."

"Keep me posted."

Then I waited.

I stood there watching other travelers pass through border control as if it were nothing. Hand over a passport, scan it, move along.

Ten minutes later, Elena texted. "Anything?"

"No. Still here."

Finally, after 20 minutes, the officer handed back my passport with no explanation. He didn't even say, "Have a good flight."

I called Elena to tell her they'd let me through, but until I was in the air, I didn't feel safe. I had no idea why this had happened, but I was positive it had something to do with the Russians.*

From that moment, I was a little spooked to travel around Europe.

And this fear was not unfounded. As you know, a little more than three months later, on the morning of May 30, 2018, I was arrested in Madrid at the Gran Hotel Inglés on a Russian Interpol warrant.

I've never been able to figure out exactly why this happened, but in the immediate aftermath, Interpol claimed that the Spanish were acting on an old Russian warrant (the one issued right after the Canadian Magnitsky Act had passed), and that Spain had ignored Interpol's directive to delete my name from their system.

The Spanish refuted this, claiming they'd acted on a brand-new warrant. Since my Madrid arrest came on the heels of Geneva, I was inclined to believe the Spanish, not Interpol. This was bolstered by a strange tweet from @Interpol_HQ, issued shortly after my release, that read, "There is not, and never has been, a Red Notice for Bill Browder. Mr. Browder is not wanted via INTERPOL channels." They were being totally disingenuous. By then, multiple notices had been circulated by Russia through Interpol channels.

The Russians reeled from this Madrid humiliation. Shortly after the

---

* And I wasn't wrong. We eventually learned that, right around this time, the most senior Swiss federal police officer investigating money laundering connected to the Magnitsky case, a man named Vinzenz Schnell, was caught taking a secret, unauthorized trip to Moscow to meet with none other than Natalia Veselnitskaya. It was later discovered that while he was actively trying to sabotage the Swiss Magnitsky investigation, Schnell went on a lavish hunting trip in Russia that was paid for by a Russian oligarch. Schnell was eventually fired and convicted in a Swiss court.

Spanish released me, General Prosecutor Yuri Chaika made a public statement: "We will redouble our efforts to get Bill Browder. . . . He should not sleep peacefully at night."

While this was alarming, I wasn't going to let Chaika's threats alter my plans. A week after my Madrid arrest, Vadim and I traveled to Copenhagen, Denmark, to meet with a pair of investigative journalists, Eva Jung and Michael Lund, at one of Denmark's most prominent newspapers, *Berlingske*.

Eva and Michael had used a massive data leak called the Russian Laundromat to discover that Danske Bank, Denmark's largest bank, had been involved in serious money laundering for at least a decade (like other leaks in this story, this one had also been obtained by the OCCRP, the NGO that had originally provided us with the Moldovan file). Over the previous year, Eva and Michael had written more than 70 articles on Danske Bank. These covered a range of suspicious payments across multiple schemes involving disparate characters like Azerbaijan's most senior leaders, corrupt Western European politicians, a Russian arms dealer, sanctioned Iranian companies, and even a cousin of Putin's, among others.

Their reporting forced Danske Bank to act. In the fall of 2017, the bank's CEO, Thomas Borgen, announced a top-to-bottom audit, to be conducted by external lawyers and accountants. The findings of this audit had still not been made public by the time we were going to meet with Eva and Michael.

We wanted to see them because we'd made some dramatic discoveries of our own regarding Danske Bank. Using data from the French investigation, the Moldovan file, and other sources, Vadim had identified 43,112 transactions showing that $200 million connected to the $230 million had been laundered through 20 shell companies with accounts at Danske Bank's lone Estonian branch, in Tallinn.

We'd had no luck engaging with Danish law enforcement and hoped that connecting with these reporters might spur the authorities.

On June 5, Vadim and I flew to Copenhagen to meet with Eva and Michael at *Berlingske*'s bustling head office, a modern building in the City Centre. (*Berlingske* was one of Scandinavia's oldest newspapers, first published on January 3, 1749; it also happened to be one of the longest continually published papers anywhere.)

Eva, a blond woman in her mid-30s, greeted us in the lobby. She led us upstairs, and we settled into a spartan conference room with IKEA-like furniture. She introduced us to Michael—tall, brown hair, toothy smile—who pulled out a chair for Eva.

Vadim took it from there. He unfolded a massive piece of paper and spread it across the table. It depicted a complicated web of shell companies showing how the money had moved from the Russian Treasury, through a series of other countries, and then into and out of Danske Bank Estonia. Vadim expertly traced his finger over the web, going over every detail with them for 45 minutes, and answering all their questions.

As he folded up the chart at the end of our meeting, Eva asked, "Would you be willing to share your information with us?"

"We'd like to cross-reference it with our material," Michael added.

"Yes, we'd be happy for you to have a crack at it," I said.

When we returned to London, Vadim gathered all 43,112 wire transfer records at the 20 companies—firms with names like Diamonds Forever International, Everfront Sales, and Castlefront (some very inspired names for money laundering shell companies)—put them in an encrypted file, and sent them off to *Berlingske*.

We didn't know when or if we would hear from them, but five days later, Michael messaged Vadim to inform him that their analysis confirmed the $200 million we'd identified, but that they'd also found an *additional $8.3 billion* of suspicious money flowing from Russia and other former Soviet states through these 20 companies between 2007 and 2015. This was far, far more than any of us had expected. By itself it represented Europe's third largest money laundering scandal *in history*.

The *Berlingske* article came out on July 3, 2018. It was a bombshell in Denmark, but where it had its most impact was internationally. Up to that point, interest in the Danske Bank scandal had been mostly limited to Scandinavia. But now interest was truly global.

These developments put even greater pressure on Danske Bank

in its upcoming audit. This was no longer just a corporate matter, it was now a *national* matter, with all sorts of far-reaching implications. Denmark has a sterling reputation for honesty—it consistently ranks second (to New Zealand) on Transparency International's annual Corruption Perceptions Index. If the country were to retain that reputation, then Danske Bank would have to come clean.

It wasn't just the Danes who were worried, though. Eva and Michael's reporting had revealed the architecture of one of the main pipes that facilitated the flow of dirty money out of Russia. This revelation would, in time, expose many more crimes committed by the Putin regime, I was sure.

There would be blowback. I just didn't know how soon it would come, or in what form.

39

An "Incredible Offer"

SUMMER 2018

Three days after the *Berlingske* article, I received an email in broken English. "I write to warn you about the assassination plot against you by the Russian security services in the foreseen future to happen. I did receive the fresh info on directly identifying you as the target for hit."

It was difficult to assess this message's credibility, but the person who'd written it—a former Russian intelligence officer living in the UK—had a reputation for making dramatic statements about assassination plots and other Russian schemes. Nevertheless, he was sober in his assessment. "It is my personal professional advice," he wrote, "which you of course are free to ignore and disregard—please, be cautious and increase your security measures."

For the most part, I didn't take this seriously. I receive a lot of these messages, and this one in particular didn't seem very credible. However, recent events had put me on edge. On March 4, 2018, the Kremlin had sent two assassins to Salisbury, England, to kill Sergei Skripal, another former Russian intelligence officer (who happened to be a double agent working for the British). The assassins used a banned Russian military-grade nerve agent called Novichok, and while they failed to kill Skripal, they still poisoned him—along with his grown daughter, Yulia, who also survived. Tragically, a Salisbury police officer and two local residents were accidentally exposed to this batch of Novichok. One of them, Dawn Sturgess, later died. She was only 44 years old.

This latest Kremlin-directed assassination attempt on British soil showed, again, just how brazen and unafraid Putin was when it came to operating in the West.

Mainly because of Skripal, I wasn't just going to laugh off this latest threat. I passed the message to SO15, London's Counter Terrorism Command, who began their own probe and risk assessment. They hadn't been particularly helpful in the past, but Skripal's poisoning and its aftermath had focused everyone's mind on the stark reality of these Russian threats. I was confident SO15 would take this one seriously.

The day after I received this message, Elena, the kids, and I returned to Aspen for our scheduled summer vacation.

Even if there had been any truth to this latest threat, world events were working in my favor. We arrived in America one week before the first summit between Trump and Putin, which would take place in Helsinki, Finland, on July 16. It was inconceivable that the Russians would attempt a high-profile political assassination on US soil in the week leading up to a major meeting between these two heads of state.

The summit was all anyone could talk about. And even though it sounded a little crazy, I couldn't help but think that I would be a topic of conversation between Trump and Putin.

I knew this sounded self-important, but as I lay in bed on the night we arrived in Colorado, I thought, *Maybe it isn't.* Trump and Putin had discussed the Magnitsky Act at their impromptu meeting at the G20 in Hamburg a year earlier, and documents recently seized from Paul Manafort by the FBI confirmed that I had been a principal subject of the infamous Trump Tower meeting. (The first thing Manafort had written was "Bill Browder." Other items included "Offshore—Cyprus" and "Browder hired Joanna Glover"—an obvious misnaming of Juleanna. "Russian adoption by American families" was the last thing Manafort wrote.)

With the lights out and my mind swirling, I picked up my phone and drafted a tweet. "I wonder if Putin is going to bring me up in Helsinki?"

My thumb lingered over the tweet button. Twitter had become one of the main platforms for chronicling my conflict with the Russians. But I didn't want to be too emotional in the moment. Elena was fast asleep next to me, but she had scolded me many times for tweeting first and asking questions later. I decided to sleep on it.

When I woke a little before 7:00 a.m., I deleted the tweet. Of course they weren't going to talk about me. They had bigger fish to fry—nuclear disarmament, the war in Syria, counterterrorism. Besides, if I had tweeted that, I would've been hung out to dry by trolls.

It was a good thing I deleted it too. Later that morning, Robert Mueller, the special counsel who had been in charge of investigating Russian involvement in the 2016 presidential election, as well as possible Russian links to the Trump campaign, made an unexpected announcement. His office was indicting 12 Russian GRU officers (the GRU is Russia's military intelligence wing), accusing them of hacking the Democratic National Committee and interfering in the election to help Trump win.

The indictment was devastating. Mueller had gained access to secret emails between Russian intelligence officers. He'd also found Bitcoin payments, which are supposed to be untraceable by their nature, that the Russians had used to fund their operations in the United States. It looked like the US government would secure iron-clad convictions—*if* these 12 Russian officers could ever be brought before a US court.

Whatever had been on Trump's and Putin's agenda before, the Mueller indictment would now be front and center, no matter how awkward it would be for both sides.

As much as I looked forward to watching the fireworks in Helsinki, I was now sure that the summit would have nothing to do with me, and in any case I had something much more important to do: getting started on this book. I'd been putting it off for months, especially with all that had happened that spring—my detention in Geneva, the Madrid arrest, Danske Bank, et cetera—but I wasn't going to put it off any longer.

At 8:00 a.m. on Monday, July 16, as Trump and Putin were sequestered away for their private meeting, I set up my laptop at the end of the dining room table, a view of the mountains to the west over my shoulder, and got to work.

Usually my kids run riot all over the house, but that day I put the dining room off-limits. I also put restraints on myself, laying my phone facedown and muting it, vowing not to turn it over to check Twitter or email.

After two hours of laborious work and less than a page to show for it—writing was harder than I'd remembered—my willpower crumbled. I turned over my phone. The screen was flush with notifications. I had dozens of messages—texts, emails, DMs, voicemails, everything.

I opened the first email. "Bill, are you watching Helsinki??"

I scrolled through my inbox. "That was the scariest, most fucked-up thing I have ever seen," one friend said. Another wrote, "If you need a place to hide, we will put you in our mountain house!"

What the hell was going on? I found the earliest email about Helsinki, from the correspondent Ali Velshi at MSNBC. The subject was to the point: "Putin talking about you now."

Fuck.

I put down my phone and went online. It didn't take long to find the post-summit press conference. The two leaders were onstage at twin lecterns, and their body language couldn't have been more different. Putin looked like he owned the place, while Trump glowered and slumped his shoulders, looking anything but presidential.

President Trump and President Putin, Helsinki, July 2018.
(© CHRIS MCGRATH/GETTY IMAGES NEWS/GETTY IMAGES)

I watched the whole thing. The shocking moment came when a Reuters reporter asked: "President Putin, will you consider extraditing the twelve Russian officials that were indicted last week by a US grand jury?"

Putin smiled and nodded confidently, looking like he'd spent the whole weekend preparing for this moment. "We can meet you halfway. . . . We can actually permit representatives of the United States, including this very commission headed by Mr. Mueller. We can let them into the country. They can be present at questioning. In this case there's another condition. This kind of effort should be a mutual one. We would expect that the Americans would reciprocate. . . . For instance, we can bring up Mr. Browder in this particular case."

I had to watch it several times to make sure that I'd heard it correctly. Somehow, Putin, standing next to the President of the United States, was suggesting swapping 12 Russian GRU officers—for me!

I waited for Trump's reaction. Surely, he would reject this out of hand.

But he didn't. "I think that's an incredible offer," he said, suggesting he *was* ready to trade me.

Rationally, I understood the gravity of the situation, but emotionally I was too shaken to take it in. It was like being in a serious car accident. I knew I'd just been injured, but I had no idea how badly.

As I tried to assess the damage, the main thing I kept coming back to was whether it was safe for me to stay in America. My original, nebulous concern that some Russian assassin might try to kill me had now been overtaken by the very real fear that the President of the United States would hand me over to the Russians.

I ran to the backyard to find Elena, who was watching our children bounce on the trampoline. I tapped her on the shoulder and motioned for her to come inside. Elena told our eldest daughter, Jessica, that she was in charge. Once we were out of earshot of the kids, I exclaimed, "Putin just asked Trump to hand me over—and Trump said, 'Yes!'"

She placed her hand on my arm to calm me, and guided me back to the dining room so we could watch the press conference together. I tapped my foot, waiting for her assessment. When it was over, I said, "I think I should leave the country. Right now."

Elena thoughtfully said, "I don't think so. Trump might be able to do this, but if he does, it won't happen overnight. At this moment, the whole world wants to know, 'Who's Bill Browder?' I think you should tell them."

She was right. Three-quarters of the messages on my phone were from news organizations asking me to come on-air. The media interest was even more intense than after the Trump Tower revelations. I started returning calls, and within an hour I was booked on more than a dozen news shows.

I threw on a jacket and tie and headed back to the Aspen Institute's small television studio. I knew that I would be stuck in that black foam-padded room in the basement of the Doerr-Hosier Center all day and late into the night.

On the drive over, my phone rang again. It was a friend from Washington with high-level connections.

I answered. "Hello?"

The man launched right into it: "I don't know where you are, Bill, but you need to stay the hell away from America. I just got off the phone with someone at Justice. He said the wheels are coming off and no one knows what the fuck is going on over there. He thinks Trump *will* hand you over."

I didn't tell him I was already in America, but thanked him nonetheless.

I reached the Institute and entered the Doerr-Hosier Center. I greeted the cameraman, Jason, whom I'd gotten to know over the previous summer, following the Trump Tower story.

As he wired me up with a microphone, I noticed that the image on the screen behind me was a video of Aspen Mountain, the gondola slowly moving toward the summit. This was the image every TV viewer would see, giving away my location. I asked Jason if he could change it, and he found a picture of a generic nighttime newsroom that could have been anywhere in the world.

CNN was up first. I asked Jason to triple-check with their producer that they would remove any location information. He confirmed they would and that all it would say, on this segment and every one that followed, was "Bill Browder."

I sat on that stool off and on for the rest of the day, appearing on CNN, Fox, MSNBC, BBC, Al-Jazeera, CBC, France-24, the Australian Broadcasting Corporation, Sky News, Deutsche Welle, and on and on.

I explained that Putin wanted me so badly because the Magnitsky Act put his power and fortune at risk. I also explained that, if he got me, he would have me thrown in a Russian prison, where I would be tortured and eventually killed, just like Sergei. These were the things I knew for certain. What I didn't know was if Trump would follow through on this "incredible offer," and, if he attempted to, whether America's legal institutions were strong enough to stand up to him.

All I could do was put on a brave face and say, "America has a rule of law, and I don't think he'll be able to hand me over." But it sure didn't feel that way.

In that moment, I—and everyone else—was grappling with the realization that everything had suddenly changed and anything was possible. In the age of Trump, it was getting harder and harder to know what to believe.

40

98–0

SUMMER 2018

I was utterly exhausted when I returned to the house late that night. Not only had I spent the previous 12 hours repeating my story to millions of viewers around the world, but I'd also had to keep my composure and not let on how terrified I was that President Trump might be collaborating with Putin to send me back to Russia.

Elena had left out a plate of leftovers for me on the kitchen counter. I pulled off the Saran Wrap, sat on a stool, and ate every bite. I then went to bed and fell into a deep sleep.

The next morning at 6:30 a.m., Elena jolted me awake, waving a piece of paper in my face. "You've got to see this, honey!"

She'd gotten up before sunrise to read the Russian news. That morning, the Russian General Prosecutor's Office had issued a list of 11 additional people that the Russians wanted the US to hand over in exchange for the 12 GRU officers. Russians love symmetry in these matters. The United States wanted 12, which meant Russia wanted 12.

I propped myself up and took the paper. The Russians wanted Mike McFaul, the former US ambassador to Russia; my friend Kyle Parker, the man who wrote the Magnitsky Act; Special Agent Todd Hyman from Homeland Security, who'd investigated the Prevezon case; Special Agents Svetlana Angert and Aleksander Schwartzman, who were responsible for the Gorokhovs' protection in New York;* Jonathan Winer, the Washington lawyer and former State Department official who had come up with the original idea for the Magnitsky Act; and David Kramer, another ex–State Department official and the former head of the human rights NGO Freedom House, who'd advocated for the Magnitsky Act alongside Boris Nemtsov and me. There were four additional names on the list, but the main common denominators were either involvement in the Magnitsky Act or participation in the Prevezon case.

What were the Russians accusing us of? The day before, Putin alleged that my "business associates" and I had "earned over $1.5 billion in Russia," "never paid any taxes," and then, to get Trump's attention, gave "$400 million as a contribution to the campaign of Hillary Clinton."† Putin went on to say, "We have solid reason to believe that some intelligence officers guided these transactions." Putin was accusing Ambassador McFaul, Kyle Parker, Special Agent Hyman, and everyone else on the list of being part of my "criminal enterprise."

This was classic Russian projection. We weren't the victims, they were. They weren't the criminals, we were. Instead of the Klyuev Organized Crime Group working with corrupt Russian officials to launder vast sums of money, it was the "Browder Organized Crime Group" working with corrupt American officials to launder vast sums of money.

Elena and I looked at each other and smiled. Once again, Putin had way overplayed his hand.

It was one thing to go after a private person like me, who wasn't even an American citizen. That might have been distasteful, but in the final analysis how many people cared about me? It was entirely different to ask for a former US ambassador, a congressional staffer, and rank-and-file DHS agents. If Trump obliged Putin, it would set a disastrous precedent. Not only would it be a total capitulation to the

---

* Perhaps wanting to make these agents appear more like spies, the Russians erroneously claimed in their official statements that Special Agents Angert, Schwartzman, and Hyman worked for the National Security Agency, not DHS.

† This was absurd, and even the Kremlin seemed to realize it. The following day, the Russians quietly revised the figure downward from $400 million to $400,000. This was also false. The actual amount was zero.

Russians, it would make it impossible for the United States to attract anyone into public service. Who would take a government position if they knew they could be handed over to a hostile foreign power at any moment simply for doing their job?

Trump should have rejected Putin's proposal in Helsinki outright. Even giving him the benefit of the doubt that he didn't understand what was going on, (which surely wasn't the case since, a year earlier, he'd drafted his son's statement citing "adoptions" as the reason for the Trump Tower meeting), his advisors should have set him straight immediately afterward. But here we were, nearly 24 hours later, and there was total silence from the White House.

I got out of bed, went to the kitchen, and poured myself a bowl of cereal. After eating, I called Mike McFaul. I'd known Mike pretty much from the day I'd first set foot in Russia in 1992, and considered him a friend. Prior to his stint as US ambassador in Moscow, he had served as Obama's national security advisor on Russia, and had been an important ally inside the US administration in getting the Magnitsky Act passed.

Mike had just landed in San Francisco from Helsinki, where he'd been working for NBC as a commentator at the summit. Similar to me, he'd learned that he was on Putin's wanted list when he'd turned on his phone and found a backlog of dozens of messages.

"Do you think there's any risk this could actually happen?" I asked him.

"No, but my lawyer doesn't think I should leave it to chance. I'm talking to people in the administration today to make sure."

"I'm so sorry you got dragged into this mess, Mike."

"It's not your fault, it's Putin's." He paused. "I always knew he hated you, Bill, but I had no idea how much."

After finishing with Mike, I grabbed my things and drove back to the Doerr-Hosier Center for another full slate of interviews.

That day, my eldest son, David, came with me. He was visiting from California and was extremely worried by these developments. There wasn't much he could do if the authorities came for me, but if they did, he could at least make sure the right people knew about it. The last time David and I had encountered trouble at the Aspen Institute, he was a teenager, but now he was a full-grown 22-year-old man. Having him with me made me feel a little better.

I also got some comfort from the fact that the Aspen Institute was kicking off the Aspen Security Forum that day. This was an international conference that would bring together luminaries from the national security establishment, as well as countless journalists. If anything did happen, it would be covered on live television and witnessed by some of the most important people in government and the media.

The Institute was abuzz that morning. Overnight, a huge white party tent had been staked to the ground on the main lawn. Tables and couches had been set up underneath it, with a small bar and stations where attendees could pick up their credentials. A suckling pig was even roasting on a spit for the afternoon barbecue.

David and I went down to the small basement studio. I introduced him to Jason. I set up for the interviews, and David sat on a couch just outside, watching my appearances on his iPhone.

After I completed a segment for MSNBC, David popped his head inside with a concerned look on his face. "Can I come in?" he mouthed.

"Sure," I said. "What's going on?"

He showed me and Jason a screenshot from his iPhone. It was of me on television. There I was against the neutral newsroom backdrop, frozen mid-sentence. But at the bottom it read, "Bill Browder, Aspen, Colorado."

In the scramble to arrange a second day of interviews, Jason and I had completely forgotten to tell the MSNBC producer not to reveal my location.

Because I lived in the UK, the assumption was that I'd been doing these interviews from London. If that had been the case, then Trump's "deal" with Putin would have been moot, since the US government had no jurisdiction in the UK.

But now everyone knew I was in America. And the US government *did* have jurisdiction.

My first reaction was to rip off the microphone, drive to the airport, and get the hell out of the United States. But I took a few minutes, and eventually calmed down. Arresting me would require Trump to issue an order to Attorney General Jeff Sessions, who would have to order the US attorney for the State of Colorado, who would then have to concoct a plausible legal justification for my arrest in the absence of an extradition treaty between the United States and Russia. This would all take time. I decided to remain in place and continue doing what I was doing.

After another interview, we broke for lunch. David and I went outside and grabbed two pulled pork sandwiches and sat in the shade under the tent. As we ate, I was approached by a succession of conference guests. Those who knew me expressed concern for my safety. Those who didn't gawked at me, as if I were at the bottom of a flaming twenty-car pile-up.

I gave more interviews that afternoon. This time, Mike McFaul jumped into the fray with his own TV appearances. He was even more outraged than I was. Back when he was ambassador in Moscow, he and his family had been stalked, harassed, and surveilled, but he had never been the target of spurious criminal allegations made by the Russian government. Now that he was, he expected an automatic and vociferous rejection from Washington. For him, the continuing silence was truly shocking.

Before returning to the Aspen Institute the next morning, I called Mike again to see how his Washington outreach was going.

"I've spoken to officials at NSC, State, and Justice. They were all very supportive—and appalled—but none were categorical that this wouldn't happen. The unspoken message is that there's a crazy uncle in the White House."

I returned to the Institute for a third day of interviews. The level of interest hadn't abated. Putin's "incredible offer" continued to be at the top of every news cycle. But still, the White House was silent.

In the early afternoon, I was preparing to go on Fox News for the fifth time in three days. Fox was notoriously pro-Trump, but on this issue, they were just as confused and outraged as everyone else. There was no daylight between them, CNN, or even MSNBC.

Just before my hit-time, the producer came over the earpiece. "Bill, we have to go to Washington for a live White House briefing. Can you stay on and we'll talk to you afterward?"

"Of course," I said.

Fox then cut to the briefing, which was underway. While I couldn't see the picture, I could hear what was going on. Sarah Huckabee Sanders, Trump's press secretary, had just started answering questions from the press pool.

A few minutes in, Maggie Haberman from the *New York Times* said, "Russian authorities yesterday named several Americans they want to question that they claim are involved in Bill Browder's quote-unquote 'crimes,' in their terms, including the former ambassador to Russia, Mike McFaul. Does President Trump support that idea? Is he open to having US officials questioned by Russia?"

This was the moment we'd all been waiting for.

Huckabee Sanders didn't waver. "The president is going to meet with his team and we'll let you know when we have an announcement on that." She added that Trump "said it was an interesting idea. . . . He wants to work with his team and determine if there is any validity that would be helpful to the process."

What the fuck? They were still thinking about this?!

I felt like the floor had fallen out from under me—again. Every reasonable person in Trump's orbit must have been telling him this was insanity, yet he was still mulling it over.

When the press conference ended, Fox came back to me and asked what I thought about this latest development. I tried not to insult Trump—I didn't want to give him any more motivation to send me back to Russia—but it was hard not to be completely incensed, and I said as much.

Luckily, everyone in Washington seemed to agree. Within moments, the State Department held its own press conference. When their spokeswoman, Heather Nauert, was confronted by a reporter on why this idea was still being considered, she said, "I can't answer on behalf of the White House"—a crazy thing for a State Department official to say, since the State Department is part of the administration—"but what I can tell you is that the overall assertions that have come out of the Russian Government are absolutely absurd."

Later that afternoon, Congressman Adam Schiff, the ranking member of the House Intelligence Committee, weighed in on Twitter. "No 'consultation' is needed to make clear that U.S. will never cooperate in Putin's crusade against Bill Browder or former U.S. officials, like Ambassador McFaul."

Then, Sen. Roger Wicker, a Mississippi Republican and one of the original cosponsors of the Magnitsky Act, wrote in a statement, "The White House needs to make clear that under no circumstances will the US government hand over former US Ambassador to Russia Michael McFaul, Helsinki Commission Chief of Staff Kyle Parker,* or any other US official for interrogation by a hostile foreign power. President Trump must also strongly oppose Putin's proposal to question British citizen Bill Browder, who bravely exposed the murder of Sergei Magnitsky and brought it to international attention. The United States will not betray those who have fought the aggression and crimes of the Putin regime."

Similar condemnations came in from every corner of Washington. The tidal wave of indignation was towering, and the Senate quickly organized a vote on a resolution calling on Trump never to follow through on Putin's "incredible offer."

The administration could sense this wave was about to come crashing down on them. An hour before the vote, the White House finally backtracked. Huckabee Sanders announced, "It is a proposal that was made in sincerity by President Putin, but President Trump disagrees with it."

This was hardly the robust rejection Washington expected. It seemed like Trump was apologizing to Putin, shrugging his shoulders and saying, "Hey, buddy, I tried, but they won't let me."

At 2:42 p.m. that afternoon, the Senate voted on the resolution.

It passed 98–0.

No one would be handed over to the Russians.

---

* Since the drama with Rohrabacher at the House Foreign Affairs Committee, Kyle had gone to work for the US Helsinki Commission.

41

$234 Billion

Twelve years earlier, in the late evening of September 13, 2006, a 41-year-old man named Andrei Kozlov, the chairman of Russia's Central Bank and one of a handful of honest Russian officials, had just finished a friendly soccer match with other regulators at Spartak Stadium in Moscow. As he made his way to his car in the parking lot, two armed men approached him and his driver and opened fire. Both Kozlov and his driver were struck multiple times. The driver died instantly, but Kozlov, who was hit in the head, chest, and stomach, initially survived. He was taken by EMTs to Moscow Hospital No. 33, where he died on the operating table. He was survived by his wife and three young children.

Three months earlier, Kozlov had traveled to Tallinn, the Estonian capital, to meet with that country's chief financial regulator. Kozlov had identified a major money laundering scheme originating in Russia and flowing through Sampo Bank in Tallinn, and he wanted help in putting a stop to it. The Estonians heard him out, but did nothing. The money laundering continued unabated.

Five months after Kozlov's assassination, Sampo Bank was acquired by a larger bank from another country.

Danske Bank.

This was the same branch of the same bank that would end up laundering $200 million connected to the Magnitsky case, as well as the $8.3 billion that Eva and Michael would eventually expose in their reporting.

Not long after the Helsinki Summit, in September 2018, Danske

Bank finally published the findings of their audit. It quantified the actual volume of dirty money that had flowed out of Russia and the former Soviet Union through this Estonian branch over a 10-year period.

The amount was $234 billion!

That's right. $234 billion. This was *28 times* greater than *Berlingske*'s figure, and more than *1,000 times* greater than the $200 million we'd identified.

This shook Danske Bank to its core. Between 2017, when Eva and Michael started reporting on it, and 2019, one year after the audit, Danske Bank lost 65 percent of its market value; its CEO, Thomas Borgen, along with most of senior management, was forced to resign;* and a major criminal investigation was finally opened in Denmark.

Tragically, the former head of Danske's Bank's Estonian branch, Aivar Rehe, committed suicide at his home in Tallinn while he was under investigation.

In the months that followed, investigative journalists unearthed two additional Scandinavian banks involved in Russian money laundering. Both were Swedish. One was SEB, which allegedly laundered $28 billion, and the other was Swedbank, which was allegedly involved in $42 billion of suspicious transactions. After these reports surfaced, Vadim confirmed that $18 million connected to the $230 million in the Magnitsky case had moved through Swedbank. Their CEO was also forced to resign.

Although this $234 billion sum was huge, it was just the amount of money that had passed through one branch, in one country, of one midsized European bank.

If we could lift the hood on every Western bank, I estimate we'd find that the amount of dirty money that has moved out of Russia since Putin took power to be $1 trillion, and possibly much more.

I'd been talking about Russian money laundering for years. But to have an independent law firm that had been hired by Danske Bank

---

* Any claim of ignorance by senior management could safely be ignored. Reporters revealed that Danske Bank Estonia had a 402 percent return on equity. This was compared to a 6.9 percent return for the entire bank.

begin to quantify just how much money was involved had profound effects in legislative bodies around the world.

Most significantly, it broke the logjam in Europe. Within two months of the publication of Danske Bank's audit, the Dutch government gathered all EU member states in The Hague to discuss an EU Magnitsky Act. I'd been frustrated with Dutch prime minister Mark Rutte—the politician who'd blocked a Dutch Magnitsky Act in 2011— but now he was finally coming through.

An EU Magnitsky Act was the nightmare scenario for Putin. Of all the things I'd been working on, this was the one he was trying to avoid the most. I'm sure the Russian government intensely lobbied against it, but to "bolster" their case, they did something even I hadn't seen coming.

On November 19, just one day before the EU meeting at The Hague, the Russian General Prosecutor's Office held a press conference in Moscow. A deputy to Yuri Chaika took the stage in front of a large group of Western and Russian journalists. Behind him was a screen glowing with a projection of impossible-to-read documents.

He announced that the Russians were filing new criminal charges against me. According to him, I had formed a "transnational criminal group" that killed Sergei Magnitsky using "a diversionary chemical substance containing aluminum compounds, leading to acute heart failure and the appearance of a natural death." He said that my "criminal group" had killed three other individuals, including Alexander Perepilichnyy, using the same technique. By his account, they had collected "enough evidence" to indict me for these "most serious of crimes." If I was found guilty, I'd face a 20-year sentence. This would be on top of the 18 years I'd already been sentenced to in absentia. Chaika's deputy promised to issue further arrest warrants for me and to seize any assets I held in Russia.

We had now come full circle. For nine years, the Russian government, and Vladimir Putin personally, had insisted that Sergei had died of natural causes, and that there had been no signs of foul play. Putin and his government repeated this over and over and over, in front of every court, with every journalist, and to every Western government.

Now, on the eve of the EU Magnitsky Act, and after the exposure of one of the main pipes of their vast money laundering network, the Russian government was claiming that Sergei had in fact been murdered, *and that I was his murderer*!

When we started investigating the $230 million tax rebate fraud, we'd had no idea that it would lead to any of these world-shaping developments or these unthinkable Russian reactions. Why hadn't Putin just thrown a few of his low-level officials under the bus for murdering Sergei? Why would he put a dead man on trial for the first time in Russian history? Why would he ruin his relationship with the West over the Magnitsky Act? Why would he hack Western elections? Why is he so committed to fomenting chaos?

Now we knew. There weren't just millions of dollars at stake. Or even billions. There was likely more than $1 trillion at stake. And Putin will do anything to protect this.

This amount of money also helped explain why so many people had been murdered. People like Sergei Magnitsky, Boris Nemtsov, Alexander Perepilichnyy, and Andrei Kozlov. It also explained why the Kremlin had attempted to kill Vladimir Kara-Murza and Nikolai Gorokhov.

As despicable as Putin and his regime's behavior is, none of this can happen without the cooperation of Western enablers. Lawyers like John Moscow and Mark Cymrot, spin doctors like Glenn Simpson, politicians like Dana Rohrabacher, and executives like those at Danske Bank—these people, along with many others, lubricate the machine that allows Putin and his cronies to get away with their crimes.

Nor can these crimes happen without the acquiescence of timid and ineffective governments that refuse to follow their own laws and stated values. Let's take Britain, just as one example. The largest amount of money associated with the $230 million crime didn't end up in New York or Spain or France or Switzerland, but right in my adopted hometown: London. This money has been used to purchase property and luxury goods, and despite all the evidence I've presented to British law enforcement, Parliament, and the British press, to this day not a single money laundering investigation connected to the Magnitsky case has been initiated in the United Kingdom.

As you've followed me through this story, you might have wondered, "The odds are so impossibly long, and there are so many risks. . . . Why does he do all of these things?"

At first, I did them because I owed it to Sergei. He had been killed because he worked for me, and I couldn't let his killers get away with it. As with the theft of my childhood flute, but on an infinitely grander and more meaningful scale, I have been compelled to get justice. As the theft of my flute showed, this inclination toward justice is part of who I am. It's in my nature. To reject it would have poisoned me from the inside.

Then, as things escalated, it also became a fight for survival. Not only for myself and my family, but for my friends and colleagues, and all the people who were helping Sergei's cause inside of Russia.

But in the end, I've done these things because doing them is the right thing to do. For better or worse, I've been obsessed with this cause since the moment of Sergei's death. This obsession has affected every facet of my life, and all of my relationships, even those with my own children. These effects haven't always been for the better.

But this obsession has also introduced me to remarkable people who have not only changed my life, but the course of history. Some of these people feature in these pages: Boris Nemtsov, Vladimir Kara-Murza, Nikolai Gorokhov, Kyle Parker, Paul Monteleoni, Juleanna Glover. Some have only been mentioned in passing: Sen. John McCain, Sen. Ben Cardin, Sen. Roger Wicker, Sen. Joe Lieberman, Rep. Jim McGovern. Others haven't been mentioned at all: Canadian MP Irwin Cotler; Canadian deputy prime minister Chrystia Freeland; British foreign secretary Dominic Raab; Dutch MPs Sjoerd Sjoerdsma and Pieter Omtzigt; Lithuanian MEP Petras Auštrevičius; Australian senator Kimberley Kitching.

This isn't meant to be an acknowledgments page. It's just meant to show that this movement has grown far beyond my obsession. It is a thing unto itself, and it is a good thing.

Most important, my obsession has created a legacy for Sergei so that his murder wasn't meaningless, unlike so many others.

At the time of writing, there are Magnitsky Acts in 34 different countries: the United States, Canada, the United Kingdom, Australia, the 27 countries of the European Union, Norway, Montenegro, and Kosovo. This doesn't take into account the British Overseas Territories and Crown Protectorates of Gibraltar, Jersey, Guernsey, the British Virgin Islands, and the Cayman Islands. New Zealand and Japan are on deck.

More than 500 individuals and entities have been sanctioned using these laws. In Russia, these include Dmitry Klyuev, Andrei Pavlov, Pavel Karpov, Artem Kuznetsov, and Olga Stepanova and her husband, along with 35 other Russians involved in Sergei's false arrest, torture, and murder as well as the $230 million tax rebate fraud.*

But not only Russians. Magnitsky sanctions have now been applied to the Saudi assassins responsible for the murder and dismemberment of journalist Jamal Khashoggi; the Chinese officials who set up the Uighur concentration camps in Xinjiang; the Myanmar generals responsible for the Rohingya genocide; the Gupta brothers, who stripped the South African government dry; and hundreds of others for similarly pernicious acts.

For every person or organization that has been sanctioned, there are thousands of human rights violators and kleptocrats who are waiting in terror to see if they will be sanctioned next. There's no question that the Magnitsky Act has altered behavior and been a deterrent for would-be murderers and thieves.

I can't bring Sergei back. And for that, I carry a heavy burden that will never go away. But his sacrifice has not been meaningless. It has saved, and will continue to save, many, many lives.

If Russia ever has a real democratic reckoning, future Russians will expand on these legal monuments by building physical ones to a true hero: Sergei Magnitsky.

For now, though, the fight goes on.

---

* See appendix for a full list of Russians sanctioned under the US Magnitsky Act for their involvement in the Magnitsky case.

Epilogue

What happened to some of the people in this story?

While many of the bad guys in Russia have been sanctioned under the Magnitsky Act, one key person hasn't—Natalia Veselnitskaya.

But she won't be coming to the United States anytime soon.

On January 8, 2019, she was indicted by the US government for obstruction of justice. Leaked emails between her and a senior Russian government official showed she had lied to the US government in the Prevezon case. She'd represented herself as a lawyer working for a private Russian citizen, but in reality, she had been working with the Russian government the whole time. In fact, the emails showed she'd largely written the Russian government's official response to the SDNY in the Prevezon case. This is the document that accused me and Sergei of stealing the $230 million, and that also refused to provide the crucial Russian banking information that the US government had requested.

Following her indictment, the Department of Justice issued a warrant for Veselnitskaya's arrest and placed a freezing order over any of her US assets connected to her work on the Prevezon case.

A few other people bear mentioning here.

In Russia, Andrei Pavlov has taken a different tack in his career. In late 2019, he left private legal practice to become a Russian government official, heading the legal department of the Depository Insurance Agency (Russia's version of the FDIC). Unlike in the West, a government position such as this can be incalculably lucrative.

In the United States, Mark Cymrot and BakerHostetler were also exposed by Veselnitskaya's emails. These showed that Cymrot and

BakerHostetler, despite their categorical disqualification in the Prevezon case, continued to provide legal advice to that company right up to the day Prevezon agreed to pay $5.9 million to settle the case. Neither Cymrot nor BakerHostetler has faced any consequence for defying the court. Mark Cymrot still works at BakerHostetler, where he continues to advise Russian clients, including Sberbank, Russia's largest national bank.

John Moscow left BakerHostetler in November 2018, to join the law firm Lewis Baach Kaufmann Middlemiss as senior counsel. Ironically, the Kaufmann in that name is Adam Kaufmann, the former New York prosecutor with whom I'd filed the original Prevezon complaint. John Moscow continues to lecture about money laundering and organized crime at the Cambridge Crime Conference.

After serving 15 terms in the US House of Representatives, Dana Rohrabacher of Orange County, California, was defeated in 2018 by Harley Rouda, a Democrat. After this defeat, Rohrabacher moved to York, Maine, where he set up a lobbying firm called R&B Strategies with Paul Behrends, his former staffer. Behrends died on December 13, 2020, at the age of 62. The cause of death was severe head trauma following a fall near his home in Virginia. A spokesman for Rohrabacher insisted there was no reason to believe that Behrends's death was suspicious or had anything to do with his associations with Russia.

As far as my friends in this story go, most of us are doing fine. Most of us.

Nikolai Gorokhov still lives in Moscow with Julia. Their daughter, Diana, is a grown woman. Nikolai is doing reasonably well, but he has paid a heavy price for the head injuries he sustained from his fall—he is slowly going blind.

Vladimir Kara-Murza continues to circle the globe advocating for Magnitsky sanctions and justice for Boris Nemtsov. Despite his poisoning, and attempts by me to persuade him otherwise, he still officially resides and spends most of his time in Russia, fighting for freedom and democracy. In early 2017, he was poisoned a *second* time. Again, he was saved by Dr. Denis Protsenko. A 2021 report by Bellingcat, a crowdsourced investigative organization based in London, identified

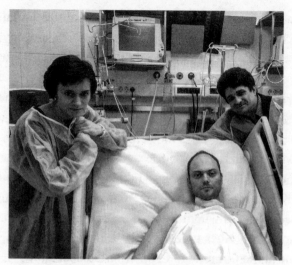

From left to right: Evgenia Kara-Murza,
Vladimir Kara-Murza, and Vadim Prokhorov.

(© VADIM PROKHOROV)

four officers from the FSB who were behind Vladimir's poisonings, including two who followed him to Kazan in May 2015. The same operatives were involved in the poisoning of other Russian dissidents and opposition figures, including Alexei Navalny.

Two people I haven't written about much in this book are Sergei Magnitsky's widow, Natasha, and son, Nikita—though they are never far from my mind.

From the moment Sergei was killed, I've been committed to getting justice, but above and beyond that, I've committed myself to taking care of his family.

The first thing I wanted to do after his death was to move Natasha and Nikita, who was eight years old at the time, out of Russia. I didn't think it was safe from them to stay. I also felt I could do a better job of caring for them if they were close by.

But Natasha was determined to remain. She felt Nikita would be better off in Russia. In the immediate aftermath of Sergei's murder, she contacted over a dozen doctors and psychologists, seeking advice about what to do with Nikita following such a traumatic experience. The consensus was that he needed a stable environment. In her mind, picking up and moving to London, where they had no family, where they didn't know the language or the culture, where they didn't have a home or school, was exactly the opposite of providing a stable environment.

As time went on, this decision became increasingly untenable. The more we exposed the people who'd killed Sergei and those behind the $230 million fraud, the more the Russian authorities looked for someone to retaliate against in Russia—and they zeroed in on Natasha.

On August 17, 2011, Natasha's doorbell rang. She was in her kitchen, cleaning up after breakfast. Nikita had already gone to school. She opened the apartment door to find a uniformed postal carrier holding a crisp telegram. She signed for it and tore it open. It was an "invitation" from the Russian Interior Ministry demanding that she come in for questioning. The end of the "invitation" read, "Failure to appear will result in delivery by force."

Natasha collapsed into a nearby chair, shaking. They wanted to question her in the posthumous case that had been opened against Sergei.

When I heard about this, I tried yet again to convince her to leave, but she wouldn't. Her own trauma was preventing her from seeing things clearly, and I had to be respectful. I couldn't force her to leave.

In spite of my misgivings, on August 26, 2011, Natasha traveled to the Interior Ministry on the corner of Bolshaya Nikitskaya and Gazetny Pereulok in central Moscow. As she approached the building, she realized that she and Sergei had passed it countless times on their way to classical music concerts at the Moscow State Conservatory only a few blocks away. The building, a handsome 19th-century structure, had no obvious signage. It was painted an inviting pale yellow.

She met her lawyer and they entered. They were escorted by an officer through a series of corridors and narrow staircases, passing dark offices and storage rooms. When they reached the office where the interrogation would take place, they found a pair of small tables facing each other. There was barely enough room for two people, let alone Natasha, her lawyer, the interrogator, and a video technician. Cabinets lined the wall opposite a dirty window, and file folders were everywhere. On the wall was an old calendar from the previous year, underneath a framed picture of Vladimir Putin.

The interrogator was a pear-shaped middle-aged woman with dyed red hair who seemed almost as nervous as Natasha. After reading Natasha her rights, the interrogator presented Natasha with a strange document. She and her lawyer read it. Natasha had been given the status of "legal representative of the indicted deceased individual." This was an entirely novel legal designation that did not exist under Russian law. Deceased individuals couldn't be indicted, therefore they required no legal representative. The Interior Ministry had simply made it up, just for Natasha.

She sat in an uncomfortable metal chair, and before the female officer had a chance to speak, Natasha pulled out a prepared statement. Reading from it, she denounced the posthumous case and ended by saying, "To continue to prosecute a deceased person is illegal, inhumane, and immoral, because he cannot defend himself. . . . I will not provide any further answers or testimony."

The red-haired interrogator ignored her and began her questioning. She started by demanding the names, addresses, phone numbers, and work details of anyone connected to Sergei or Natasha.

Natasha stared at her stone-faced and didn't say a word.

The interrogator then asked Natasha to acknowledge the legitimacy of the case against her dead husband.

Again, she didn't answer.

The interrogator asked the same question using different words.

Still nothing.

Seeing that she was getting nowhere, the interrogator dangled a carrot. She told Natasha that if she cooperated, she could claim damages from the state. Natasha knew there was no way the state would ever acknowledge any wrongdoing in Sergei's death, or pay a single ruble in damages.

Finally, the interrogator asked Natasha straight out to plead guilty on Sergei's behalf.

This was ultimately what they wanted. If they could pressure Natasha into denouncing Sergei, they could declare him a criminal, wrap everything up in a neat little bow, and nobody in Russia would have any reason to chase the real culprits behind the $230 million fraud.

Natasha didn't respond.

She endured two hours and thirty-nine minutes of questioning before the interrogator decided to call it a day.

Just as she and her lawyer stood to leave, the interrogator leaned over, opened a file cabinet, grabbed a piece of paper, and slid it across the table. Natasha's lawyer picked it up. It was a new summons, demanding Natasha appear for more questioning on August 29. This one also stated that "Failure to appear will result in delivery by force."

Natasha left the building, her emotions swirling. She swore to herself that, regardless of the threats, she would never willingly return to any Interior Ministry building.

When I heard about what happened, I tried to convince her to leave yet again. I couldn't understand why, but she still refused.

On August 29, she sat in her apartment, nervously waiting for the Interior Ministry to come and "forcibly deliver" her. But they didn't.

Over the next year, the Russian authorities continued to summon her, and she continued to ignore them. In all, she was summoned six more times—the last one demanded she appear for eight straight days of questioning.

Every time she refused, she risked being carted off, never to see Nikita again. She'd finally had enough. Whatever disruption moving to London would have on Nikita, her arrest would be far, far worse.

On September 20, 2012, Natasha and Nikita boarded a plane for Heathrow. Once they arrived, they were safe. I could now protect and take care of them properly.

The first thing we did was find a good school for Nikita. He was accepted at the Hampton Court House School, in Surrey, a London suburb. We then rented them a flat in nearby Teddington. Once classes began, Natasha started working full-time with us on the Magnitsky campaign, in our offices.

Slowly and steadily, Natasha and Nikita began the long and difficult process of healing without their wounds being constantly reopened in Russia.

Over the ensuing years, Nikita grew from a boy to an impressive young man. He learned to speak English perfectly, and even translated for his mother and grandmother whenever they met with politicians in the United States and around the world. He was an excellent student with high grades, and above all he was an empathetic, charming young man. We were all very proud of him.

Watching him grow, I thought he should go to an Ivy League university. Given his unique story and grades, he had a real shot. I thought of how proud Sergei would be if his son was a Harvard or Princeton alum, and I made it my personal mission to make that happen.

I found London's best guidance counselor for US universities to advise us. Nikita, Natasha, and I regularly met with the counselor to discuss the application process, what extracurriculars he should focus on, how to write a great essay, preparing for the SATs, and much more.

Although I wasn't his father, like many parents of high-achieving 17-year-olds, I became obsessed with this process. As the application deadline approached, we agreed to meet at the office to discuss Nikita's essays with Vadim and Ivan. The entire brainpower of our operation would be there to help.

When Nikita arrived, he looked a little sheepish. Before we got down to work, he asked if he could have a quiet word alone.

We went into a conference room, and he said, "Thank you for everything, Bill, but . . . do I really have to do this?"

"What do you mean?"

He took a moment before saying, "I don't really want to go to Harvard or Princeton."

This took me by surprise. I'd never considered that he would want something else. "Okay," I said slowly. "What do you want to do instead?"

"I want to study art."

"You can study art at Harvard, I'm sure of it."

"No. I've looked into it. I want to go to a school that specializes in illustration, animation, design. That's what I want to do."

I realized in that moment that this whole Harvard-Princeton thing was my fantasy, not his. Of course, he should follow his heart—not someone else's.

I also realized in that moment that Sergei would have been proud of Nikita for standing up for himself and telling someone like me his real feelings.

I was proud of him too.

I dropped my grandiose plans and let him take the lead. He got into the school of his choice, and in the fall of 2022, Nikita Magnitsky started his junior year at one of America's top art and design schools, pursuing his dreams.

In the end, I'm sure that is all that Sergei could have hoped or asked for.

With Nikita Magnitsky and Canadian prime minister Justin Trudeau, just after the passage of the Canadian Magnitsky Act, November 2017.

(© HERMITAGE)

Links and Legal Documents

Russian Untouchables, Episode 1, Artem Kuznetsov, June 2010
  tinyurl.com/2p8pv6kk

Russian Untouchables, Episode 2, Pavel Karpov, July 2010
  tinyurl.com/46m49j39

Russian Untouchables, Episode 3, Olga Stepanova, April 2011
  tinyurl.com/2wsuxysy

Russian Untouchables, Episode 4, The Magnitsky Files (Dmitry Klyuev),
  June 2012
  tinyurl.com/55jxab9b

Hermitage complaint against Olga Stepanova and Vladlen Stepanov,
  Switzerland, January 2011
  tinyurl.com/3768vdeh

Video clip of Dmitry Klyuev at the OSCE Parliamentary Assembly, Monaco,
  July 2012
  tinyurl.com/2wkba6jf

"Following the Magnitsky Money," OCCRP, August 2012
  tinyurl.com/7uh25mt3

Hermitage complaint against Prevezon and Denis Katsyv, New York,
  December 2012
  tinyurl.com/5dwb434t

SDNY complaint against Prevezon, September 2013
  tinyurl.com/49tn3kt7

Memorandum of Law to disqualify John Moscow and BakerHostetler from the
Prevezon case, September 2014
tinyurl.com/mv968tfn

Natalia Veselnitskaya Facebook post, October 2014 (English translation)
tinyurl.com/4xmdbac4

Confidential letter given to US congressman Dana Rohrabacher by Russian
deputy general prosecutor Viktor Grin, April 2016
tinyurl.com/2njpas6b

US indictment of 12 GRU officers from Special Counsel headed by Robert
Mueller, July 2018
tinyurl.com/yzbz5a98

Paul Manafort's notes from the Trump Tower meeting, July 2016
tinyurl.com/4pz84bd7

US indictment of Natalia Veselnitskaya, January 2019
tinyurl.com/sdd94u8s

List of Russians connected to the Magnitsky case sanctioned by the US
Government
tinyurl.com/2juae2c2

Acknowledgments

This book portrays only a small fraction of the work that has gone into getting 34 countries to pass Magnitsky Acts, as well as convincing 16 jurisdictions to open criminal money laundering investigations connected to the $230 million fraud that Sergei exposed and was killed over. (If I were to tell the whole story, the book would probably be 10 times longer and likely unreadable.)

Accomplishing all of this has taken an army of lawmakers, journalists, activists, lawyers, NGOs, investigators, prosecutors, editors, and friends, among many others. I'm going to do my best to list them below but will exclude a few groups intentionally.

For obvious reasons, I'm not going to mention anyone who has provided confidential assistance. People like whistleblowers, sources, and certain friends. You know who you are, and I hope you know that words cannot express my gratitude.

I'm also not going to list journalists or members of law enforcement. I'm eternally grateful for the work that they've done, but it's crucial to state that they've done this because it was their duty, not because they had some "loyalty" to me or anyone else.

Some of the people listed below are readily recognizable, but most of them, who have labored behind the scenes for years, you've never heard of.

I'd like to begin with the country of my birth, the United States, and then move to the country I currently call home, the United Kingdom. In each section, I've done my best to list names alphabetically by surname.

In the United States, I would like to thank Michael Abramowitz, Karl Altau, Attorney General John Ashcroft, Anders Åslund, Robert Berschinski, Ellen Bork, Cindy Buhl, Dr. Robert Bux, Ted Bromund, Chris Brose, Senator Benjamin Cardin, David Crane, Charles Davidson, Patrick Davis, Lars de Gier, Sophie de Selliers, Sarah Drake, Grant Felgenhauer, Thomas Firestone, Enes Kanter Freedom, Jeffrey Gedmin, Juleanna Glover, James Goldston, Maggie Goodlander, Michael Gottlieb, Thor Halvorssen, Hans Hogrefe, Gulchehra Hoja, Nathaniel Hurd, Uri Itkin, Nils Johnson-Shelton, Robert Kagan, Robert Karem, Jonathan Karp, Garry Kasparov, Orly Keiner, Michael Kim, David Kramer, Katrina Lantos Swett, Carolyn Leddy, Duncan Levin, Senator Joe Lieberman, Nikita Magnitsky, Representative Tom Malinowski, Christopher Mangum, Paul Massaro, Randy Mastro, Senator John McCain, Meghan McCain, Ambassador Michael McFaul, Representative Jim McGovern, Juan Méndez, Katya Migacheva, Mark Milosch, Tanya Nyberg, Spencer Oliver, Priscilla Painton, Hana Park, Kyle Parker, Julia Pettengill, Lisa Rubin, Randy Scheunemann, Stefan Schmitt, Nate Sibley, Neil Simon, Mason Simpson, Susannah Sirkin, Representative Chris Smith, Kimberly Stanton, Bernie Sucher, Jordan Tama, Piero Tozzi, Fred Turner, Ed Verona, Lindsey Weiss Harris, Senator Roger Wicker, Jonathan Winer, John Wood, and Natasha Zharikova.

In the United Kingdom, I would like to thank Baroness Rosalind Altmann, Lord David Alton, Lisa Amos, Lord Donald Anderson, Anne Applebaum, Lord Ian Austin, Courtenay Barklem, Robert Barrington, Lord Richard Benyon, Olga Bischof, Ian Blackford MP, Peter Bottomley MP, General Sir Adrian Bradshaw, Tom Brake MP, Sabrina Brasey, Daniel Bruce, Malcolm Bruce MP, Chris Bryant MP, Robert Buckland MP, Barbora Bukovská, Ivan Cherkasov, Anna Chernova, Christopher Chope MP, Lord Timothy Clement-Jones, Lord Ray Collins, Claire Coutinho MP, Peter Dahlin, Luke de Pulford, Jonathan Djanogly MP,

Anand Doobay, Anton Drel, Mark Ellis, Ben Emmerson QC, Catrin Evans QC, Carla Ferstman, Maya Foa, Andrew Foxall, Nusrat Ghani MP, Jamison Firestone, Jonathan Fisher QC, Edward Fitzgerald QC, Roger Gherson, Helen Goodman MP, Margaret Halton, Stephen Hayes, Henrietta Hill QC, Jonathan Hill, Eliot Higgins, Margaret Hodge MP, George Ireland, Bianca Jagger, Natalia Kaliada, Steven Kay QC, Alicia Kearns MP, Hugo Keith QC, Baroness Helena Kennedy QC, Eduard Khayretdinov, Mikhail Khodorkovsky, Stephen Kinnock MP, Vadim Kleiner, Maya Lester QC, Davis Lewin, Maria Logan, Edward Lucas, Imogen MacLean, Denis MacShane MP, Arthur Marriott QC, Ian Marshall, Stewart McDonald MP, Edward McMillan-Scott MEP, Andy McSmith, Alan Mendoza, Neil Micklethwaite, Andrew Mitchell MP, Jasvinder Nakhwal, Jessica Ní Mhainín, James O'Brien, Tim Otty QC, Vladimir Pastukhov, Alexandre Prezanti, Watson Pringle, Dominic Raab MP, Daniel Rathwell, Geoffrey Robertson QC, Benedict Rogers, Lord Jeffrey Rooker, Jago Russell, Mark Sabah, Jürgen Schurr, Bob Seely MP, Anisha Shakya, Jason Sharman, Laura Simmonds, Rupert Skilbeck, Iain Duncan Smith MP, Clive Stafford Smith, Joe Smouha QC, Mark Stephens, Dr. Charles Tannock MEP, Peter Tatchell, Sue Thackeray, Flavia Trevisani, Tom Tugendhat MP, Rebecca Vincent, Monique Villa, Patrick Walsh, Antony White QC, Andrea Wong, and Martin Woods.

Following these two countries, I'm going to proceed alphabetically by country.

In Australia, I would like to thank Kevin Andrews MP, Michael Danby MP, Andrew Hastie MP, Chris Hayes MP, Jordan Heng-Contaxis, Senator Kimberley Kitching, Francis Leach, Senator Nick McKim, Senator Christine Milne, Senator James Paterson, Senator Marise Payne, Senator Janet Rice, Tonya Stevens, and Senator Peter Whish-Wilson.

In Austria, I would like to thank Dr. Friedrich Schwank.

In Belgium, I would like to thank Piet Blondé, Karel de Meester, Eva Palatova, Andrew Rettman, Alice Stollmeyer, Joris van Cauter, and Guy Verhofstadt MEP.

In Brazil, I would like to thank Ricardo Mioto and Jorge Oakim.

In Canada, I would like to thank Dean Allison MP, Senator Raynell Andreychuk, James Bezan MP, Lincoln Caylor, Jonathan Cooperman, Irwin Cotler MP, Charlie Feldman, Chrystia Freeland MP, Senator Linda Frum, Hedy Fry MP, Garnett Genuis MP, Peter Kent MP, Tom Kmiec MP, Marcus Kolga, Alexei Kovalev, Hélène Laverdière MP, Michael Levitt MP, Howard Liebman, John McKay MP, Rob Nicholson MP, Rob Oliphant MP, Senator Ratna Omidvar, Bob Rae MP, Murray Rankin MP, Andrew Scheer MP, Brandon Silver, Arif Virani MP, and Borys Wrzesnewskyj MP.

In Cyprus, I would like to thank Christos Pourgourides MP.

In the Czech Republic, I would like to thank Jakub Janda, Jan Lipavský MP, and Jaromir Štětina MEP.

In Denmark, I would like to thank Michael Aastrup-Jensen MP.

In Estonia, I would like to thank Marie Edala, President Toomas Ilves Hendrik, Andres Herkel MP, Riina Kionka, Prime Minister Mart Laar, Silver Meikar MP, Eerik Niiles-Kross MP, Mart Nutt MP, Kristiina Ojuland MEP, Mailis Reps MP, and Jaanus Tehver.

In Finland, I would like to thank Jessikka Aro, Pia Kauma MP, Joel Kontro, Leena Majander, and Henrikki Timgren.

In France, I would like to thank Safya Akorri, Pauline Benay, William Bourdan, Agnès Callamard, Mireille Clapot MP, Daniel Cohn-Bendit MEP, François Croquette, Emmanuel Daoud, Senator André Gattolin, Raphaël Glucksmann MEP, Eva Joly MEP, Axelle Lemaire, Noël Mamère, Laurent Muschel, Delphine O MP, Philippe Robinet, Laëtitia Saint-Paul MP, Günter Schirmer, and Senator André Vallini.

In Germany, I would like to thank Henry Alt-Haaker, Marieluise Beck MP, Jaka Bizilj, Bernd Fabritius MP, Rebecca Harms MEP, Ambassador Christoph Israng, Gyde Jensen MP, Sergey Lagodinsky MEP, Sabine Leutheusser-Schnarrenberger MP, Barbara Lochbihler MEP, Markus Löning, Andreas Nick MP, Norbert Röttgen MP, Manuel Sarrazin MP, Marina Schuster MP, Christoph Strässer MP, and Oliver Wallasch.

In Iceland, I would like to thank Jonas Sigurgeirsson.

In Ireland, I would like to thank Ivana Bacik TD, Senator Pádraig Ó Céidigh, Jason Corcoran, Remy Farrell, Brendan Howlin TD, Mary

Lou McDonald TD, Catherine Murphy TD, Ann Phelan TD, Senator Jim Walsh, and Senator Barry Ward.

In Italy, I would like to thank Laura Harth, Matteo Mecacci MP, Senator Roberto Rampi, David Sassoli MEP, and Antonio Stango.

In Japan, I would like to thank Professor Akira Igata and Shiori Yamao MP.

In Jersey, I would like to thank Senator Philip Ozouf.

In Kosovo, I would like to thank Muhamet Brajshori.

In Latvia, I would like to thank Minister Jānis Bordāns, Lolita Čigāne MP, Sandra Kalniete MEP, and Valdis Liepiņš.

In Lithuania, I would like to thank Vilija Aleknaitė-Abramikienė MP, Laima Andrikiene MP, Petras Auštrevičius MEP, Leonidas Donskis MEP, Andrius Kubilius MEP, Gabrielius Landsbergis MP, Vytautas Landsbergis MEP, Žygimantas Pavilionis MP, Dovilė Šukytė, and Emanuelis Zingeris MP.

In Luxembourg, I would like to thank Anne Brasseur MP.

In Moldova, I would like to thank Igor Munteanu MP.

In Montenegro, I would like to thank President Milo Đukanović.

In the Netherlands, I would like to thank Leonoor Broeder, Coşkun Çörüz MP, Ingrid de Caluwé MP, Esther de Lange MEP, Kathleen Ferrier MP, Pieter Omtzigt MP, Kati Piri MEP, Marietje Schaake MEP, Sjoerd Sjoerdsma MP, Göran Sluiter, Sophie in 't Veld MEP, Barend van der Have, and Barbara van Straaten.

In New Zealand, I would like to thank Simon O'Connor MP and Louisa Wall MP.

In Norway, I would like to thank Ivar Amundsen, Aage Borchgrevink, Carl Bore, Gunnar Ekeløve-Slydal, Ola Elvestuen MP, Bjørn Engesland, Peter Skovholt Gitmark MP, Knut Arild Hareide MP, Morten Høglund MP, Trine Skei Grande MP, and Ingjerd Schou MP.

In the Philippines, I would like to thank Maria Ressa.

In Poland, I would like to thank Adam Bodnar, Sonia Draga, Anna Fotyga MEP, Ryszard Kalisz MP, Pawel Osik, and Radoslaw Sikorski MEP.

In Portugal, I would like to thank Ana Gomes MEP and João Soares MEP.

In Romania, I would like to thank Cristian Ghinea MEP, Adrian Prisnel MP, and Stefan Voinea.

In Russia, I would like to thank Yevgenia Albats, Maria Alekhina, Roman Anin, Alexander Antipov, Valery Borshchev, Vera Chelischeva, Evgenia Chirikova, Masha Gessen, Nikolai Gorokhov, Sergei Guriev, Andrei Illarionov, Vladimir Kara-Murza, Mikhail Kasyanov, Eugene Kiselev, Yulia Latynina, Dmitry Lipkin, Natalia Magnitsky, Tamara Morschakova, Dmitry Muratov, Alexei Navalny, Boris Nemtsov, Mara Polyakova, Olga Romanova, Oleg Ruchka, Lilia Shevtsova, Olesya Shmagun, Sergei Sokolov, Zoya Svetova, Nadya Tolokonnikova, Alexei Venediktov, Petya Verzilov, Lyubov Volkova, and Irina Yasina.

In Serbia, I would like to thank Ivan Cvejic and Orhan Dragaš.

In South Africa, I would like to thank Premier Helen Zille.

In Spain, I would like to thank Ruperto Guerra, Juan Carlos Gutiérrez, Juan Fernando López Aguilar MEP, Fernando Maura Barandiarán MP, Javier Nart MEP, José Ignacio Sánchez Amor MEP, and Senator Jordi Xuclà.

In Sweden, I would like to thank Sofia Arkelsten MP, Walburga Habsburg Douglas MP, Gunnar Hökmark MEP, Mats Johansson MP, Oscar Jonsson, Kerstin Lundgren MP, Christer Sturmark, Martina Stenstrom, Caroline Szyber MP, Katarina Tracz, and Hans Wallmark MP.

In Switzerland, I would like to thank Andreas Gross MP, Florian Irminger, Hikmat Maleh, Markus Mohler, Hillel Neuer, Mark Pieth, Elena Servettaz, Carlo Sommaruga MP, and Daniel Tunik.

In Taiwan, I would like to thank Wang Ting-Yu MP.

In Ukraine, I would like to thank Serhiy Kiral MP and Maria Lilichenko.

I may have forgotten some names (and misspelled a few, too!), and if I have, please forgive me.

As I wrote earlier in this book, and as you can see, this is no longer a movement driven only by me and our small team, but one that has taken on a life of its own. It has been an honor to work with each of you, and to call some of you friends.

Sadly, the situation with human rights abuse and kleptocracy in our world only seems to grow darker and more intractable. I'm sure I'll be working with many of you to meet new challenges in the days and years to come as, together, we continue to fight for justice and the rule of law.

But for now, I'd like to thank you again.

About the Author

BILL BROWDER is the founder and CEO of Hermitage Capital Management and was the largest foreign investor in Russia until 2005. Since the murder of Sergei Magnitsky, Browder's advocacy has led to the passage of the Magnitsky Act in 34 countries. These laws have the power to sanction human rights abusers and kleptocrats all around the world. He holds a BA in economics from the University of Chicago and an MBA from Stanford Business School. He lives with his wife and children in London.